D0842325

The Smile of
the Gods

A THEMATIC STUDY OF
CESARE PAVESE'S WORKS

The Smile of the Gods.

A THEMATIC STUDY OF CESARE PAVESE'S WORKS

By Gian - Paolo Biasin

Translated by Yvonne Freccero

Cornell University Press

Ithaca, New York

Alla tribù,
con "un falò di bene"

Acknowledgments

The Italian original of two sections of this study has already appeared, in somewhat different form, in *Modern Language Notes*, LXXXI (January 1966), pp. 1–21 ("Lo straniero sulle colline: Cesare Pavese"), and in *Italica*, XLIII (June 1966), pp. 141–166 ("Il rapporto Io-altri nei romanzi 'politici' di Cesare Pavese"). An earlier version of Chapter 8, "The Smile of the Gods," was published in *Italian Quarterly*, X (Fall 1966), pp. 3–32.

Professors Charles Singleton and John Freccero followed this work, fondly, in its successive stages; without their encouragement, advice, and friendship I would never have been able or willing to finish it. I want to thank also all the friends (especially Piero Pucci) who read the manuscript and contributed their criticism and suggestions.

Yvonne Freccero survived a flood and some minor disasters to complete the translation, including all the passages from Pavese's works not already translated. Existing translations are identified following the first quotation from each work: I have made some passages closer to the original. The changes appear in square brackets. I also wish to thank Arnoldo Mondadori for permission to quote a few lines of Eugenio Montale's poems.

GIAN-PAOLO BIASIN

Ithaca, New York
April 1968

Contents

The Smile of
the Gods

A THEMATIC STUDY OF
CESARE PAVESE'S WORKS

Introduction

"Words are tender things, intractable and alive. . . ."

CESARE PAVESE

In 1936, when Cesare Pavese's first book was published, a collection of poems entitled *Work Is Wearying*, the Italian literary scene was composed of various movements that derived partly from French symbolism and partly from German impressionism, and that, aside from their distinctive characteristics, could be considered the last lingering effects of romanticism.

In the poetry of that period we find the long lines and intimate tone of the crepuscular poets, the agitated pan-Europeanism propounded by the review *La Voce*, the futurists' verbal experiments, the poetic fragments of the impressionists, the extreme classicism of another review, *La Ronda*, and the shadowy "essentiality" of the hermetic poets (Eugenio Montale's *Cuttlefish Bones*). Taste and attitudes, however, were primarily dominated by D'Annunzio's "sensual love of the word." Thus, the literary scene was rich and alive on a subjective and lyrical level, consciously expressing or unconsciously testifying to the fundamental separation of individual and world. Italian poetry, in particular, rejected any contact with the political and social reality of its time (fascism and the rise of the *bourgeoisie*), or else adopted only its most extreme and superficial aspects, such as the nationalism of F. T. Marinetti or of D'Annunzio.[1]

The prose of the period also reflects the same conditions as the poetry; if anything, it reveals an even more pronounced rejection and escapism, especially in comparison with the excessive, autarchical, and rhetorical optimism of official Fascist culture. Svevo's interior analysis, Tozzi's psychological naturalism, Pirandello's atomistic relativism, all express the same basic division between self and world, between individual and society; moreover, even the "*prosa d'arte*" testifies to such a separation. Among the few authors who clearly and consciously drew from their *condition humaine* and the social and historical situation are Elio Vittorini, Corrado Alvaro, Carlo Bernari, and Alberto Moravia, whose *The Time of Indifference* was published in 1929. Meanwhile, in the field of political thought and philosophy, Benedetto Croce represented an authoritative and dignified voice of criticism and independence, whereas the more politically engaged but less famous Antonio Gramsci and Piero Gobetti were "disposed of in due course."[2]

This was the cultural background of Italy in the thirties, and Cesare Pavese was of course profoundly influenced by it; but his own most important contribution was his studies of American literature, which came as a breath of fresh air. His doctoral thesis was an application of Crocian criticism to Walt Whitman; his essays and translations introduced Sinclair Lewis, Sherwood Anderson, Edgar Lee Masters, and Herman Melville to Italian readers. For an idea of the touching enthusiasm with which Pavese attempted to understand the American authors, their language—especially their slang—their culture, and their society, one should read his many letters to his friend in Chicago, Antonio Chiuminatto. For example:

Dear Mr Chiuminatto,
I'm befuddled, all in a daze, with your titanic kindness. I'm now seeing the world only through a veil of pink sheets, all bristling with slang phrases which are meddling together, re-echoing and staring at me from everywhere. I've got now I can no more take a pull out of a bottle together with my gang, without thinking I'm going on the grand sneak. And how flip I get sometimes! And how many keen mamas I'm looking after! And how . . . so on. My whole existence has got a slang drift now. You could almost say I'm a slang-slinger (Ha!). . . .[3]

These were "the times in which we discovered America," Pavese wrote later,[4] emphasizing the significance such a discovery had had for him, as for Cecchi and for Vittorini— America as "the gigantic stage where the drama of everyone is performed more openly than anywhere else,"[5] America "as political allegory"[6] and certainly not as escape, America as a literary model, "the ideal antithesis to the climate of the *"prosa d'arte"* and hermetic poems . . . and at the same time a linguistic experimentation parallel to the European one but grafted on to a fantastically younger and more vigorous trunk,"[7] in short, America as a rediscovery of Verga's regional realism, for his American studies convinced Pavese that "certainly, without its provincial writers a literature cannot be strong."[8]

From the beginning Pavese wanted a literary revival. With *Work Is Wearying* he attempted to destroy the contemporary conscious or unconscious vision of the relationship of self and world, individual and society, treating this relationship from a positive and objective viewpoint. His efforts were destined to partial failure, especially since Pavese's own nature was in conflict with his reason and will. But there is no doubt that his work, when taken in its entirety, expressed and interpreted with painful clarity the crises and despair of modern man.

Pavese was born at Santo Stefano Belbo, in Piedmont, on September 9, 1908. As a child in a lower-middle-class family, he spent his summer vacations in the country, but all his education took place at Turin. His years in classical high school under the guidance of Professor Augusto Monti, a follower of Gobetti's, were particularly important. In 1930 he took his degree in letters at the University of Turin. Beginning in 1933, he was one of the first contributors of the Einaudi publishing house. During that period he was in love with a woman of strong character who was involved in the Communist party, then a secret organization; in 1935, as the result of some politically compromising letters addressed to her and discovered by the police in Pavese's house, he was arrested and imprisoned (*"confinato"*) at Brancaleone Calabro, a small town even more remote and isolated than Eboli, where Christ stopped.

Pavese's experiences during his ten months' imprisonment left a deep mark on him, all the more so because, on his return to Turin, he found that the woman he loved had married someone else. There followed for Pavese a period of terrible crisis, but he survived it and devoted himself entirely to his literary and editorial work. From that time on, even during the Second World War and the Resistance, and during his brief stays in Rome (1945–1946, 1950) and in Milan (1946), Pavese's life was essentially a private one, punctuated by the publication dates of his various works, which followed one another more and more rapidly, each one more nearly perfect than the last.

For a few years, right after the war, Pavese was a member of the Italian Communist party but soon became disillusioned and left it; politics never really interested him. Instead, as the director of the Einaudi cultural series, he made a noteworthy contribution to the diffusion in Italy of famous ethnological and critical works. In 1950 he won the Strega Prize for *The Beautiful Summer*. On August 27 of that year he committed suicide in a hotel room in Turin.[9]

Ever since, his death has troubled readers and critics, for as Fulvio Longobardi says, "It is up to the living to bury the dead: they sometimes return at night; . . . They ask our reason for going on: we know why they are dead, but we don't know why we are living."[10] We know, perhaps, why Pavese preferred death to life, and indeed much criticism has been devoted to understanding his inner motivations up to his fatal decision.[11] Yet "we don't know why we are living," and Pavese's work, which is more alive, tender, and disturbing than ever, keeps confronting us with fundamental questions about ourselves, about the world.

As Roland Barthes says, "Death has another importance: it denies the reality of the author's signature and makes the work a myth: anecdotal truth endeavors unsuccessfully to become symbolic truth. . . . By destroying the writer's signature, death establishes the truth of the work that is an enigma."[12] Certainly, Pavese's work helps us to understand the human reasons for his need to write, for his suffering (his "exemplary" suffering), and for his death;[13] yet his writing remains fundamentally enigmatic, rich in a symbolism, significance, and ambiguity that are no longer directly related to the author, and that, perhaps, more directly concern us.

My intention is to examine the "enigma" of Pavese's work, to reveal through a thematic and diachronic study the dialectic of prefiguration and memory contained in the poetic images, and to delineate the stages of Pavese's self-discovery in his search for an absolute. But this study, as it probes further, will try to ascertain the significance of Pavese's work for the understanding of ourselves in our time.[14]

1

Where Myths Are Forged

". . . the endless races of working people and farmers
and seamen."

WALT WHITMAN

"Avrei voluto sentirmi scabro ed essenziale
siccome i ciottoli che tu volvi. . . ."

EUGENIO MONTALE

In his first book Pavese attempted to write a type of poetry
that would be "an expression of essential facts, rather than the
usual introspective abstraction"; moreover, he attempted to
write a "narrative" poetry that would be "objective" and
therefore "epic"—not an easy undertaking, as we shall see.[1]
Objectivity implies both an extension of interest beyond the
self to include environment and social structure, factors nor-
mally excluded from the aristocratic ivory tower of poetry;
and a wealth and immediacy of subjects that contrast sharply
with the essentiality of poetry. Furthermore, epic poetry is
concerned with facts not problems. Much later Pavese wrote
in reference to his early work and to the cultural atmosphere
in which it was produced: "At a time when Italian prose was a
languid conversation with oneself and poetry a painful silence,
I was talking in prose and verse with peasants, laborers, sand-
blasters, prostitutes, prisoners, working women, youths."[2] Ac-

tually, the most obvious and immediate characteristic of *Work Is Wearying* is its extremely sensitive portrayal of a class of society that can hardly be called "poetic." It was a noble effort to show unity and coherence in a society and era so lacking in both qualities that their outstanding characteristic was the complete alienation of self from the world.

Pavese chooses to be, to use Malcolm Cowley's description of Walt Whitman, a "proletarian bard," and in his early poetry he celebrates the humble, difficult life of "that level of society which is usually called the people," among whom "laughter is more open, suffering more acute, and speech more sincere."[3] But since Pavese, like Whitman, is also an idler, "in the sense that all poets are idlers,"[4] there are innumerable picturesque figures in *Work Is Wearying* that serve as counterpoint to the workers: the old tramp, the drunken old lady, the boy who runs away from home, the ragamuffin, the idiot, the beggar, the street musicians; in them we savor the atmosphere of inns and dives, of vagrancy, of idle conversations that last till dawn, "before the cock crows." The title *Work Is Wearying* suggests in fact both *homo laborans* and *homo ludens*, and foreshadows a whole group of themes that Pavese later explored more deeply.

But it would be wiser to go beyond such a dichotomy and examine more thoroughly the themes and meaning of *Work Is Wearying*. In his appendix, "The Poet's Job," Pavese himself tells us of the experiences that carried him from "a lyricism which was somewhere between emotional release and a further probing" of the early attempts of his youth "to the clear, calm narrative" of "Southern Seas," and from there to the more complex "fantastic relating" of images, "which was the subject matter of that narrative" and in which was to be found "his personal perception of reality."[5] Later, in another appendix, "Concerning Certain Poems Not Yet Written," he will

re-examine the whole work and find an order and structure in
it, and treat it therefore as a *canzoniere*, explaining its meaning
"as the adventure of an adolescent who is proud of his countryside and imagines the city to be the same, but finds loneliness there and turns to sex and passion for comfort. This
merely uproots him and increases the distance between him
and both country and city, driving him into a more tragic
solitude, which is the end of adolescence."[6] In even more
peremptory tones he writes in his diary: "This is one of the
many interpretations of the poem. The village becomes the
city, nature becomes human life, the boy becomes a man."[7]
We will follow the path indicated by Pavese and, accepting it
as a first working hypothesis, will examine the poems of *Work
Is Wearying* from a thematic point of view.

The solitude of which he speaks is to be found everywhere
in his work, either explicitly or as a psychological and environmental premise. Explicitly, it appears as early as "Southern
Seas": "One of our ancestors must have been truly alone
. . . / to have taught his family such silence." The theme is
picked up again in "Ancestors"[8] and transferred from the
ancestral world to that of love. "Betrayal" begins with the
affirmation "This morning I am no longer alone"; "Deola's
Thoughts" ends with the ambition "To be alone, if she
wants, / in the morning, sitting in a café. Not to look for
anyone." The same themes—immobility and silence—recur
and intermingle throughout "Mania for Solitude" as a corollary to the character's solitude; and in the poem "Work Is
Wearying" we find the agonizing cry "Is it worth being
alone, if one becomes more and more lonely?" The doubt
becomes a certainty in "Deola's Return": "We are frightened
of being alone. But we want to be alone." In "Habits" a friend
appears whose "greatest enjoyment was once to be alone" but
who now "would like a home / which was perhaps more dear

to him." And finally the sentence "Man, who is alone . . ." appears insistently throughout many of the poems.[9]

Solitude is implicit, on the other hand, in the descriptions, no matter how brief, of the city. The city will become very important inasmuch as in Pavese's work there are attempts, from the very beginning, to escape isolation through love and political engagement, in order to communicate and to mature. When such efforts at integration fail, one is left in even greater isolation, which in the poems leads to disgust and eventually suicide. Similarly the early poetry of Pavese's youth ("premises which throw light on all that comes later") acquires a special importance—"those basic arguments of a hypothetical and ever new tomorrow," which "remain the true, the least debatable and speculative," as Emanuelli says in his introduction to some of the unedited works of Pavese.[10]

The empty haunting perspectives of lampposts appear regularly in the descriptions of the city in the early youthful poems, for example, February 1, 1929:

> White lights, along dizzying avenues,
> wind into the distance, without a sound
> without a living creature.

And March 30, 1929, as a direct prelude to the poem at the beginning of *Work Is Wearying:*

> Under the silence of enormous lights
>
> . . . . .
> the crowd shuffled
> to and fro over us.

Similarly in "Southern Seas":

> The city has taught me endless fears:
> a crowd, a street has made me tremble,
> sometimes even a thought glimpsed on a face.

I can still feel the scornful light in my eyes
of the thousands of street lamps over the endless shuffling.

These descriptions either are set against an evanescent background of mist, as in "Landscape VI,"[11] or they form the
setting for hard work ("Discipline") and the distractions of
pleasure ("Scorched Lands")—the poles of Pavese's inspiration. Thus, the cafés, avenues, and squares of Turin provide
the background first of all for sad, youthful, or mercenary
love affairs ("Deola's Thoughts" and "The Country
Whore"): then for more and more passionate and lyrical love
("Later" and "A Memory"). In its last stages this love develops into the theme of a masculine sense of responsibility toward one's children, as in "Fatherhood" and "Motherhood"
—a tragic theme for Pavese because of the family he never
had, the family that stands between the self and others, between the individual and society, and is therefore the link
with the more direct political and social experience of his
other poetry. It reminds us of Masino, the unemployed workman of "Idleness"; of the released prisoner who "tomorrow
will resume / work with a few companions" in "Green
Wood"; of those killed and imprisoned by the Fascists in "A
Generation" and "Revolt"; and of "the unsmiling buildings,"
"the hunger of others" measured "against one's toils," and the
"injustices everywhere" in "Smoking Cheap Cigarettes."[12]

The failure he experiences in love and politics, on the other
hand, is reflected in the desolation of poems such as "Deola's
Return," in which disgust with life is blended with sad resignation in the face of destiny (another of Pavese's themes):

We shall try
to get up in the morning and put away the disgust
of the night, to go out with the same old step as before. . . .
We shall look at the passers-by with the dead smile

of one who has been beaten down, but does not hate or cry
out
because he knows that for a long time past fate
—all that has been or will be—is in the blood,
in the murmur of the blood.

"The Star" expresses with even more bitterness and clarity the
disgust with life that each new day brings:

There is nothing more bitter than the dawn of a day
in which nothing will happen. There is nothing more bitter
than uselessness. In the sky hangs wearily
a greenish star, surprised by the dawn.

Finally, "Agony" and "Paradise On the Rooftops" witness
the ultimate result of failure to communicate with others: the
first poem transcribes the thoughts of an attempted suicide,
interspersed with images of the morning and of colors felt like
a keen pain;[13] the second is the description of a suicide that
took place in a room:

There is no need to leave the bed.
Only dawn will enter the empty room. . . .
Memories become lumps of shadow
flattened like embers
in the hearth. Memory will be the flame
which only yesterday was blazing in eyes now
extinguished.

These poems are later echoed in his novel *Among Women
Only:* Rosetta is filled with disgust one morning and tries to
commit suicide but is saved; later she succeeds in committing
suicide under the same circumstances as in "Paradise On the
Rooftops," circumstances that are identical with those of
Pavese's death. (We are reminded, too, of "The Cats Will
Know," one of his last poems, in which the cats are messen-
gers of death.) Thus the tragic circle of solitude is closed.

In the same statement that was the starting point of our analysis, Pavese spoke of an "adolescent . . . proud of his countryside," thus pointing out and emphasizing two other themes of *Work Is Wearying* (and the works that followed): infancy-adolescence and countryside-nature, both of which are important because they define temporally and spatially the spiritual and imaginative world of Pavese. These two themes evoke on the one hand Pascoli and on the other Pirandello and play a large part in characterizing the decadent Italian culture in which Pavese found himself. The first theme, which appears in "Southern Seas," is based on the mediation (in Girardian terms) between the young boy and his cousin: the young boy is imaginative and a dreamer, eager for the exotic, and his admiration for his cousin begins when the latter sends him a card "with a huge greenish stamp of ships in a harbor":

> Everyone was astonished
> but the boy, now grown up, explained eagerly
> that the card came from an island called Tasmania
> surrounded by a deep blue sea, seething with sharks,
> in the Pacific, to the south of Australia.[14]

He continues in his usual contemplative manner; "thoughts and dreams" are the fabric of his life. The cousin is seen as "a giant dressed in white / moving calmly, sun-tanned face, / taciturn," and is the incarnation of the myth of return, which becomes more and more obviously a search for oneself (though not necessarily a discovery of oneself); this search marks the beginning and end of all Pavese's work:

> . . . Life should be lived
> far from home; you make your fortune and enjoy yourself
> and then, when you return home, like me at forty,
> you find everything new. The Langhe hills do not disappear.

It is perhaps worth stressing that "Southern Seas" contains other characteristic themes too, such as a certain superior attitude toward women (who are less "serious" than men), a habit of wandering over the hilltops, and a taste for olfactory perceptions, rather than audial or visual, in the mellow landscapes:

> A smell of earth and wind envelops us in the dark,
> lights in the distance: farms, cars,
> which can scarcely be heard; and I think of the strength
> which this man has given me, snatching it from the sea,
> from distant lands, from the silence which endures.

Aspects of infancy-adolescence appear in other poems: the relationship between adult and boy is the subject of "The Boy in Me"; "the idea of a distant land," the fascination of the exotic, is at the core of "Mediterranean"; the similarity and differences between city and country crowd a boy's memory and perceptions in "Poetics" ("some remain boys / too long"). One last aspect, in many respects the most important, is expressed in "Myth," in which the passage of time and awareness of death form a shadowy counterpoint to the unconscious, triumphant happiness of the young boy, in the magically luminous lines:

> There will come a day when the young god becomes a man,
> effortlessly, with that dead smile of the man
> who now understands. . . .
> Some morning one wakes up and the summer is dead,
> yet one can still see the tumultuous splendors
> of yesterday, and in one's ears is the roar of the sun
> turned to blood. The color of the world has changed.
> The mountain no longer touches the sky. . . .
> The huge sun has gone, and the smell of the earth
> and the open road, colored with people
> who knew nothing of death. No one dies in summer.

If anyone disappeared, there was always the young god
who lived for everyone and knew nothing of death.
Sadness was like the shadow of a cloud above him.
The earth was amazed at his step.

Here summer is very closely and symbolically linked with
infancy, and even phrases such as "The mountain no longer
touches the sky" contain a symbolism that far exceeds the
image-story, and echo many lines of *Work Is Wearying*,
where infancy and the hills are coupled as a lyrical *leit motif*.
In similar expressions the hills of infancy, of the myth, become
the hills of maturity and of death, the hills which span the
whole arc of Pavese's work.[15]

The countryside, therefore, with the recurrent image of the
hills (still mainly descriptive, yet evocative), is the chosen
background for the development and intensification of
Pavese's experience of the world. He is searching somewhat
confusedly in the countryside and in nature for a principle of
self-identification, with the raw spontaneity of nakedness in
"Dina's Thoughts" and "Atavism," and more discreetly in
"Landscape V":

Do they have meaning, those great slopes thrust into the sky
like houses in a big city? They are naked. . . .
To cover houses and stones with greenery
—so that the sky will make some sense—black, black
roots must be thrust deep into the darkness. . . .
Bodies too are made of black veins.[16]

Pavese is fascinated by the violence that he sees in the
countryside, and which has a mysterious bond with the violence of man. Both have a common root (a frequent theme in
mythology) and develop along similar lines, one in the poetry
of myth and the other in that of destiny, from *The Harvesters*
to *Dialogues with Leucò*.

Certainly one of the most interesting poems for the present discussion is "The Goat-God,"[17] in which for the boy "who comes in the summer . . . the countryside is a land of green mysteries": the she-goats and snakes "with their sinuous trace along the ground," the bitches and girls, all share in common "the green mysteries" of sex that attract the wild goat, the big dogs, and the peasants. These have a strength both vital and destructive; for animals it can all be reduced to instinct and release, but for man the release comes from work, a way of controlling chaos, of possessing nature and its mystery. Let us look at the description of the totally animal orgy beneath a motionless, emblematic moon, a fantastic and Dionysian orgy enveloped in nocturnal howls:

> And the bitches are barking beneath the moon,
> because they have heard the he-goat leaping
> over the hilltops and have sniffed the scent of blood.
> And the animals stir in their stalls.
> Only the larger and stronger dogs bite at their ropes,
> and one of them breaks free and runs after the goat,
> who sprinkles him and intoxicates him with a blood redder
> than fire,
> and then they all dance, balanced on their hind legs and
> baying at the moon.[18]

Man acts as counterpoint; admittedly he too has violence but, what is more important, he has love, joy, and his work, so that he dares to answer the moon with his little bonfire. The last two lines conclude precisely with a judgment on the creative and directing function of work, which sets the seal on the preceding images:

> They make their women pregnant, the peasants, and go on
> working.
> They go out walking day and night and are not afraid
> of digging in the moonlight or of burning

weeds in the dark. This is why the land
is so beautifully green, and when plowed, has the color
at dawn, of sunburnt faces. They harvest,
they eat, they sing; they husk the corn,
they dance and drink. Young girls are heard laughing
when someone remembers the he-goat. Up there, on the
                                        hilltops,
in the woods, among the stony crags, the peasants saw him
looking for the she-goat and butting against the tree trunks.
Because, if an animal doesn't know how to work
and exists only for siring, it likes to destroy.

Work in the fields in the dazzling, stifling sun is the theme,
too, of "The Widow's Son":

The sun beats down on the farmyard and on reddened,
blinking eyes. A crimson cloud veils the stubble
sown with yellow sheaves. . . .
Women run impatiently through the deserted rooms
ordered about by a nod and by eyes, which
follow them solitary from the bed. The big window
which encompasses the hills and the lines of trees and the
                                        wide sky,
sends back the faint hum from everyone working.

As for the violence of nature, it reminds us of the surrealist
atmosphere in "The Sad Dinner," which is both soft and
dazzling: "More diffuse than the moonlike yellow, which has
a horror / of penetrating the woods, is this tireless longing, /
the feel and taste of things that harass the dead. / Other times,
the rain torments them in the ground. / " Or else we think
of the dead husband "with his skull cracked by the sun" in
"August Moon," where again blood, shadow, earth, and moon
are woven into a poetry of fear, grief, and horror:

            The moon rises and throws a slight shadow
under the contorted branches. The woman in the shade

leers in terror at the huge face of blood
that coagulates and floods every fold of the hills . . .
     and already the shadow of the tree
seems on the point of shrinking and being swallowed up, too.
She rushes out, in the horror of the moonlight,
and the murmur of the breeze on the rocks follows her
and a slender outline that gnaws at her feet,
and the pain in her womb. She bends and steps back into the
                             shade
and throws herself on the rocks and bites her lips.
Beneath her, the dark earth is bathed in blood.

In "Jealousy (2)" on the other hand, we have man's violence:
a woman is killed by her husband, who wanted to leave a
mark on her, but his grip "extinguished her smile." Finally,
the theme of violence is resumed in at least one of the poems
of *Earth and Death* and is a prelude to Pavese's pages on the
Resistance in his last novels:

> You don't know the hills
> where blood has been shed.
> Everyone fled,
> everyone threw away
> weapons and name. A woman
> watched our flight.
> Only one of us
> stopped with clenched fist,
> gazed at the empty sky,
> bowed his head and died
> beneath the wall, in silence.
> Now he is a bloodstained heap of clothes
> and a name. A woman
> is waiting for us in the hills.

But Pavese also found an indescribable sweetness in the
countryside, of both nature and humanity, as we can see in

the contemplative landscapes, in the scents and flavors, in the sounds that reflect so many memories and human presences. Typical of this is "The Night," where it is hard to say whether the echoes one detects are more of Leopardi (in the broad serenity of the landscape) or of Montale (in the powerful and sweet contemplation of memory):

> But the windy night, the limpid night
> only lightly touched by memory, is remote,
> is a memory. . . .
>   Through the empty window
> the boy gazed at the night on hills
> fresh and dark, and was amazed to see them heaped together:
> lovely and limpid immobility. Between the leaves
> rustling in the dark, the hills appeared
> where all the things of daytime, the slopes,
> the plants, and the vines were precise and dead
> and life was of a different kind, of wind, of sky,
> and leaves and nothingness.

We have already mentioned the "smell of earth and wind" in "Southern Seas." The same sort of perceptions are also found in "A Season":

> On windy evenings a smell of moisture is scattered in the air
> the smell a young body has
> under too many clothes. A smell of sodden ground
> which returns with every March.[19]

Or we see the memory-taste transference in "Landscape VIII": "A summer of voices. Every face contains / the taste of a fruit that is overripe." And in "Summer (2)": "There is the same taste / in your eyes and in the warm memory." Again we turn to the lovely "Canzone" in which country and city, nature and man, are inseparable aspects of one world, of a single reality:

The clouds are tied to the earth and to the wind. . . .
Even the trees suffer and die beneath the haze;
man bleeds and dies—but sings of joy
between earth and sky, the great wonder
of city and forests.

Images of nature grow into a human identification, as in that
of the loved woman in "Nocturne":

You are like a cloud
Glimpsed between branches. There shines in your eyes
the strangeness of a sky that is not yours.
The hill of earth and leaves cuts off
with its black mass your lively glance,
your mouth is the outline of a gentle hollow
among the distant slopes. . . .
But you live elsewhere.
Your tender blood is made elsewhere.
The words that you say have nothing to do
with the harsh sadness of this sky.
You are just a gentle white cloud
that one night became entangled in these ancient branches.[20]

Finally, even the sound of a voice is subsumed to the natural
surroundings (as in "The House"):

Alone man listens to the ancient voice
to which his ancestors listened in former times,
clear and thoughtful, a voice which like the green
of the ponds and hills deepens with evening. . . .
The secretive sound of a woman's voice
on her doorstep at dusk.

These quotations from Pavese's poetry suggest the identification of nature with woman that becomes the fundamental
theme of the collection *Earth and Death*—an identification
whereby nature's mystery is equated with the difficulty of

understanding women and of attempting communication, a difficulty breeding fear and anxiety. It has been said that Pavese's poetry developed and changed from an objective vein to lyrical contemplation:[21] this is particularly true if we consider the two volumes *Work Is Wearying* and *Earth and Death* quantitatively; but perhaps it would be more accurate to say that both strains coexist from the beginning of the first volume, even if the lyricism is submerged in it and definitely limited to the objective and "social" intent of the "proletarian bard." It is only later that he will show himself as poet pure and simple. The dry lyricism of *Work Is Wearying* will be resumed in *Earth and Death*, and finally, in *Death Will Come and Its Eyes Will Be Yours*, with a fundamental difference, however: the story-image will become symbol-image. "It is a question of describing—whether directly or imaginatively is unimportant—a reality which is not naturalistic but symbolic," Pavese wrote at the end of "Concerning Certain Poems Not Yet Written," the reflections that he felt "concluded . . . the search in *Work Is Wearying*."[22] As a partial rebuttal of Pavese's statement, it would be worth rereading one of his first poems, "Grappa in September," in which the free transmutation of images—morning, mist, water, tobacco, grappa, air, fruit, women—describes a naturalistic reality and hides a symbolic reality of maturity, "ripeness":

> Mornings go by clear and deserted
> on the banks of the river, which becomes foggy at dawn
> and grows dark green, waiting for the sun.
> The tobacco, which is sold in the last house,
> still damp, at the edge of the fields, is almost
> black in color and has a juicy taste: it has a bluish vapor.
> They also have grappa, the color of water. . . .
> Only women are to be seen at this hour. The women do not
>   smoke

and they do not drink; they only stand in the sun
and feel it warm on their backs, as if they were fruit.
The air, raw with mist, is only sipped
like grappa; everything gives off an aroma. . . .
And the tobacco is tinged with grappa. Thus the women
are not the only ones to enjoy the morning.

Nevertheless, Pavese's ideas (especially on metrical form)
are certainly valid for most of the poems of *Work Is Wearying*.[23] Typical of this recurring idea of naturalism-symbolism
are the poetical descriptions of the woman in "Encounter"
(*Work Is Wearying*) and of the woman in "In the Morning
You Always Come Back" (*Death Will Come and Its Eyes
Will Be Yours*):

> Among the women she is very young:
> As I think of her, a distant memory surprises me
> of childhood spent among these hills,
> so young is she. She is like the morning. In her eyes there
> beckon to me
> all the distant skies of those far-off mornings. . . .
> I have created her from the depths of all the things
> that are dearest to me, and I cannot understand her.

> The breath of dawn
> at the end of empty streets
> is in your mouth.
> Your eyes the grey light,
> sweet drops of dawn
> on the dark hills. . . .
> You are the light and the morning.[24]

Another of Pavese's motifs is woman-earth, sometimes, as in
Work Is Wearying, showing a similarity between woman and
earth, sometimes, as in *Earth and Death*, identifying one with
the other.[25] For example, in "Night Pleasures" the woman's

body has "the heat of the earth," "the smell of the earth"; in
"Jealousy" the old man likes to uncover his woman the way
"he breaks open the earth." The parallel is continued in some
of the poems of *Earth and Death:* "sure / as the earth,
dark / as the earth," and "Like rock and grass / like earth you
are secretive." But suddenly we are aware of a different
streak, an identification achieved through images that seem to
put the best of D'Annunzio (especially "Rain on the Pine-
wood") to the service of Pavese's tormented symbolism: "the
olives of your glance" and "You always have secret
eyes / running water glimpsed between the brambles." We
gradually reach a complete identification of woman with
nature:

> You too are a hill
> and a stony path
> and a game among the canes,
> and you know the vineyard
> that is silent at night.
> You speak no words. . . .
> You are the earth and the vineyard.
> A blazing silence
> will burn the countryside
> like bonfires in the evening.

It is an identification rich in poetic motifs, which recur again
later, such as the hill, the vineyard, the bonfire, and most of all
silence—perhaps most meaningful of all because it springs
from darkness and on the one hand emphasizes the impossibility of communicating, of understanding, of possessing and, on
the other hand, heralds death, the death of the poet:

> You are the earth and you are death.
> Your season is darkness
> and silence. . . .
> you are only pain;

you have it in your eyes and in your blood,
but you have no feeling. You live
as a stone lives,
you endure as the earth endures. . . .
They are rings on the water.
You let them disappear.
You are the earth and you are death.

Thus, not only earth, silence, and darkness but also woman's
eyes and breath and blood have a deep poetic resonance; if we
look at yet another poem, in *Death Will Come and Its Eyes
Will Be Yours* we shall see the poetic counterpoint of Endymion's tale in *Dialogues with Leucò*:

. . . as a little girl you played
under a different sky,
you have the silence of it in your eyes,
a cloud which gushes forth
like a spring from the depths. . . .
                              Like
grass moving in the wind
you shiver and laugh,
but you, you are earth.
You are a ferocious root.
You are the waiting earth.

It is in the most tormented poem that the preceding motifs are
brought together:

Death will come and its eyes will be yours—
this death that keeps us company
from morning to night, wakeful,
deaf, like an old regret
or an absurd vice. Your eyes
will be a meaningless word,
a stifled cry, a silence. . . .
                    O fond hope,

on that day we too shall know
that you are life and you are nothingness.

Notice that in these later poems eyes and silence have become very closely connected (it is in fact the silence of
death); and notice the almost Leopardian invocation to the
"fond hope," which has no future, because it is vain: "You are
life and you are nothingness." For this reason, in "You, Wind
of March," Pavese will write: "Hope makes you writhe"; the
violent paroxysm of the verb attempts to express all the anguish and desperation "of him who can no longer hope for
you." Even hope is a prelude to death: dying will be "like
seeing a dead face / reappear in the mirror, / like listening to
lips which have closed. / Silent we shall descend into the
abyss." Thus is silence sealed off. It is in the eyes of another
that Pavese sees death *within* himself, precisely because "one
does not kill oneself for love of *a* woman, but because love—
any love—reveals us in our nakedness, our misery, our vulnerability, our nothingness."[26] For this reason we must go as far
back as *Work Is Wearying* to find the poetic consequence of
the tragic impossibility of breaking the barrier of self, the
impenetrable essence of the "other"—an impenetrability revealed in the very appearance of the loved one, as in "A
Memory":

There isn't a man who manages to leave a mark
on this woman. Whatever has happened fades like a dream
gone in a morning, and only she remains. . . .
                    All alone she smiles
a most ambiguous smile as she walks along the street.

We find that same smile again in "The Cats Will Know":

The cats will know,
face of spring,
and the gentle rain,

the hyacinth-colored dawn
that tears apart the heart
of someone who no longer hopes for you,
are the sad smile
you are smiling all alone.

In *Dialogues with Leucò*, too, there is someone who "is smiling all alone" and who brings death—Aphrodite, the goddess of love, "she who came from the sea," as he writes in two of the poems of *Earth and Death:* "You Always Come from the Sea" and "You Have a Face of Sculptured Stone." Notice that the despair caused by such a smile is accompanied by the heart-rending sweetness of the one who smiles, expressed by poetic motifs such as the woman's step and the rain in "Later": "Her secret body walks through the street at this hour / with her step, but a gentler rhythm; the rain / comes down with that same beat, light and weary." And the same theme is repeated more lyrically and passionately in "The Cats Will Know":

Still the rain will fall
on your gentle streets,
a light rain
like a breath of air or a footstep.
The breeze and the dawn
will blossom gently again
as under your footstep
when you return home.
Among the flowers and the window sills
the cats will know.

The theme of the March wind appears in "A Season": "Clothes become wind on March evenings / and cling and flutter around the women going by." This theme is taken up again in "From C. to C.": "You . . . wind of March," which is also the title of one of the following poems, tensed between brilliance and pain:

> You are life and you are death.
> You came in March
> over the naked earth—
> your shudder lasts.
> Blood of spring
> —anemone or cloud—
> your light footstep
> has violated the earth.
> Pain begins again. . . .
> Hope makes you writhe
> and awaits you and calls you.
> You are life and you are death.
> Your step is light.[27]

But there can be no doubt that, of life and death, it is death which love brings to Pavese, because love reveals death within him. A final example is to be seen in the last fragile lines of "Last Blues, to be Read Some Day," where there is, as it were, an echo of a distant thought written in his diary by a man "who has *no idea how to live*":

> Some one has died
> long time ago—
> some one who tried
> but didn't know.[28]

The analysis of *Work Is Wearying* has brought us far beyond the initial period of Pavese's work, allowing us to identify basic themes that are present right to the end of his work, and showing us some of the lines of development: first the "narrative poetry" with its long lines, its powerful objectivity, the proletarian epic with its coarse and picturesque characters; side by side with it, moments of "imaginative poetry," still with the long lines of Whitman and the Italian crepuscular poetry, expressing a lyrical and virile subjectivity. Later, on the one hand we have seen a very personal, lyrical-symbolical poetry, luminous and painful, and on the other we shall see the whole narrative creation in which Pavese's view of the world is expressed in all its complexity and nuances.

It seems almost as if Pavese understood the impossibility of creating an epic for which he lacked "both the strength and temperament,"[29] or, above all, for which the necessary historical and cultural conditions were missing. The transition from *Work Is Wearying* to narrative can perhaps be most clearly explained by applying György Lukàcs' philosophic and literary theory of the novel, as interpreted by Lucien Goldmann:

Between, on the one hand, epic, which expresses the correspondence of the soul and the world, of interiority and exteriority, i.e., that universe in which answers are given even before questions can be formulated, in which there are dangers but no mortal perils, shadows but not darkness; in which meaning is implicit in every aspect of life and need only be formulated, not discovered: and, on the other hand, tragedy, which is the literary form of pure essence, of solitude and the negation of any life at all, there stands the novel, the dialectic form of the epic, of solitude within the community, of hope without future, of presence in absence. To use an image of Lukàcs', between the epic which is the literature of infancy and youth, and tragedy which is the literature of consciousness and death, the novel is the literary form for virile maturity.[30]

These words seem to have been composed expressly for Pavese, especially the final reference to "virile maturity," the aspiration of all his life and work. In the course of an analysis of Pavese's novels, the following chapters will examine the themes that are already to be found, "sometimes hinted at and sometimes expressed in images," in *Work Is Wearying*, thus encompassing the monolithic unity of which Pavese writes:

I feel sure of the fundamental and lasting unity of all that I have written or will write—and I am not talking of an autobio-graphical unity or unity of taste, which are trivialities—but of a unity of themes, vital interests, the monotonous obstinacy of one who feels sure that the very first day he has found the true world, the eternal world, and can do nothing but revolve around the great monolith and take off chunks and work at them and study them in every possible light.[31]

2

Solitude

"Naked and alone we came into exile."

THOMAS WOLFE

From his very first story, "Land of Exile," Pavese introduces characters who reflect a certain world view, a *condition
humaine*. The narrator of "Land of Exile" begins: "When a
sudden, unexpected turn of events in my job [hurled] me
down to the far south of Italy, I felt very [lonely]."[1]

The totally subjective affirmation of the narrator-character,
rendered faintly dramatic by the verb "hurled," which would
seem to contain an existential dismay, corresponds from the
outset to the spiritual condition of the narrator-author;
Pavese's diary and letters bear ample witness to the tragic
importance of solitude in his own world view, not to mention
in his own life. We have only to quote a peremptory sentence
from his diary: "Solitude every man knows, cold and immutable," and the letter Pavese sent to "the lady with the harsh
voice" when he was in confinement at Brancaleone, in the
south of Italy: "Every morning, just like the first day, the
sting of solitude wakes me up."[2] The preceding quotations
should not be regarded merely as an interesting biographical
reference but as evidence of Pavese's treatment of solitude,
even in the most intimate and private matters, as an inescapa-

ble *condition humaine.* His characters, therefore, become emblematic, universal.

The narrator of "Land of Exile" goes on to say that the security of having someone thinking of him in the "great world" gave him a "tacit detachment from everything" around him, "so that my very boredom encouraged me to indulge in daydreams," while the people around him were "an unknown race, living its own life on its own land," thus emphasizing, with the repeated possessives, the impossibility of any kind of participation rather than a wish to be excluded. In fact, when Otino asks: "Are you a prisoner, too?" the narrator answers: "We all are, here, more or less";[3] and he emphasizes this by attributing to everybody his own sense of the temporary nature of things, which derives from his solitude:

In this respect, certainly, it was an unfriendly place. Even the men seemed aloof, not identifying themselves with the village or their street, as if they did not belong there. They seemed to lack roots, and their persistent vivacity betrayed a physical uneasiness.

Even though later he feels he is no longer alone, because he and Otino have sorrow in common, the narrator experiences "distress" and "remorse," which, instead of being transformed into active solidarity, only aggravate his desire to go away, i.e., to leave Otino alone with his grief over his wife's unfaithfulness.[4] Otino says of her:

Even when I was there I never knew how to take her from one day to the next. She never let me know what was in the back of her mind. Not that she bossed me about, but she kept on and on. The only time I had any peace was when I saw her crying.

Otino's words are very important for a full understanding of Stefano's psychology in *The Political Prisoner*, especially as the source of the fear that provokes and conditions his every attitude and feeling.

Even if the final sentence of the story—"I moved on to follow my destiny"—seems somewhat rhetorical and ingenuous, yet it has a foreboding flavor, since the last view the narrator carries with him is of the bare hill. Finally, we are already aware of the unusual combination of a first person narrative, melancholy and evocative, with a rapid, broken, and interrupted dialogue: "a rhythm of alternating prose passages and dialogue"[5] by which the dialogue emphasizes and sustains the narrative, which subsides into "decadent" impressions: "The sun was still beating down, giving a red glow to the drab dejection of the thick plants and the nearby houses" or the narrator's impressions of the butcher's shop where the prostitute Concetta is housed in secret: "As I went through the dark shop I caught sight of two disembowelled kids hanging from hooks over a tub." Here what impresses us most is not the Rembrandt hues of the picture, but the feeling of physical disgust they arouse; the same disgust prevents Stefano, in *The Political Prisoner*, from taking the prostitute Annetta and teaches him renunciation.

Again, in the second of the short stories, "The Evil Eye," the imaginative center of the story is the idea and portrayal of solitude, the solitude of the errand boy Berto, a character like Melville's Bartleby, who obsesses everybody with his presence, who torments colleagues and superiors with the anguish and the "dumb nakedness" of his huge eyes, "strangely deep-set, glinting beneath their lids like a well."

I was often conscious of his eyes on my back. When I turned to meet them they would give me a painful smile. This grimace of his frightened me, gave me a feeling of almost physical discomfort. Always, below the surface, there was the lurking anguish, the pitiful loneliness of his eyes. What must the colors of the world look like, seen through those eyes?

Later on the question gets a terrifying answer:

Towards morning I remembered with a shock just where I had seen an agonized look like his. It was on my own face, reflected in a windowpane, when I was a boy and my father had chased me out of the house, yelling at me and [kicking me]. . . . Of all the thoughts that ran through my mind at that time, the most cheerful one was to throw myself in the river. Berto had exactly the look of a man who had done so. . . .

Berto does not have the evil eye: he is the incarnation of solitude and death that everyone carries within him, buried or submerged, and for that reason he will continue to "have that look" even if the manager of the bookstore yells at him to stop it and fires him.[6]

The third short story, "Wedding Trip," does in fact repeat almost *verbatim* the thoughts inspired by the eyes of Berto the errand boy: "that we should jump into the river together. Such ideas didn't bother me—I was used to them—" thus creating a brilliant link with that other theme, the impossibility of communication among human beings, and of a willed solitude.[7] The story, even in its jeering and cruel title, therefore, picks up the thread both of Otino's wife in "Land of Exile" and of Stefano's attitudes in *The Political Prisoner* and examines their various aspects more deeply. For the moment it is sufficient to mention the principal ones. First there is the contrast between reality and fantasy (or between action and contemplation), fundamental because it is also at the root of the protagonist's solitude: "Now that I, shattered and full of remorse, have learned how foolish it is to reject reality for the sake of idle fancies, how presumptuous to receive when one has nothing to give in return, now—Cilia is dead." But meanwhile, the following is almost an echo of "Southern Seas": "For me, good fortune has always meant adventure in far-away places—a liner crossing the ocean, arrival at some exotic port, the clang of metal, shrill, foreign voices—I dreamed of it all the time." Or yet again: "Now, all I wanted—and how I wanted it—was to look around and get to know in my heart of hearts this unknown city. That was precisely why I had come."

The second aspect, no less fundamental, is the intentional and egoistic way in which he cuts off every human contact:

I always did everything like a fool, a man in a dream, and I did not realize the sort of man I was until the end, when even remorse was useless. Now I can glimpse the truth. I became so engrossed in solitude that it deadens all my sense of human relationships and makes me incapable of tolerating or responding to any tenderness.

In fact, after describing his wife Cilia's smile and happiness, the narrator explains his own reactions: "I felt a twinge of jealousy at this sign of a happiness I did not always share. 'She's married me and she's enjoying it,' I thought."

Finally we should note that in this story the transition between dialogue and narrative is more balanced and harmonious than in "Land of Exile," for the dialogue actually reflects the inadequacy of the few words exchanged between Cilia and Giorgio, while the first-person narration is an intimate and indispensable key to those words and hence is highly successful in its descriptive and psychological tone: for example: "I passed many evenings thus, alone in the room, waiting for Cilia, pacing up and down or lying on the bed, absorbed in that silent emptiness as the dusk slowly deepened into dark." Or:

Such thoughts entrapped me whenever the day was foggy and the sun looked grey. If, on the other hand, there was a lovely day when the air was clear and the sun blazed down on my head, or a perfume in the wind enfolded and enraptured me, I would linger in the streets, wishing that I still lived alone, free to stroll around till midnight and get a meal of some sort at the pub on the corner of the street. I had always been a lonely man, and it seemed to me to count for a great deal that I was not unfaithful to Cilia.

The theme of solitary wandering from tavern to tavern (developed in a quick dialogue in the story "Friends" and elsewhere) will be continued with nuances and variations, against both city and country background, throughout Pavese's work, providing a stream of poetic images that reveal one constant characteristic in many different characters.

The subject of the story "Wedding Trip" is taken up again in "Suicides," but the search for solitude in the latter has far more tragic results than in the earlier story.[8] "Suicides" deals with a couple, of which the man "preferred to be alone"; he, as narrator, explains his solitude, which appears mainly in a feeling of alienation from the world around him:

There are days when the city where I live wakes in the morning with a strange look. The people in the streets, the traffic, the trees —everything seems familiar but as if seen with new eyes, like those moments when one looks in the mirror and asks oneself: "Who is that man?" For me, those are the only days in the whole year that I really enjoy. . . . I am not made for storms and struggles: and if, on certain mornings, I go down full of zest for a walk around the streets, and my [stride] seems a [challenge], I repeat that I ask nothing more of life than being allowed to watch [it].

To *watch* life without taking part in it. Why? Here is the answer:

I have no great vices, (unless, indeed, my timorous shrinking from life's battle and my quest for serenity in solitude are the worst vices of all), but nevertheless, I know how to be astute with myself and keep my self-control when I enjoy what little pleasure life allows me.[9]

. . . as for me, all I have ever done is to suffer from a vast, inept lack of confidence, and to react against other people, when I come into contact with them, with stupid cruelty.

And again: "So, having been treated unjustly, I revenged myself, not on the guilty one but on another woman, as happens in this world." We see annoyance and cruelty provoked by the presence of the unloved person:

I did not repulse her. When I got up, though, my head was aching. I felt irritated by Carlotta's air of happiness as she prepared coffee for me, humming to herself. . . . My bitterness [was not directed towards her, but towards] any restraint, any [enslavement] that our intimacy tended to create in me. Since I did not love her, it seemed to me monstrous that she should have even the slightest claim on me. There were days when it made me shudder to address her as an intimate friend, an equal. I felt degraded. What was this woman to me, that she should take my arm?

Hence, again there is fantasy:

After all that warmth and affection inside, the keen air waiting for me out of doors stimulated my blood; only I would have rather stayed by myself, smoking and thinking, conjuring up a very different awakening and a different companion.

The lucidity of these introspections is of great assistance in outlining Pavese's themes, which are less explicit in his longer novels, more submerged, more subdued than in his short stories, but, precisely because of this, the lucidity prevents the complete fusion of sentiment and imagery and detracts from the harmony of the narrative. In fact, this type of introspection, with its rational ideas, prevents the direct expression of a determined state of mind through poetic images that reflect it.

The theme of solitude is also found in the *divertissement* "*Si parva licet*," in which Pavese has these words spoken by Adam, first of the human race and therefore mythical archetype: "This forest is all Eve. . . . It gives me shade, it gives me shelter, it gives me food and fresh air, but no confidence. O Lord, I wonder if you understand what it means to be alone." Finally, the psychology of the prisoner is to be seen in the short story called "The Intruder":

That morning I saw myself as if enclosed in glass; no longer imprisoned by walls and bars but isolated in a void, a chill void that the world knows nothing about. This was the real punishment: that the world rejects a convict. What I longed for was not so much to be free, but that the world should come into my empty void and bring it color, give it warmth with words and gestures. Reading was not enough, my cellmate was right; what I needed was that someone, at least, in the world should think of me, send me a message now and then; not that everything should vanish in that dreadful, unnatural nothingness.

With his solitude, his isolation, his imprisonment, his seeming to be "enclosed in glass," the prisoner of "The Intruder" is a direct forerunner of *The Political Prisoner*, the first novel in which Pavese develops his world view (as he begins to form it through his characters) in the abundant and varied motifs.

Stefano knew that there was nothing unusual about the place; the inhabitants lived their daily lives, the earth produced; there, as on any other coast, the sea was the sea. Stefano felt happy by the sea; on first arriving he imagined it as the fourth wall of his prison, a huge wall of color and coolness behind which he would be free to move about and forget the prison cell. . . .

For some days Stefano contemplated the hedges of fig trees and the faded horizon as if they were strange realities; that they composed the invisible walls of his cell was the most natural part about them. . . . The arid fields, the vegetation, the sea with its changing moods, however, seemed strange to him at first. He could not take his eyes off them and they were continually in his mind. But as the memory of his real prison life faded, even these presences receded into the background.[10]

At the beginning of the novel the hero is a political prisoner who looks on the reality around him as something remote and strange: a combination of objects, scenes, persons and panorama, whose strangeness is much greater than that of new surroundings, never seen before, and so acquires a more universal, symbolic meaning.[11] Stefano is described in the middle of a large empty cell, rarefied space, in which a crystalline atmosphere isolates the objects around him even more by outlining their vitreous clarity. makes them more distinct, larger, and gives them a faintly obsessive strength. ("He could not take his eyes off them and they were continually in his mind.") It gradually wears away and dissolves in memory until eventually these objects are lost and become vague "presences" that form the "background" of Stefano's solitude. Stefano, however, accepts his condition passively, and his spiritual attitude is as limited by the "shutting-in of his horizon" as is his field of vision. In this connection we see the emblematic value of some of the descriptions:

Where the windows coincided—though they were usually closed —the onlooker from the road got the impression that the building was perforated and filled with sea. The luminous panel stood out clear and intense like a patch of sky seen from a prison window.

And again: "The low window opening on to the blue expanse of the sea had seemed to him the narrow, age-old window of the prison of this life."

Stefano, therefore, appears solitary, introspective, and dwarfed in a landscape without perspective, with its violent colors in daylight or darkness, always foreign to him:

The gloomy, cavelike entrances under the low doors, the dark faces, the reserve of the women even when they came out into the street to empty their earthenware pots made a contrast with the bright atmosphere outside that increased Stefano's feeling of isolation.

There is no connection or contact between Stefano and the world; in fact, just the opposite, he even feels a kind of hostility in the things around him, for they reflect his own solitude: "Sometimes it would be as far as the seashore, but this bathing naked and alone in the green Mediterranean depressed him and caused him to dress hurriedly in the already chilling air." Stefano's temporal situation also derives from his isolation; he is a character who does not live his *durée* but seems to be suspended in an atemporal limbo, monotonous and colorless, from which others are excluded:

Once more he felt a twinge of that physical loneliness that had never left him all day amid the festive throng and the strange sky above him. The whole day Stefano had been isolated as if outside time itself, pausing to gaze at the narrow streets open to the sky.

Or, as in the poem "Grappa in September": "The days were so long now that you only had to pause a moment and look around you to have the feeling of being isolated outside time altogether."

In reality it is Stefano who is excluded from the life of the others. Whatever contacts he has with the inhabitants of that tiny Southern town, casual or intimate, reflect the basic alienation that prevents Stefano from any simple, direct human participation and forces him to take refuge in memories, fantasy, futile desires, and moreover deprives him of the joy and pain of memory and concrete desire. See, for example, the conversation in the tavern: "They all exchanged glances, mollified or amused as the case might be, but Stefano felt the joke was beyond him and tried to weigh and assess [their] glances." Or again:

No one makes a home of a prison cell, and Stefano never forgot the invisible walls round him. As he played cards in the tavern surrounded by the cheerful or tense faces of the other men, he sometimes saw himself alone and precarious, wistful at the thought of the invisible wall separating him from these casual acquaintances.[12]

Later, a passage recalls the basic situation of the prisoner in "The Intruder" when he feels himself "enclosed in glass": "There was only one answer, and it brought a smile to his lips: the invisible walls, the habit of the prison cell that cut him off from all human contact. Those were his nightly fears."

When they relate to him the amorous going-on of the village people, Stefano does not listen to them with the curiosity or indifference one could expect of him; his reaction is ambiguous and significant, as it characterizes his own particular state of mind, an acute and tormented sensitivity, unable to remain on the plane of reality, preferring his own mental categories.

Stefano's lips formed themselves into a smile and he rose to his feet with the pale sea behind him. His smile expressed disillusionment, for, on his first arrival he had believed in the innocence of this country village; but this belief was merely his reluctance to hear about the sordid acts committed by others. It was the lighthearted tone of the narrator rather than the particular incident that disgusted him. It [prevented] him [from loving] the other people [comfortably] as simple objects.

It is clear from the quotation that Stefano's mental categories echo a whole "decadent" education (the "innocence" of the village is the equivalent of the "barbaric" qualities which D. H. Lawrence or D'Annunzio found in the South); but even more important is Stefano's reluctance to uncover the *sordid*, i.e., to accept the facts of life, an attitude that culminates in the convenient "reification" of others.

Even his memories, brief and unexpected as flashes of lightning—"the villas of his childhood days, closed and deserted in the land of memory," the drunks who come "roaring down the hill and on past the villa below," the sound of a voice unexpectedly in the prison—dissolve in a detached self-contemplation:

But deep in his inmost heart he was troubled by the other memory, his desperate longing for a solitude that was just coming to an end. What had he done with that death and that regeneration? . . . The clouds, the roofs, the closed windows, everything at that moment expressed quiet and peace; it was all as it had been when he had come out of prison. What then? It was better to stay there dreaming of going out than not to go out in reality.

This contemplation is as much in the present as in the past; each is transfused in the other by virtue of the visual power of the *dédoublement de soi*, the interior analysis of Pavese's predecessors Pirandello and Svevo:

Even Stefano himself had quietly transformed every memory and every word, and when he occasionally received a picture postcard showing a piazza or a landscape he had previously known, he could not credit that he had ever set eyes on the place in question. . . . The wine made him mellow and gave him the quiet courage to see himself from his solitude living in that country the way he did. The self of a few moments back was like the stranger of his previous life, nay, the stranger who had once inhabited a prison cell.

Stefano's fantasies become the most important part of his life, and he transforms the whole of reality into them: "He imagined the whole world as a prison in which everyone is shut up for the most various but all valid reasons, and he found the notion comforting." Even objects and specific people are transfigured; the old beggar is an example:

Perhaps the mere sight of the old man and this link with him—familiarity with his deformity and his monotonous lament—would finally make him concerned and distressed. But Stefano gave rein to his imagination instead, and gradually on that scorched [road] he had a vision [of the old man like] an outlandish, vaguely horrible object, something like a stunted and intricate Indian fig tree, human and with limbs attached instead of branches.

The preceding description alone indicates the difference between Pavese's completely subjective lyricism and the objective, open lyricism of others such as Carlo Levi in *Christ Stopped at Eboli.* In fact, whereas Levi interprets the inmost reality of the South in an elegiac and imaginative tone (remember the *"monachicchi"*), it is obvious that Stefano's absorption in fantasy is a *protection* that saves him from coming to terms with the old beggar's human substance—"his deformity and . . . his monotonous lament."[13] Thus, the figure of Concia is fundamental to the complete comprehension of the psychological mechanism imprisoning Stefano. Concia is a servant "he had seen before walking along in the village—the only girl in point of fact. She stepped in a sprightly, almost cheeky dance, raising her brown, goatlike face with each upward swing of her hip. Her confidence amused him." (Notice the adjective "goatlike"; its "barbaric" force recalls the primitive, poetic world of *Work Is Wearying.*) In the whole novel Stefano speaks to her very rarely and is content to gaze at her fondly as he did the first time he saw her: "He allowed his imagination to play with the young woman in the seclusion of his ramshackle house, conscious of a sense of freedom and detachment, for the strange nature of the person in question liberated him from every pang of desire." Every little sense impression makes him think of her ("The tobacco itself was brown—like Concia's neck") in a tireless process of idealization and association, which even in style reveals the profound "decadence" of such an attitude; for example, the water jar with its "damp slender side" "rose-tinted like a flushed cheek," is transferred almost unnoticed into thought and desire of Concia:

With the water came an earthy taste that felt harsh against his teeth; he enjoyed this more than the water; it seemed to be the taste of the vessel itself. It suggested something wild and goatlike and yet smooth. It was all somehow mixed up in his mind with the color of the geraniums [on the window sill of Concia's house].

Later, in "Intimate History" we shall see that the window sill with geraniums is a poetic and lyrical motif that takes the narrator back to his own childhood, to his father and his village. But meanwhile, the following passage reveals explicitly Stefano's attitude:

Even the low, squalid rooms, with their ancient cupboards festooned with red or green paper, the creaking wood, the floors strewn like a stable with maize tufts and olive branches, all this brought back to his mind her goatlike face, her low forehead, a sort of brutal, timeless intimacy.

Precisely because she was "the lover of a foul old man and the flame of the village lads," precisely because Stefano never touched or possessed her and therefore never really knew her, but merely gazed at her fondly and made her the object of his fantasies, Concia acquires much greater prominence; she is in exactly the opposite position of Elena, the young widow, who is meek and servile, with whom Stefano, though they have a physical relationship, cannot succeed in forming a true human relationship, because of his fear and his intrinsic inability to let himself go.[14] This antithesis, therefore, is a clear example of the ironic and relentless law that makes of Stefano the master of Elena and the slave of Concia:

Elena had come and had secretly withdrawn. All her strength, thought Stefano, lay in this humility, the humble submission which appeals to the affection and sympathy of the strongest. Better Concia's uptilted face, shameless and unsympathetic though it was, better those brazen glances. But perhaps Concia, too, could on occasion produce those faithful-hound looks.

Concia becomes the pretext, the alibi for the *mauvaise foi* of Stefano, who does not want to feel "parts of himself at the mercy of" others, and who cannot bear that Elena or anyone else should have "the right to cast reproachful glances at him"; he prefers to remain alone, isolated in his ivory tower, untouched by others' misery, sheltered and secure in his own harmless and futile dreams. His first reactions to Elena are characterized by an increase of cruelty:

Long silences ensued filled with glances from her, and Stefano felt both gratified and embarrassed. The woman blushed at her own obstinacy; her husky voice fell silent, as she yearned for a kind word. Stefano looked on, troubled. . . .

As Stefano made his way up towards the houses by the dusty hedge, his thoughts went back to the barefoot maid of the geraniums and he wished he could have embraced and kissed her instead of Elena. . . .

Stefano slept heavily and woke up in the chill of the dawn, glad to be alone. As he prepared to go out, he reflected that next time he would have the lights out so that he would not have to smile, and he could imagine it was the young, barefoot girl beside him in the bed.

The fantasies woven around Concia are constantly preventing Stefano from feeling any true love for Elena: at the most he feels distress or tenderness, but never complete abandonment, never a union of their lives. Stefano's attitude is significant and would appeal to Denis de Rougemont: "Stefano would have liked her [Elena] to come in the morning and slip into his bed as if she were his wife, then vanish again like a dream that requires neither word nor compromise." This one sentence sums up the characteristic attitude of many of Pavese's characters when they are confronted with love (especially those in *The Beach* and *The Devil in the Hills*, as we shall see later); a longing for love in itself, and therefore for one's own being in love: a narcissism that opposes love to marriage, as De Rougemont claims in *Love in the Western World*, from the Middle Ages to the present. Nevertheless, Stefano's claim is absurd and irreconcilable with reality. Consequently, "Elena's slight hesitations, her timid way of speaking, her mere presence in fact, caused him a guilty uneasiness." Moreover, "it still rankled that he had entreated her, had spoken to her, and had given evidence—false though it was— of sincere and tender feelings. He felt vile and smiled a wry smile"; finally,

that dull sadness arising out of their intimacy made her hateful to him and brought back to his mind her clumsy gestures. If on some occasion Elena had only dared one gesture, one word of genuine possessiveness, Stefano would have [pushed her away from himself].

Being so hard to please, Stefano reaches the point of loathing the moments of joy that he still gives to Elena, and of regarding the external manifestations with a detached disgust, however slight they may be: "Even more than by her harsh voice, he was repelled by the sensual and contented smile, which [for some moments spread on] those lips and [on the eyelids nailed down to] the pillow."

But when Stefano does not feel threatened, instead of feeling uneasy, bitter, sad, or full of hate, he is able simply to enjoy the company of Elena in the same way he enjoys the countryside or other encounters: he reduces everything to things, bodies, presences that cannot touch him:

It seemed odd that these sensitive remarks should be coming from someone covered by that rough brown skirt. . . . In the rather sweet, goatlike smell that arose from the stove, Elena seemed more in her element, becoming the average good housewife, the rather drab presence you tolerate, along with the chickens, the broom, the housemaid.

Stefano, with his "impassive closing of the mind to every word, the most secret enticement," really expresses a fear of being hurt by the world:

. . . every pleasure, every contact, every abandonment to feeling should be shut up in his heart as in a prison, kept under control as if it was a vice, then nothing would show outwardly, and nothing should depend on external events; neither things nor people would have any more hold over him.

Similarly, this fear is expressed in his attitude of constant contemplation, which not only loathes the present concrete reality but even the remote possibility of an action that might realize his fantasies: such an action would encounter too many uncertainties, too many chances of delusion, especially with regard to Concia:

If Giannino really had no eyes for her, there was no further excuse and he [Stefano] ought to try his luck. He hoped in a dim way that it was not true; [he told himself] that Giannino had seduced her, or at [least] had had her in his arms under a staircase during a visit he was paying to the other woman. If indeed no one else had ever desired her, his previous imaginings had all been childish and deserved the sarcasm from the rest of them.

Thus, Stefano makes no move whatever toward Concia, but continues to daydream of her, even while he is with the meek widow: "Stefano remained with his eyes closed and tried to imagine the same slow words falling from Concia's lips, and as he lightly touched Elena, he thought of Concia's brown arm." It will be noticed that "the refined emotion of superimposing on one woman the image of another so as to possess one in the other"[15] is typical of D'Annunzio, but in Pavese, it assumes a softened and almost sorrowful tone. Only at the end of the novel does Stefano understand that "to be really alone it needed so little; abstinence was enough."

Concia's role in Stefano's sentimental life, therefore, corresponds to Giannino's role in his broader social and political life: both Giannino and Concia help Stefano in the same way to remain detached from the world, a prisoner of his own solitude. When an unknown anarchist writes a note to Stefano asking to meet him—a human contact, some solidarity—Stefano refuses, then cannot find anything better to do than analyze the words and style of the message with the detached air of an elderly literary critic instead of the grateful humility of one companion in misfortune toward another:

Stefano at present was passing in front of Concia's house, and his thoughts were on the wind-swept prison up there in that tiny space cut out in the sky that overhung the sea in the serene emptiness of the morning. Another wall had added itself to his prison; this time it was composed of a vague terror, a guilty anxiety. Up there, on that low parapet, sat a man, an abandoned comrade. It would not involve him in much risk to go and visit him and speak [a] word. The appeal had mentioned "solidarity"; there emerged then, wrapped though it was in that fanatic and almost inhuman jargon, which would have been expressed in the old days in the form of a precept, milder but no less serious, an invitation to visit "the imprisoned." There was something that caused him to smile in those words "frank discussion" and "rights" . . . but his amusement was not enough to overcome his remorse. Stefano [admitted he was a coward].

Instead, once more Stefano prefers another kind of solidarity, if one can call it that: that of the uninterrupted memory he has of his friend Giannino, strong and silent, imprisoned for seducing a girl. A solidarity or an "identification,"[16] therefore, consisting only in contemplation, which can even be extended to include the anarchist, in fact happens: "Stefano ate a few pieces of tart and then made his way home, comparing his own solitude with that of the anarchist up in the old village." There is, too, the following passage, where in his very contemplation the two worlds, dream and reality, collide irreconcilably:

Stefano even envied the anarchist stuck over there where he could see the plains, horizons, and the seacoast looking like a tiny toy across this stretch of open, and in the distance the blue patch of the sea; everything would have for him the beauty of an unexplored country, like a dream. Whereas he himself saw merely the squalor of the narrow streets and windows, the four hovels rising perpendicularly above the abyss, and he felt ashamed of his own vileness.

Nevertheless, though Stefano finds solidarity and "identification" with two other human beings, he does not go beyond recognizing his own inability to act and his own detachment "lightheaded and irresponsible, almost like the whine of a mosquito." Alone and isolated, he tends to project his own condition on the outside, making himself the center of a world, the whole of which is a prison and seems, at the same time, unreal, alert as he is to capture the most subtle sensations created by his sensitive fantasy:

Even this detail reminded him of his prison cell where, whoever presented himself at the door was allowed to enter and speak to him. Elena, the goatherd, the boy who bathed, even Giannino could enter like so many jailers. . . . The quiet summer had slipped by slowly, silently like a daydream. Among so many faces, so many thoughts, so much distress, so much peace, nothing remained except curling waves like blue reflections sweeping over a ceiling. And even that arid country . . . had soon ceased to affect him and had become unreal, like Elena's face intersected by the window bars. The illusion and the smell of that whole summer had insinuated themselves into his bloodstream and into his room in the same way as Concia had slipped in, even though her feet had never actually crossed the threshold.

In the light of the preceding reflections the feeling of precariousness that obsesses Stefano acquires an even greater prominence. Although it is the result of his situation as a political prisoner, it is above all an aspect of the *condition humaine*, an aspect essential for the authenticity of the tragic hero: "Stefano knew that his constant anxiety and tension arose from [the temporary], from his dependence on a scrap of paper, the suitcase that stood open on his table. How many years would he remain [down] there?"[17]

From such an attitude Stefano gets a dizzying sense of emptiness, of the absurd, at the bottom of which he sees himself:

The whole country and the life there seemed a kind of game to him, of which he knew the rules and could follow the progress without actually participating, master as he was of himself and his strange lot. . . . But Stefano very quickly realized that the game that life there had become could vanish like the illusion it was. . . . During the whole excursion he had taken comfort in the illusion that his bedroom, Elena's body, and the beach he walked on every day composed so minute and absurd a world that he had only to put his thumb in front of his eye to blot it all out. And yet that strange world, seen from an even stranger place, [contained him, too].

On the formal plane, Stefano's habit of constant contemplation corresponds to an evocative and elegiac style, centered on memory and on the past, alert to associations of images and ideas, nuanced in tone, and without any of those leaps from narrative to dialogue which we noticed in "Land of Exile." For example:

The sea, which he saw only as a background to his thoughts, was as lovely as it had been during his first days there. The little waves rippled at his feet with [lips] of foam.

The slanting rays of the sun penetrated the air and were filled with smoke like shot silk.

Her lips were gay and soft, as if [laying] back on a pillow.

They came to a stop in front of the inn underneath the [fragile] glow from the first lamppost in the street, now empty of children.

It had been such a day of white clouds, the only ones visible in the sky beyond the iron bars, that had made him dream of their shadows on the unseen earth below.

To images such as these we could apply a passage from the diary:

[They are made for broadly constructed works, because they are just a glance to external things during the attentive narration of facts that have *human* importance. They are like a sigh of relief, a glance through a window. Precisely because they seem decorative details in a hard context, they prove the unconscious austerity of their creator: they imply his natural incapacity for "feeling" a landscape. Through them, he clearly and honestly uses nature as a means, as something inferior to the substance of the story.][18]

This is not in contradiction to Pavese's image-story, for the passages quoted do seem to "convey the naturalistic state of mind, in which case the glance through the window becomes the substance of the whole construction."[19] If this "interpretation of the state of mind in terms of images" needs confirmation, it can be obtained from the imaginative (contemplative) inspiration invested in the following passages:

Stefano would have liked to sit down and see the dawn break among these peaceful surroundings. . . . The scene changed as they walked along, and it was no longer dawn rising forth from the things around but events themselves taking charge. But Stefano enjoyed fresh air only from a window or a doorstep.

The shadow of the station at that hour lent the piazza a certain coolness, between a shaft of sunlight which fell from the glazed "No Entry" door and across the peaceful, shimmering railway lines. The platform was a leap into the void. Like Stefano, the stationmaster, too, lived under this void, moving to and fro on this borderland of leavetakings, in the unstable equilibrium of the invisible walls. The black trains ran along by the sea as if [they were scorched by] the dogdays they had passed through, towards remote and level distances.

Or let us look at the gentleness of this other scene, which reminds us of Mena in Verga's *The House by the Medlar Tree:*

They went out in the still, clear air without saying a word. When they were on the terrace road, Stefano turned to look at the house and saw that one of the windows showed a light. [In front of the pale sea, it looked like] the lantern of a fishing boat, lit up ready for sailing.

Or finally, a tenderness like Pascoli's in the description of the beginnings of spring:

The strange thing was that although it was still winter, there were signs of spring. Some of the boys went along barefoot with their scarves round their necks. Green shoots could be seen in the ditches that bordered the bare fields; and the almond tree stretched its pale branches against the sky.[20]

Truly, "an air of another place, another month and another life," fitting a novel whose hero lives, above all, in contemplation and memory.

Later, when Pavese describes the cold lack of communication among the *bourgeoisie* (in *The Beach, The Devil in the Hills,* and *Among Women Only*) and, in a dialectically opposite way, his efforts at political and human participation (especially in *The House on the Hill*), he will turn his attention to the external world, but his intimate reasons for solitude, which are both self-imposed and predestined, will remain the basis and premise of his lucid and desperate analyses.

3

Violent Types

"The wild is not picturesque but tragic."

CESARE PAVESE

The events and characters in some of Pavese's short stories embody a world and a way of looking at life that are very different from those so far analyzed. Solitude seems forgotten or at least relegated to the background, whereas violence becomes an ever stronger element, until it finally dominates —open and brutal violence revealed in man's gestures and words; the wild violence of nature, often cloaked in obvious sexual images; the violence of life and death, which share a common mystery in man's blood.

The core of "Summer Storm," with the Po River for background, is the implacable correlation between the violence of the river current whipped up by a sudden cloudburst and the insolent and disgusting cynicism of the two unscrupulous characters Aurelio and Moro. The latter, just out of prison, is a "bony young fellow with large dirty feet and reddened hands," his skin as "pale as the belly of a fish," and "a flash of ill-temper" gleaming in his eyes.[1] The climax involves rape on the dredger in the middle of the river and two girls drowned (the second under the impassive eyes of the two assaulters). The tension of this story is clearly modeled on the more striking and superficial aspects of such writers as Caldwell or Faulkner, but its roots are deep and go back to certain aspects of decadent culture, such as D'Annunzio's, which have been absorbed by Pavese and re-elaborated by his own sensibility. In fact this tension in the story appears superimposed and forced and stands apart from the completely fragile and intimate beauty of the few and revealing descriptions, such as the following: "[Frightened] clouds were piling up [high above], and a [feeble] flash of lightning darted across the sky [like a throb]." This gap reveals in the author a deep, unresolved, and unconscious ambivalence toward violence. His attitude is generally considered to be the result of a clinical condition of impotence, and it will recur in various forms throughout Pavese's work, but here it seems particularly obvious and direct.

"Gaolbirds" too, is a short story written from an unusual angle; it centers around the escape from prison of Rocco, a man who had murdered because of jealousy, and who goes to visit Concia, the wild and faithless girl for whom he committed the crime; he takes her violently, feeling both love and hate, then renounces his vendetta with an emphatic gesture:

Rocco turned to the window. "Look here," he said dryly. He held up the knife. "Take a good look at it. I was going to give it you in the neck. You knew it, too. But it's not worth the trouble. Watch." He took the point between his fingers and threw it, shining, high in the air among the olives.[2]

Calmly Rocco returns to prison of his own free will, back among all the other characters, each described with his individual characteristic: the sorrowful, exemplary severity of the "political" priest; the good nature and kindliness of the warden Ciccia; the cunning of his son Cicciotto; the petulance of the other prisoners. Throughout the story verbs such as "whine," "strangle," "moan," and "bleed" are constantly re-peated, but most conspicuous is the contrast between Rocco's moonlit flight among the olive trees of the Southern coast, and the vividness of the sun with its stains of color and dirt inside the prison. The moon, in particular, presides over the meeting of Rocco and Concia, bathing it in an ecstatic light: "Outside the crickets were chirruping and the moon was shining farther over the flagstones of the threshold, leaving a deeper shadow across the wall where they stood."

The moon is the central image in a much later story, "The Field of the Dead," in which violence is completely immersed in a "metaphysical" atmosphere: "Probably [the assassin] wondered what the clearing would look like in the daylight and tried to strip the scene of its lunar horror and imagine it as any place under the sun, framed by hills in the background like the whole city."

The moon is also the key image in "Festival Night," the first story in which Pavese begins to explore his native country, the Langhe hills. There is no doubt it is an exploration: both the boy Biscione and the Professor contribute to it, each in his own way; the former with the frankness and curiosity of his youth, the latter with the gravity of a stranger. And the exploration is centered on the harshness of an unrewarding work and of the countryside, of life and the world. So that Biscione can utter the paradigmatic words: "The world is full of people who threaten and are respected"; and we are not surprised to find him armed and ready to strike, if only in self-defense, like Cinto in *The Moon and the Bonfires:*

Biscione loosened his belt and took out the billhook. He bran-dished it for a moment in the shadow of the wall. The great hooked blade was cold, but the smooth horn handle, broken at the tip, was still warm from his trousers. With a laugh he drew it across his cheek and the chill of it made him shiver. Then, silently, he whipped it through the air at the full length of his arm. If the Padre had had a goiter, like Gosto, that blow would have sliced it off. Biscione remembered when he had cut a grass snake in two. What a stroke! And the two pieces went on wriggling. A snarl escaped him.

Naturally the powerful and inexplicable attraction of sex is felt, too, by the boy; woman reappears as a mysterious being: "Biscione saw one of them once with a man, when he went to tread grapes at the Rossi's place. He says they were lying together behind the bushes in the Pratone, towards evening. They were doing what dogs do. He heard the woman laughing."

The Professor, for his part an idler like Whitman,[3] sits apart from the others and smokes his pipe in silence, observing the Padre, who is strong as a tree:

The Padre again began rubbing his fists on the sack hanging from his neck. They were huge brown fists, streaked with black in every crease, under the nails and around the wrists. They looked like wood or shrivelled meat. Below the edge of the sack protruded his bare feet, and those, too, were knotted, covered with earth and twisted like roots.

There is nothing in this passage to recall the imaginative description of the old beggar whom Stefano meets in *The Political Prisoner:* behind the hard concrete words is the hard concrete reality of the work the Padre is doing, preparing the manure with the help of his farm boys, and the Professor is watching and almost tempted to join in, in a sort of Dionysian intoxication:

Some semi-solid, semi-liquid splashes from the stinking flood even reached as far as the schoolmaster. He felt his head swimming as the fumes stung his eyes and nostrils, the distant music rang in his ears, and a wild impulse seized him to shed his shoes and stockings, strip off his clothes, and plunge into the heaving mass, leaping and shouting, his beard flying in the wind. But he didn't bat an eyelid, except for the tears that streamed from his enflamed eyes.

The power of the countryside is admirably expressed here in the Professor's reaction to all its smells and to the sounds and colors of the celebration in the noisy, picturesque inn:

In the cool night air, mellowed by the fumes of wine, he watched the comings and goings of the customers. It was stifling in the large room and the noise was deafening. The thick curtain of smoke swirled as men shouted to one another, all of them streaming with sweat. Around the tables were groups of carters with their red woollen sashes; old men from the country, their [hats] over their eyes; [clumsy] young hooligans; all holding glasses, sucking up their drinks with wet lips, banging on the tables, yelling, surrounded by a litter of waste paper and puddles of wine. Outside it was festival night, by God!

The exclamation ("by God") at the end of the description emphasizes and encompasses all the vigor and violence of this rural world on a festival day, and they are in fact revealed right afterwards to the silent observer as he sits apart near the door:

Outside the door, where a ruddy light was shed by a lamp hanging from the architrave, a brawl had started between two deep-voiced country bumpkins. They stood there, their laboured insults inaudible above the noise of trumpets, the cries and the interminable trampling of feet, panting like a pair of bullocks. Stubbornly they persisted for a while, undeterred by the uproar around them.

Later the Professor is listening to the blonde woman, a poor lion-tamer from the amusement park, who is unburdening herself to the waitress in the middle of the general confusion. He listens unperturbed, yet he shows interest and compassion:

". . . yet I'd put up with it all if it wasn't for the stink," she went on, breathlessly. "For six years all I've smelt is that stink. And everywhere we go the people stink, too. Blaring music, deafening noise, drunks, people with their mouths wide open, yelling, drinking."

The Professor, after drinking "the wine of meditation," can explain his own satisfaction with the discovery of life in the country, hard as it is, to the worried Padre, a satisfaction that on the formal plane is expressed in the serenity of the countryside. In the opening of the story color and sound are perfectly fused and metaphoric language transforms violence into serenity:

Over the threshing floor, smooth and firm as a marble table, the evening air was rising, fresh and cool. When the setting sun has only just dropped behind the brow of a hill, the earth around the base of it seems to glow with a light of its own, a clear, serene radiance emanating from the stones and the bare soil. In the still air behind the cowshed, snatches of dance music could be heard, borne by the wind and broken by the distant hills, as if shrill voices were quarrelling far away. . . .

The bursts of music were more frequent now, more ethereal, throbbing in the tranquil air, freeing themselves in the sky from the tumult, the excitement, and the wine that gave them birth—a sound as pure, as remote from humanity as the voice of the wind.

The Leopardian touch of another description, therefore, does not surprise us:

As he stood holding up the lantern, running his eyes over the sacks, the store of corncobs, the blades of scythes stacked in the corner, there reached him on the still night air the faint sound of a song from some far-away farm, a [grave], deep voice that hardly broke the silence and softly died away in the distance.[4]

Thus, in "Festival Night" we meet characters who live, work, suffer, and sing; country people, quick and genuine, ready to use their hands (all except the Professor); people who are an integral and essential part of a natural background that is both violent and idyllic.

The exploration of this background becomes a sexual exploration in "First Love,"[5] going back in time to childhood roots when the narrator discovers as a boy the difference between city and country, after the manner of Vico, with his senses:

Before I knew Nino it never struck me that the boys I ran shouting around the streets with were ragged and filthy. Indeed, I actually envied them for going barefoot. One of them could even walk over corn stubble without being hurt, while my pale, city-dweller's feet cringed from the very thought of treading the cobbled streets.

The boy feels nothing but unconditional admiration for Nino, who makes him feel ashamed of his rustic habits; and he begins to put on airs with his old friends just as Nino does with him:

After that, I divided my time accordingly. Almost every morning I sneaked off to the goat pasture with the ragamuffins I had been friendly with at first. I stuffed them with exciting tales of the city [that little by little became like my own farm, where] extraordinary adventures happen[ed] on the trams or in lifts. Every now and then I would stop to chase a goat, peel a wand, or hunt grasshoppers.

These relationships (in which we see *in nuce* the Hegelian dialectic of master and slave as interpreted by Girard in his theory of mediation) will gradually change in the course of the story as the boy gets to know Nino better and as they both become dominated by an adult before whom they are both inferior.

The boy, moreover, is not very brave: when he is invited into the garden by Nino, he notices—in parentheses, significantly—that "the dog was now tied up at the back of the villa." Because of his mildness the other characters appear even more violent and vicious. Look at Nino, a bully, who is spiteful and plays mean tricks: "Nino had gone with the others to make a bonfire in the Mulini's field, and when he saw a chance he had pushed the blacksmith's son right into the fire. Now that lad was out to catch Nino and threatening to slaughter him."

Most of all we should study the figure of Bruno, the adult who dominates the boys' lives and through whom they are introduced to sex. The way in which Bruno is first presented indicates, even visually, his importance: "Nino appeared on the doorstep with a curly-haired man wearing a scarf round his neck, a red belt, and Wellingtons. His sleeves were rolled up and he filled the doorway. Nino appeared at his elbow." Moreover, Bruno had a leather arm-guard around "his square wrist," which he used "to bash in the face of any cheeky blighter," as he explained to them:

"You give him a sideways blow, overhand, so as not to hurt your fingers, and it acts like a boxing glove. One night at Spigno there was a fellow who walked by the car—I was parked by the station —and he spat into it. Just spat and ran away. You must never put up with spitting, because a man who spits is afraid. I shot after him and split open his face. Like this. See how it works?"

His first action is decisive for the relationship between the two boys:

There was a smile in his voice as he said to Nino, and to me, "So you've made friends, eh?" He gave me a wink and took my hand, but I broke away. He shook my forearm forcibly two or three times, then said: "Nino, don't pick a quarrel with this one, for he's stronger than you."

In a world based on force, Bruno becomes a model for the boys to imitate: quick, self-assured, fascinating, and feared; this is how he reacts to a joke in rather poor taste by Nino, his accomplice in a little amatory excursion: "Without saying a word, Bruno gripped Nino's wrists in one hand and held him up like a rabbit, screeching and kicking. With the other hand he thrashed his bottom. His lips were tight together, and every blow made Nino scream."

But Bruno's physical violence is nothing compared with the violence of things. Soon the boy learns with ill-concealed disgust what sexual life is all about, and his first discovery is made in the stable, or rather outside the stable, in bewilderment:

I still hung around, trembling with fear at the animal groans that broke into the open air, followed by gurglings as if the creature was dying. Then came excited voices; the woman gave a sudden exclamation, followed by the splashing of water and the jingle of a chain. I thought about the [swollen] mass of the cow's belly as I had seen it a day or two before.

This discovery is followed by an even greater one, that human beings, too, are like animals. (It was not for nothing that Bruno called the girls "heifers," and one recalls Biscione, when he is describing the two people in each other's arms who "were doing what dogs do.")

So we went forward, too, and rejoined Nino, who was supporting himself on the board that held the window frame and staring through the filthy glass. I tried to look in, too, but saw nothing because my eyes were still dazzled by the sunshine. But something was moving inside, in the darkness.

Then I could make out a white [form] lying and a man just breaking away from it; a man with a red kerchief. It was Bruno, and the woman was Clara. There was a kind of golden sheen over her bare body. The dusty panes [covered] the scene [with] a kind of mist. "She's white," the smith's son whispered.

The place where this timorous discovery is made is an abandoned hut at the bottom of a vineyard, another image that acquires a symbolic value. And the boy's pain is all the more desperate for having been, throughout the story, silently in love (with a vague, unknowing love) with Nino's sisters, especially Clara with her sunshade, a bright happy little figure whom we have already met in the poem "The Young Teachers" and who reappears against a distant and tragic background in *The Moon and the Bonfires:*

As I reached the villa, one of his sisters was coming out, the fair one with the dazzling white skin. I had watched her cycling past and thought how pretty she was. Now she laughed, rested her hand on my head, and asked me what was the matter. I told her I was looking for Nino.

"Why?" she persisted.

"There's a newborn calf," I stammered, red-faced. She looked at me, took her hand away, and laughed aloud. "Is it a pretty little thing?" she asked.

I didn't know what to say. She laughed again, turned away, and called: "Nino." I heard an answering voice. She waved her hand, barely glancing at me, and went on her way, opening her parasol.

Clara's role in the world that the boy is exploring is emphasized by Pavese himself when he writes in his diary, on the topic of rusticity, or "rustic classicism":

A rustic [background, formed] not by country folk or peasants but by girls with a sunshade. The Roman ruins please you because the reeds and poppies, the dry hedges on the hills, somehow link them with your childhood; also because history (Ancient Rome) and pre-history (Vico: blood sprinkled on the hedgerow or in the furrow) are in harmony with this rusticity, making it a world in itself, consistent from birth to death.[6]

Like the things from childhood, therefore, the sunshade is linked to a world that will only be seen and judged from a historical perspective later; but meanwhile it is included, and by contrast integrated, in a life and a reality which are described powerfully and sorrowfully. In "First Love," as in the other stories examined in this chapter, the predominant element without a doubt is violence, beside which contemplation or idyll, solitude or love, remain secondary, like the counterpoint to a resounding music. The synthesis of these short stories could be the graphic sentence "with love or with hate, but always with violence,"[7] which will be fully developed in the coherent and implacable rhythm of the novel *The Harvesters*.

The first contact of Pavese's characters with the world is with violence: it is precisely the painful discovery of that violence that was secretly dreaded in the solitude of isolation, in the protective seclusion, in the shelter of contemplation. Fundamentally it is the proof that those solitary fears are well-founded. The effect of such a contact is magnified by the particular background of the event: the country, where everything is more openly violent than amid the hypocrisy of city life, as if it were a reflection of the ancient primitive world: "The peoples who practiced the most frequent, most atrocious human sacrifices were those who lived by agriculture (matriarchal civilizations). Shepherds, hunters, artisans were never cruel like tillers of the soil."[8] Thus, the violence of the countryside contains an element of the atavistic, the barbaric, the mythic. Here are concentrated the ethnological interests of Pavese, the reader of Vico; but we also find the literary echoes of Pavese, the admirer of D'Annunzio (especially of *Jorio's Daughter*) and the translator of American writers (especially Anderson).

The city remains in the background, an occasional reference, an as yet untried possibility, in order to give greater prominence to the exploration of the country; and the country, particularly in *The Harvesters*, is both the world, and to a certain extent "I," for as he describes it, as he lives in it, the city man Berto assimilates it, and through it learns to know himself. Berto is not like Stefano in *The Political Prisoner*. He has a different bearing, a self-assurance, a certain cunning, a security, a self-possession that Stefano lacked. Let us look at his encounters with Talino and Vinverra for example:

"Let's get this straight. Over there is a machine. I'm here to look after that machine, not to act as nursemaid to you, nor to animals even more crafty than you are. Can't you see you're making a nuisance of yourself? Go and burn down houses! Nobody here is such a goat as to account to you about where he goes or what he does."[9]

Then there are his encounters with women: with Michela, his friend Pieretto's fickle friend; with the cashier at the café in the town square; above all with Gisella. We see his ability to form friendships immediately in the taverns in the town, to start up a conversation with everyone (like Nuto in *The Moon and the Bonfires*), to feel warmth even toward the police:

I was thinking of those poor wretches who had to prowl around all night after [wise guys] like Talino and me. I could see them going up and down those hills all day and all night. Even for them, what a life! Quite apart from the probable chance of a bullet from some lout who was even more stupid than the rest. And all because a fool like Talino took it into his head to set fire to another man's home.

Yet, at heart there is a faintly perceptible resemblance to the Stefano we knew: for example, when Berto feels compassion for Gisella, who wants to be kissed; or in the passages where he describes the countryside, revealing his lyrical nature. Above all we realize that he neither wants to nor can kill

Talino, when the latter appears in front of him after his crime and escape:

"It's a police matter, now," I was thinking. "Now that Gisella is dead, as long as I get back to Turin, that's all I care about. He'll have to go to prison, and that rests with the police. What a fool the man is! Why didn't he escape?"

At that moment I seemed to see him attacking Gisella, who was screaming, while he, like a beast, was breaking her back and holding her down. He must have seen in my face what I was thinking, for I saw how he was trembling and twisting his fingers. But I had already spoken to him.

Berto's attitude does not imply either refusal of responsibility or cowardice; rather, he has renounced violence, or better still, he has renounced the world of the peasant, a rejection of the violent world of action.

Berto, in the first lines of the novel, literally comes out of prison and, in company with his friend Talino, feels bewildered and in an unfamiliar place, in sun-drenched streets:

We were walking on like a couple of bullocks with no idea where we were going, he with his red kerchief round his neck, his bundle and his rough corduroy trousers. . . . Talino started laughing as though we [were alone] grumbling and laughing and taking up all the pavement. Passers-by kept bumping into him, for Talino was shambling along as though he were the only man in the place.

The first danger signal, however, is already hidden beneath this bewilderment of Talino's, who is actually much more cunning than he appears, with an atavistic, primitive cunning; Berto, the mechanic, suffers by comparison. But cunning apart, Talino's words already indicate the violence of the rural life from which he comes:

"I'm not going back to the country," he said. "My father'll slay me." Great big fellow though he was, he sounded as scared as if he were still being grilled by the police, and he wiped the sweat from his neck.

And Berto will see the father in action with his own eyes, in a scene which is reminiscent of Vico:[10]

Everyone gave a cry, for Vinverra had taken off his belt and was slashing away at Gisella as if she were shoe leather. But Gisella did not run away; she buried her face against Adele's side, yelling and twisting like a snake, while Adele sheltered her baby with her arm. The old man did not say a word; his cap had dropped off and he went on beating her.

Violence, however, at least at the beginning, is subordinate to the revelation of the world of the peasants, the country. It is a progressive and total revelation of all the aspects of this world: places, colors, sounds, smells, people, animals. This revelation begins with the very first descriptions in which, for example, Talino's bewilderment in the city turns to self-assurance and joy as soon as he reaches the market:

But what fine red chillies the women were selling! Then we came to the watermelons and I began to feel thirsty. From the way everybody was shouting, especially the women, it seemed to be a local market. "Take a good look at them, Berto," I said to myself as I strolled along. "This is the sort of people you'll have to mix with from now on."

Looking out over the market from the arcades was like looking at a beach. There were stalls selling shirts, knitted things, caps and berets that made me sweat even to look at them, for in the country everything is thick, from [the skin of feet to] the corduroy of trousers. And Talino marched firmly on, bumping up against people, planting his feet wide apart so that dogs could run between his legs, and not even wiping his neck on the red kerchief that hung in a triangle over his shoulder.

There is an implicit boldness about the descriptions of the threshing floor of the farm, and the crickets and the smells:

The first thing I noticed was one of a pair of double doors standing open underneath a hayloft; then a team of oxen stock still in front of a cart; then some women moving about inside. Talino waved his bundle and began to shout. . . . The women by the cart stood staring at me, and an old woman appeared at the door of the house, while the dog came sniffing round me. I, too, was sniffing, enjoying the scent of the hay. . . . Far away in the distance the hill ended in that bare patch I had seen before. I began to notice the smell of manure and the sound of the crickets. . . .

The fine thing about the country is that everything has its own smell, and the scent of hay always goes to my head—a perfume [with which] women, if they had any sense in their veins, [should lie down].[11]

People are seen in relation to their surroundings, animals or things: thus, Talino is compared to a calf or a goat,[12] and Gisella reminds the protagonist, more subtly, of fruit:

At mid-day they came to call me and we sat down to another meal of [minestrone] soup, anchovies, and cheese. That's how these women grew so fat, but Gisella, who now smiled at me, [seemed instead to be made of fruit]. When I had finished I asked Talino if he hadn't any apples, and he took me into a loft where the whole floor was covered with them, all red or turning brown, [like her]. I picked out a good one and bit into it. It tasted sharp, as I like apples to be.[13]

The same motif of apples returns in a truly poetic passage to explain Berto's state of mind over the girl's death: "I went off by myself into Gisella's apple loft, picked out the best fruit I could see, and bit into it frantically."

Not only the rustic and hard aspects of the country are seen but also the idyllic side of it in passages that might almost be called Arcadian:

I was so tired that I could hardly keep on my feet, and I flung myself down at the edge of the first field I came to, in the shade of some acacias. I looked all around me, at the trees in the distance and the clear sky overhead. In the midst of those trees was a house, and as I lay smoking, there came to me on the wind the sound of voices and the barking of dogs. . . .

As I walked along under the trees and jumped across ditches, I could hear someone singing in the distance. Echoes flung back from the hills seemed to float in midair, like the music of a band playing on windy nights.

The same state of mind is found in the wandering musicians who go around the hills at night, for the Feast of the Assumption—a favorite motif of Pavese's, which is found as early as *Work Is Wearying* and which is resumed later, especially in *Festival Night* and *August Holiday*. But with night came vague, ancestral fears and worries:

It was pleasant to be lying there close to the earth. There were more crickets than stars, and every now and then the dogs up on the hill gave tongue. I fancied somebody was creeping round behind me, somebody who had come up close without my seeing them in the dark. The reeds on the other side of the road creaked and rustled. I had always thought that fear in the night was caused by cold, but there it was quite warm and yet I felt my flesh creep all the same.

. . . and for a moment there was nothing but the darkness, the flicker of lightning, and the sound of crickets. Then, suddenly, a voice was raised beyond the far side of the farmyard, a shrill voice like that of a madman—or a woman. It gave a long howl and then died away into silence. The dog woke up and broke into a perfect frenzy of barking. . . .

And on to this motif of the fear and anguish that come by night is grafted the whole pattern of the country as violence, of sex as violence, and of the country as sex—a pattern developed and achieved in a complex symbolism of recurring images: vineyard, moon, hill. These are not the basis but the actual substance of the tragic action. From the moment when the train takes them out of Turin into the country, Berto and Talino see "a big hill shaped like a woman's breast" and this hill is constantly brought to our attention in the story itself as a sexual image or symbol. There are many examples of this, such as the following:

But Gisella did not come, so I smoked another cigarette. The stubble showed patches of white or black, according to how the moonlight fell across it . . . I felt sleepy too. Then the clouds were gone, and the whole landscape lay in a sea of moonlight, so that, behind the farm, I could see the dark [nipple] of Monticello.

Without the whole pattern of these images it is perhaps not possible to gauge fully the sanguinary impact of the implacable sun, of the summer sun that greets Talino and Berto when they come out of prison, that follows them into the country, and that beats out the rhythm of their interminable days and almost seems to provoke and justify the violence:

There we stood with the blazing sun pricking our skin, he with his great ugly cap and six days' growth of beard. As I watched him coming toward me in the bright sunshine, the thought struck me that the shedding of blood seemed less shocking in the country than in the shadow of a house in Turin. Once I had seen blood on the tram [tracks] after an accident, and it was terrifying. But here, the idea of someone sinking down and pouring out his lifeblood on the stubble seemed more natural, as in a slaughter-house.[14]

The threshing scenes particularly, "in the middle of dust and sun," are totally immersed in a glaring light, in a dazzling atmosphere from which inevitably violence must emerge:

His voice was sneering, sweat was streaming down his face, and the veins of his neck throbbed with the effort he was making. The sheaves were heavy, and Talino pitched them down on my head as if they were pillows, but I kept hard at it, and after five or six trips through the doorway there was a red haze before my eyes. In my mouth was the taste of grain, dust, and blood, and I was sweating. . . .

"Now they can whistle and shriek as much as they like! They can blow up the machine, for all I care," I thought, as I looked out and saw two of the men, burned a fiery red by the sun, stuck up there on top of the sheaves where the dust scorched worse than fire. "It's having to do work like this that turns their heads and changes them into beasts."

After Talino's crime, the note of violence is blended with the elegiac note of Berto's grief, while the threshing continues:

What with the noise of the machinery and the hot sun and the dust, I could hardly keep awake. The sound went up and down, up and down; the blazing sun was as hot as my engine; all the men were plunging in their pitchforks or carrying away the sacks or jumping out of the way of the flails, and I was thinking: "Damn Ernesto! He's probably upstairs. I expect she's dead, but it all goes on, just the same. If she isn't dead, perhaps she can hear that we're threshing the corn and remember where she is and fall asleep. She can't still be in pain, now."

And again, "by holding my breath I could hear the dull roar of the blazing sunshine, as if it were a fire." The characters of *The Harvesters* move in such a framework, under an implacable light. Talino, fearful of his violent and authoritarian father, is characterized by his crude country attitudes, a mixture of stupidity and cunning, but most of all by his outbursts of brutality:

Suddenly Talino lost his temper and shouted at them. They all stopped, even Gisella, who was talking to the old woman. . . . The darkness seemed to press down on us and I could hear the old man's breathing. From the threshing floor came the sound of the dog jumping about. Then I heard the crickets. A little toddler moved and Talino swore at her: "Carolina, I'll kill you."

The fact that Talino had set fire to the Grangia keeps recurring in the story, as if to remind us of the violence and the myth. (In a later story, "Festivals," the protagonist kills an old man in order to take possession of his beautiful horse with a red hide like the leaves of plane trees, and then sets fire to the stable; but the horse runs away and the peasants "say that the horse is roaming the woods, and sometimes they hear him along the hilltops."[15] It has almost become an apparition of a wild and mythical being.)

There is, moreover, a series of apparently casual actions in the story (reminiscent of Tozzi's *The Farm*) that prefigure Talino's crime and finally are seen as warnings of an irrevocable act. For example, when Gisella looks at Berto suddenly after their arrival at the farm: "Choosing his moment, Talino stood up and went round behind the girl who was looking at me. He thrust a hand under her chin and made her jump. Everybody laughed." Even though it is only a joke and Talino rubs a pepper in his sister's face, those two verbs "stood up" and "thrust" have an obscure menacing force that is out of proportion to the joke; and even Gisella's jump of surprise is repeated later in a much more serious and explicit scene: "Talino came bustling forward, carrying four pitchforks, and threw them under the cart against Miliota's legs, so that she had to jump back quickly to save herself from injury." The effect, which is so reminiscent of Tozzi, is heightened too by the dream Berto has after discovering the cause of a scar on Gisella's body, a wound made by her brother with a farm implement:

I was so tired that as I slept I seemed to be falling down a well, while Talino, Gisella, Pieretto, and a crowd of other people leaned over the top; I was falling and falling; I seemed to be falling all night long. I grew so terrified that I couldn't think, and I stretched out my hand to feel if there were rakes stuck in the bottom of the well. "They'll run you through," I said in my dream, and my head swam.

In the light of such precedents, Talino's final "epiphany," as he is blinded by his incestuous jealousy, seems the inevitable conclusion of a fatal tragedy that has long been repressed, and emphasizes, in retrospect, the apparently insignificant actions that preceded and heralded it:

A sudden ferocious glare blazed up in Talino's eyes; he jumped back to give himself room, and before we knew it he had driven the pitchfork into her throat. In the sudden stillness I heard a great gasp from everyone there, then Miliota's voice calling across the farmyard: "Wait for me." Gisella let the bucket fall and the water spilled over my shoes. I thought it was blood and leapt aside. Talino sprang away, too, and we heard Gisella's voice come bubbling up in her throat. "Holy Mother!" she gurgled, then coughed until the pitchfork dropped away from her neck.

Gisella is one of Pavese's most successful feminine creations; apart from having a personality of her own, she incarnates so many themes, from that of Concia's wildness in *The Political Prisoner* to Santa's symbolism in *The Moon and the Bonfires.* Gisella is the only one of the three sisters who is really a woman, concerned with her appearance and graceful in her movements, sensual and genuine, meek and proud. The first time Berto sees her she is tidying her hair "furtively." They like each other and reveal in looks a silent but intense mutual attraction:

"But aren't you afraid of the men at the Prato?" she asked, in amazement.

"I wasn't afraid by the well," I answered, and Gisella stared at me without a word.

And again:

Gisella [had promised me that she] was going to meet me in the field before nightfall; Gisella had a way of responding with such flashing eyes that she could have set fire to the Grangia, like Talino. . . . Her leg was sunburned, but strong. "Pull your skirt up," said I, not moving any closer to her. "It depends on the knees." She laughed, and her eyes pierced me through [to the marrow].

Gisella is sensual like the country and the animals around her: "Her mouth [was all] desire, her hair was in her eyes." We can smell her odor of sweat mixed with hay; even in her work her sensuality is irrepressible and attractive:

Gisella placed the pail underneath a cow and began milking her, handling the teat as if it were her own. It made my mouth water to see her leaning forward like that.
    . . . I haven't said this before, but when I was watching her milking in the cowshed, I cupped my hand round the teat and her fingers as well, pulling with her until the milk came. "Be good," she whispered, her smiling lips close to my ear.

In words that are almost brutal, Berto says of her, at the time he was about to take her, that "she was streaming with sweat, as wet as a tongue," but then adds: "She walked like a man, looked straight at you," words which are really a compliment from a man like him and indicate the girl's pride.

But the true importance of Gisella is that the whole world Berto has discovered converges in her: Gisella is a part of the countryside in which she lives, of the earth on which she has worked, has made love, smiled, and suffered. She is life and death: see for example the motif of the *polenta* (maize pudding) on the kitchen table:

Back at the farm we found the rabbit all ready for us, with a dish of chillies and a fine boiled pudding that Gisella turned out onto a board. I remember that pudding as clearly as if I could see it now, for later on that evening no one had time to cook anything and I swallowed a couple of slices of it cold. By that time it seemed to me to taste of blood, and my teeth were chattering. There was a bowl of blood on the table before my very eyes, and my heart was in my mouth, even colder than the pudding. But that was later. Now at midday, the pudding, the rabbit, and the chillies were all piping hot. The children clamored for more and the girls seemed as if they would never stop eating. Especially Gisella! What an appetite she had! She devoured the pudding with her mouth and me with her eyes.[16]

Or an image which literally unites within it life and death:

The bloodstains could still be seen in the doorway of the shed. "It's [nothing] strange," I reflected. "Every day blood is spilt on the roads. The ground soaks it up, and we think no more about it. But to look at it now and realize that this mud patch is Gisella's warm lifeblood [that] ebbed away turns me cold with horror."

Blood is like the vital sap of a land immersed in the heat of summer, and perhaps this is why Gisella is not so much the expiatory goat of everyone's cunning and violence, as the sacrificial victim of a much older and inexplicable rite, where sex and blood, nature and death form one inexorable whole for man. Gisella really does appear as a sacrificial victim, like a Greek figurine, when Talino has "butchered her as if she were a rabbit," striking her on the throat: "Gisella lay there as if she were dead. They had stripped off her blouse, and her breasts were bare. Where she was not covered with blood, she was naked."

Gisella is a victim who carries with her on her body, in the long scar, the visible sign of her destiny: "You are life and death." Even Talino, we see, is only following his own destiny, already deeply marked in his character and revealed by insignificant acts, which are yet so very significant. Similarly, the sisters, patient and tough, endure a bestial life without the

light of intelligence and redemption. And Vinverra, the
father, is no less fatalistic than the others in his violence, in his
gloom, in his submission to the necessity of work: after saying
to Berto that from the first he has smelt that bowl full of
Gisella's blood, he concludes: " 'Something was bound to
happen . . . and we had to get the corn threshed.' " A sentence of Lukàcs comes to mind apropos of these destinies:

From the contingent to the necessary, this is the path of every
problematic man, this is the goal where everything becomes necessary, where everything expresses man's essence, nothing else but
this, and expresses it perfectly and completely, where everything
becomes symbolic, where everything, as in music, is only what it
means and means what it is.[17]

So in this essential and symbolic whole Pavese has fixed the
final result of the fatalistic acceptance of so many events,
which are mere chance for the peasants who do not possess his
epistemological awareness. Like Edgar Lee Masters, he has
seen "the inexorable oneness of the actions, thoughts and relationships which go to make up a destiny, and has organized
them to a rhythm which is that same destiny,"[18] a rhythm
which reaches its most intense agitation in Gisella's death
scene, where so many mythical images throng together. After
an atrocious and interminable death-bed agony, during which
the fire of that summer sun gradually dies away with the heat
of Gisella's body, comes a moment of calm and solemnity
when she dies, facing the hill on whose summit Talino had
burned a house, making a huge bonfire of it under the
moon:

The window was wide open and I could see the Grangia and the
moon. They were all kneeling in a circle round the bed in the
light of two or three candles, praying and fingering the beads of
their rosaries. The women of the family had their heads shrouded

in their black veils as though they had just returned from mass. Between the candles and the moonlight, there lay Gisella on the bed, all swathed in bandages, with a white dressing on her forehead, but her nostrils and her mouth were black.

In the whole book the images assume an increasingly clear and explicit importance; they become progressively stronger and more poetic, stretched to the point of becoming a style in which are blended "realism's wealth of experience and symbolism's depth of [meanings]."[19] A closer look at this statement makes us aware of how much thought Pavese had given to it; besides emphasizing the realistic and symbolic aspects of the narrative and clarifying their position in the poetic link that binds them, it reveals the particular character of the language used in *The Harvesters:*

The *symbol* . . . is an imaginative link forming a network that underlies the discourse. I am talking of recurring points of contact ("epithets," as in the classic example of 6th November) that indicate a persistent, imaginative significance in one of the material elements of the story (a tale within a tale)—a secret reality coming into bloom. For example, the "breast" in *Paesi tuoi*—a true epithet expressing the sexual reality of that countryside.

No longer an allegoric symbol, but an *imaginative symbol,* an additional means of expressing the "fantasy," the story. Hence the dynamic quality of these symbols; epithets that appear and reappear in the story are *characters* in it, adding their effect to the complete materiality of the discourse; not substitutes that rob reality of its very breath and lifeblood.[20]

By emphasizing the complete materiality of the discourse, Pavese helps us to understand its symbolism; the dialect or slang expressions, the syntactic and grammatical breaks are the sole root from which can grow a more complex and truer vision of reality. They express the most striking aspect of a reality which reveals its secret.

The same can be said of Berto's interior monologue, a monologue that is unusual precisely because it "should not be regarded as peculiar to him alone, but as though it were in the third person. By its very naturalism, it must become a reveal-ing *way of thinking*."[21] All of which means that Berto, in the middle of this dizzying atmosphere of blood and spasms of violence in which the story unwinds, manages to keep a cer-tain sweetness, a grieving compassion, and flashes of lyricism in his images of the countryside (as I have tried to show in the preceding analysis). To quote Pavese, who shows he has learned Verga's lesson well:

I did not write in imitation of Berto—the only one who says anything—but translating his meditations, his wonderment, his raillery, as he would have expressed them himself, *had he spoken Italian.* I introduced errors of syntax only to indicate occasions when his own spirit grew scornful, involved, or tedious. I wanted to show, not how Berto would write had he forced himself to speak Italian (that would have been dialect[al] impressionism), but what his own words would be, had they been changed into Italian by some new Pentecost. In short, his thoughts.[22]

There is no doubt that Berto expresses his reactions very effectively when confronted with the violence all around him: when he emerges from the isolation which imprisoned Stefano and discovers the world of the farm, Berto comes in contact with a cruel and bloody reality (even though it is genuine and full of humanity) to which he cannot belong: yet he moved and suffered in it for a brief period interrupted by a tragic destiny.

From now on, in Pavese's work, the existence of violence will appear only in the background, almost surreptitiously: but it can still be recognized in sexual relationships (from Mina in "The Idol" to Nora in *The Moon and the Bonfires*); it appears in the descriptions of the Resistance and the war; it is traced to its various mythological origins and incarnations; it is transfigured and admired in nature (for example during the storm in *The Devil in the Hills*): in short, it is an element that recurs and underscores the themes and problems that express Pavese's search, a secret spring that is both existential and stylistic. By rejecting in *The Harvesters* that violence to which he feels vaguely attracted, Pavese is making a fundamental choice and thereby gains an essential knowledge of himself and his style.

4

Attempts at Love

> "Our friend lived in the city like an adolescent—and he lived like that up to the end."
>
> NATALIA GINZBURG

Berto in *The Harvesters* emerged from solitude to find himself in a world of violence and tragedy, but other Pavese's characters face different problems. Love becomes the center of some of the short stories, and it is delineated with increasing intensity. Until now love has always appeared as a consequence or a marginal aspect of solitude ("Wedding Trip," "Suicides") or of violence (*The Harvesters*); now it becomes the main preoccupation, the imaginative and psychological center around which the characters' conception of life in all its many aspects is articulated—love as a desperate passion, or as the regaining of a precarious balance in solitude, or as the destruction of innocence. Thus, nowhere does love constitute a solution; on the contrary it aggravates the fundamental problems of man—his own maturity and communication with others.

The premise for these attempts at love made by Pavese's characters can be found in a passage from the diary:

The greatest misfortune is loneliness. So true is this that the highest form of consolation—religion—lies in finding a friend who will never let you down—God. Prayer is giving vent to one's thoughts, as with a friend. Work is an equivalent to prayer, since ideally it puts you in contact with some[one who will use it]. The whole problem of life, then, is this: how to break out of one's own loneliness, how to communicate with others. That explains the persistence of marriage, fatherhood, friendship.[1]

Pavese's words reveal extremely clearly the tragic theme of his life: the vicious and impossible circle of communication between the self and others, in which religious yearning, and to an even greater extent creative work and love, constitute so many unsuccessful efforts constantly repeated until his death. The stories we shall examine, with their many variations in theme, are evidence of the existential and artistic complexity of the Pavesian attempts at love.

In "The Idol," Guido, "accustomed to living alone,"[2] describes his progressive degradation as a result of his love for the prostitute Mina, tender and inflexible, "pitiless and adorable," set against the grey, closed-in atmosphere of the city— first Turin, then Milan, "huge and strange." Guido is a dreamy, contemplative young man, a weakling; Mina's relationship with him is typical of one person's mastery over another, with the resulting mediation indicated in the title. There is a passage from Pavese's diary that should be mentioned in this context, an extremely Hegelian passage that is very apposite to this story but also indicates a whole conception of life: "Both types [of women—those who exploit and those who let others exploit them] confirm the *impossibility* of human fellowship. The[re] are servants and masters, not equals."[3]

When Mina finally marries and leaves Guido for good, the latter is bewildered and confused, aimless:

For a long time I felt shattered, as when I used to cry myself to sleep when I was a child. I thought of Mina and her husband as two grown-ups with a secret. A boy can only watch them from a distance, unaware of the joys and sorrows that make up their life.

His reactions remind us vaguely of Svevo's characters, who, being contemplative like him, are therefore shut off from real life and at best can only admire and imitate others less pensive and more active than themselves; one thinks of the protagonist of *The Confessions of Zeno*, of whom it has been said that "he seems not to exist but to know, while those around him exist and are unaware of it," and that "all normal human relationships are impossible for him, for, lacking the principle of life, he cannot communicate with those around him any more than he can communicate with the stones or the stars";[4] or the protagonist of *As a Man Grows Older*—he too is in love with a prostitute and is a succubus to a friend, to the point that even his way of walking, talking, and gesticulating is affected by him (in fact "he needed props to feel secure"). Same symptoms under different words: "What, for Svevo, is *senility*, to me seems adolescence," Pavese notes in his diary; and again, "there is something sadder than growing old—remaining a child."[5]

It is to avoid this "senile" adolescence that other Pavese characters are so decisive about their amorous experiences and plunge headlong into life. This is the case with Lidia in "The Three Girls." She leaves the country and comes to the city, bringing with her an ancient wisdom and innocence:

I don't envy these city girls. I grew up running barefoot among the vineyards, then I was kept at school. My father is a simple farmer who still spreads the manure himself, but it seems to me that I know a lot more about life than they do. I don't consider men are disgusting or [unpleasant], but then I don't run round after them like a cat.

Lidia, in her wisdom, understands the character of the people around her with a sharp precision, for example Mrs. Ugolina's, which she describes so brilliantly: "Now and then I catch glimpses of a certain bitterness that surprises me, so well does she keep it hidden behind [the benevolent sigh of a wise lady]." Armed with this innocence, she sets about exploring the world and herself amid the city environment:

Whether I'm up in my room or down in the street, I'm thrilled by the fresh, clear light, the sunshine and shadows, people walking up and down on the pavement. But even that isn't all. There's the surprise and delight of realizing I'm a woman, independent, owing nothing to anyone, being able to look a passer-by in the eye and know I'm his equal. But more than anything else, it is a quiet tenseness, [almost an intimate anxiety, a longing, an absurd] expectancy. . . . It's great fun and gives meaning to the bustle in the street, the colors, everything around me.

But it must not be thought that the antithesis between country and city is that clear and absolute; in fact, Lidia's innocence was acquired the hard way from an experience of love that took place in the country almost with the instinctive force of a natural element:

Sometimes even now, if I wake in the night, clutching my pillow with burning hands and too terrified to move a finger, I remember what it was like then. Again I feel uprooted, miserable. I see myself skipping eagerly across the field, stopping every now and then with my heart in my mouth and my nostrils flaring, terrified by what I was doing, but even more terrified at the thought of not doing it. Giusto would stroll along, whistling, and smile at me, calling me: "Poor little kid." He would slip his arm around my waist, feeling the wild beating of my heart. How he flattered me! Then he wandered into the glen: I followed him.

This experience is accepted with fatalism, a fatalism that becomes increasingly pronounced in Pavese's work:

When I think of the danger that nearly engulfed me, and how I was saved by instinct, by some unconsious power, I really believe that everything happens to us as it will. We can do nothing about it; judgment and will-power are just words. No one can lose himself or save himself, but as we are born, so we shall always remain.

Moreover, it is an experience in which the link between city and country is shown in its substantial ambiguity:[6]

Giusto wanted to use me; instead, what happened is that in his hands I became a woman. What gave him power over me was my own desperate need to get away from the country and come to the city, to know myself better, as I had dreamed of doing at school. He found me [daring] and fearful; he only had to raise his hand to imagine he had seduced me. But the real truth is that any pleasure I felt from his crude intimacy and cold eyes was like looking at myself in a mirror.

The scene in which Lidia re-evokes her liberation, the magic moment when she became aware of her own strength compared with Giusto, who is no longer the master, has a particularly poetic resonance because it contains so many of Pavese's favorite images:

It happened one day as I was walking through our vineyard on my way to the path by the chestnut trees; it was already late in the afternoon, and a big translucent moon was rising over the plantation . . . All at once I knew I was free. I paused, held myself straighter, asking myself what Giusto meant to me. I smiled to myself, imagining him waiting there alone, looking so ill-tempered, crafty and uncouth, and I heard myself laugh[ing silently]. Suddenly I felt an urge to test him, to wound him, and I took a step forward. Then I stopped and smiled once more, while the bats darted to and fro across the moon. I rised my arms as a baby does, then burst into shrieks of laughter like a silly girl and turned to go back. I was alone; [I] was enough for [myself]. I even forgot my spiteful impulse to see how Giusto liked being jilted. I was free and on my own.

That is how "the fever which had burned in [her] blood all that summer" ends; later, in the city, Lidia is able to find in her blithe affection for Nanni a serene equilibrium, a peace that has something idyllic about it: "As I listened, it always surprised me that he expressed his thoughts so plainly and simply. With him, I seemed to see myself reflected in a mirror, hearing him calmly discussing things I would say only to myself."

The preceding passage can be compared with and explained by a reflection taken from Pavese's diary:

But why it should be better to *be in communication with another* than to be alone, is a mystery. Perhaps it is only an illusion, for one can be perfectly happy alone, most of the time. [It is pleasant now and then to have a pitcher to pour oneself into and then drink oneself from it since] what we ask of others we already possess within ourselves. The mystery is why it is not enough to drink and fathom our own individuality alone; why we should have to *repossess* ourselves through others. (Sex is merely incidental; what it gives is momentary and casual: we [aim at something more hidden and] mysterious, of which sex is only a sign, a symbol.)[7]

Sex seems to have a metaphysical character for Pavese; it is not the act in itself that matters but its existential significance: the self gains its own being by mirroring itself in another's existence; or rather, sex has the inadequate and precarious function of linking (once more) the contingent to the necessary.

But Lidia's peace constitutes one happy excerpt and one unusual conclusion among the experiences with love of Pavese's characters. Amalia's in "The Cornfield"[8] have a very different ending: she too, like Lidia, is a girl from the country and wants to become a city-dweller: "When Amalia washed herself, shut up in the kitchen, standing in the washtub, she felt she was scouring off the taint of the land and the vineyard." Her timid love for the cyclist Remo, however, is destined to failure from the beginning; he fascinates her, not so much with his ways as with the help of the civilized life of the city: we see for instance the scene in the restaurant "where they were served by waiters in white jackets":

"I'm a poor country girl," Amalia babbled as she drank her iced white wine. "You've seen where I live, haven't you? My father planted corn all round the house, as if it were a shed. If you really love me you ought to set fire to the place. At the very least, burn the corn, root it out, so that I never set eyes on it again."

But after making love to Amalia on a canvas cot in an attic, Remo then loses interest in her; and Tonino, by destroying the cornfield, cuts off her last peasant roots and consecrates symbolically the destruction of Amalia's innocence. It is easy to imagine her destiny from now on; it will be like Ginia's in the novel *The Beautiful Summer*.

There are three short stories posterior to that novel ("The City," "The Houses," and "The Summer") that in retrospect throw light on its urban setting, rhythm, tone, and significance. It is worthwhile examining them in detail.

In "The City" a country-boy narrates in the first person his initiation into city life.[9] He portrays his relationship with Gallo, his "guide and master," as one of implicit and therefore typical mediation. Gallo stands out in this story because of his balanced and virile personality, his calm, self-assured character, like the cousin in "Southern Seas," Candido in "The Sea," and Nuto in *The Moon and the Bonfires*:

Scarcely a night went by that we didn't sit drinking and playing cards till morning. Gallo taught me how to enjoy myself without losing my temper; not that he'd give me lessons, but it was enough just to watch him when he dealt cards, or laughed over a glass, or eagerly threw open a window for me to feel ashamed of my rages.

It is Gallo who likes to stroll at night over the hills, to go into taverns, meet friends; his tastes inevitably influence those of his young friend, who unlike him is avid to identify with the city:

It was so good to know that at certain times all one had to do was enter a café, stop in a doorway, or whistle in an alley for old friends to turn up, and one would agree and go off and have fun. It was even a pleasure, in company, to think that that night or the next day I would be happy to be alone; or that when I went home alone all I would have to do is go out to find a group of friends. But when April came, and then May, I missed the long nights spent in drinking, singing, arguing in some out-of-the-way tavern, the walks with Gallo in the cool of dawn, the last chat under the window.

The narrator of course does not have the same character as Gallo; his attitude towards women, for example, is the same as Stefano's in *The Political Prisoner:* "The idea of bringing a woman into the house who could assert rights on me and my peace disturbed me." And later, when Gallo has gone away and one of his old girl-friends goes to sleep with the narrator, in the big room on the top floor, a scene is repeated which is already familiar to us: "The next day, as if she knew my tastes, [Giulia] went away early. I stayed in bed thinking of Maria." The narrator of "The City" resembles Ginia in *The Beautiful Summer* in his external and environmental aspects, whereas in character he is much more like the figure of the painter in the novel. Nevertheless, these aspects are important, especially for the poetic background they create; the following description, for example, resumes in a more intimate and personal tone the sentiments and thoughts of Ginia and reflects her aspirations for a little "paradise on the roof tops":

I would throw open the window overlooking the roof tops every morning, listening to the faint noises that rose from down below.

In the limpid air the dark, uneven roofs looked like an image of my new life: fleeting hope about a rough base.

In "The Houses," too, the most interesting element is its evocation of city background, made by "one man alone who works"—a typical expression, a continuation of many in *Work Is Wearying*. Among his memories of youth in this evocation, he introduces a friend Ciccotto, the young servant girls, the workers, houses and streets of Turin—the background to his solitude:

That was the first afternoon I wandered around the empty city. The idea that I knew Lina then, and that at that moment Ciccotto was making love, upset me, excited me. I was a little drunk. I was young and everything seemed to me so easy. I didn't know yet that I was happy because I was alone.

Many motifs and attitudes link the third story, "The Summer," to the novel *The Beautiful Summer*—from the love that is joyous but lasts only a season to the exploration of the city, which reflects the presence of the loved one (again a description that is very similar to one quoted already from "The Three Girls"):

Dawdling in the streets in the evening, I would enjoy the passersby, the colors, the moments, knowing someone was waiting for me. I know that my hands and my body had something tender and alive, just like the clouds, the air, and the hills on those calm summer evenings.

And again, another lovely reflection, the tone of which reminds us of Gozzano, which could have been made by Ginia in love:

These evenings the summer didn't lose its strength, since we knew that each of us was thinking of the other. Every customary meeting struck my heart with this certainty and with scarcely a stir would make it overflow. Then the light rippled, and I saw it like a recent memory, as if I had come unexpectedly into a different summer, beyond bodies and voices, and the room I had left would be like a shadow which discreetly received me. Everything, as it took place, became a memory, because it happened within me before it happened without.

All of objective and temporal reality becomes subsumed into the sphere of the self—a participation, an extremely subjective contact, and therefore fragile and precarious as a precious and unreal spell. In *The Beautiful Summer*, which is a novel and not a short story or lyrical fragment, the spell is broken, and what dominates there is the strength of things.

Life was a perpetual holiday in those days. We had only to leave the house and step across the street and we became quite mad. Everything was so wonderful, especially at night when on our way back, dead tired, we still longed for something to happen, for a fire to break out, for a baby to be born in the house or at least for a sudden coming of dawn that would bring all the people out into the streets, and we might walk on and on as far as the meadows and beyond the hills.[10]

The beginning of the novel *The Beautiful Summer* is all centered on the motif of the "festival night" transposed from the country to the city: though the background has changed, the presentation of *homo ludens* rather than *homo laborans* remains the same. One could almost say that *homo ludens* is better able to reveal his true essence, with its simple and sacred flavor—a comparison of holidays and workdays that goes back to ancient times, a superstitious-religious contrast between *fas* and *nefas*. The festival night is thus pervaded with a joyous sense of the unexpected, of adventure, which is characteristic of youth, ready for life, unaware of death, carried away by happiness. This happiness is fragile, composed mainly of words: Ginia abandons herself to words in order to overcome the crises that seize both her and Tina, the lame girl who "did not get enough to eat at home," a figure belonging to a reality that does not permit of dreams.

The festival night is not the only country motif transferred to the city: Guido, the painter who was originally from the country, says: "But I am only really happy on the top of a hill," and later the country is pinpointed as the place of original innocence as opposed to the present gloominess and corruption, like the mythical and ambiguous escape from the closed horizon of the city:

Guido had said, "You ought to see me in the country. It is the only place where I can paint. No woman is as beautiful as a hill." Ginia was happy because Guido had not taken the model on and intended, instead, to make a picture that was to extend all round a room as if the wall was open and they would see hills and blue sky on every side.

The passage is particularly important in that Guido does not want to return to the country; he only wants to reproduce it in his own surroundings, thereby both changing its nature and accepting his own no longer innocent condition as a city-dweller. In the following dialogue Pavese more or less consciously caricatures *The Harvesters:*

Guido spoke of the hillside he wanted to paint; his idea was to treat the subject as if it was a woman lying extended with her breasts in the sun and he was going to give it the flavor and taste of women. Rodrigues said, "It's been done before. Change it. It's been done."

. . . Then Guido held forth: "But no one has ever combined the two; I am going to take my woman and stretch her on the ground as if she was a hill against a neutral sky."

"A symbolic picture then. In that case you paint the woman, not a hill," snapped Rodrigues.

When one experience is exhausted, the writer must turn to another. *The Beautiful Summer* is the story of the discovery of a world completely different from the sensual and violent world of the country, nevertheless a world in which the characters become aware of the reality of city life in a way that is not unlike that of the protagonist of *The Harvesters*, in other words primarily through the senses. For example, Ginia's sense of smell is strongly impressed by the painter's surroundings, which are new to her: "A smell of freshly mixed gesso and varnish filled the empty studio." The sense of smell is also very important in rousing Guido's and Ginia's love:

"There's none of that smell of varnish here that you get in other painters' studios," said Ginia.

Guido got up and began to slip on his jacket. "It's turps. A good smell." Ginia did not know how, but suddenly she saw him in front of her and felt a hand on the nape of her neck, and all she could do, like a fool, was open her eyes wide and bang her hip against the table. Red as a live coal, she heard Guido close to her, saying, "The scent you have under your arms is nicer than turpentine."

And then again: "While they were in the middle of washing the paintbrushes, Ginia paused a moment, enraptured: the smell of the turps brought back the memory of Guido almost as if he was there."

Hearing and sight are also important means of grasping reality, for example in the description of Guido's studio in the evening, which is pervaded with an acute sensitivity to sounds and colors, to silence and darkness, with a subtle tension noticeable in things:

Guido was still walking up and down and seemed to be everywhere at once; the thin floor vibrated under his boots. They were all talking at once, but Ginia suddenly noticed that Amelia was silent, though she saw the cigarette, and that Rodrigues was silent as well. There was only Guido's voice filling the room, explaining something, she could not make out what, because [she was straining her ears in the direction of the sofa]. A light from the lamps outside came through the windows like a reflection from the rain, and she could hear the rain splashing and pouring on to the roofs and guttering. Every time both the rain and the voices ceased, it somehow seemed colder. Then Ginia strained her eyes into the darkness trying to see Amelia's cigarette.

Since the story has painter's quarters for its background, it is to be expected that the most vivid and significant of the poetic motifs should be based on sight. For example, the colors are an integral part of the joy inspired by the city at the beginning; they are an element in the discovery of the city and at the same time a sign of Ginia's innocence and self-assurance:

They left after twelve o'clock and were pleased to find themselves among people again and to walk along properly dressed and see the lovely colors in the street that came from the sun—it was undeniable, though they did not know how—since they disappeared at night.

Ginia will have the same serene impression at the beginning of her affair with Guido:

Just then the alarm went off; she was awake already, thinking of so many things in the warm cosiness of her bed. As dawn broke she regretted that it was now winter and you could not see the lovely colors that accompanied the sun. She wondered if Guido, who said that colors [meant] really [everything], was thinking the same thought. "How lovely," said Ginia to herself and got up.

Above all, sight constitutes a true and real *poétique du regard*, by means of which Pavese unfolds the whole story of

Ginia, of her hopes, her discomfitures, her decadence. It is useful to examine Ginia more closely, watch her move through the streets of the city, in cafés, in rooms, and get to know her as she gets to know herself. In the beginning Ginia, who is working in a dressmaker's shop and whose brother works at night and sleeps in the daytime, is used to being alone and even likes solitude:

In the middle of the day—Severino turned over in bed when she came in—Ginia laid the table. She was always desperately hungry and chewed slowly, at the same time listening to all the household noises. As is usually the case in empty lodgings, there was no sense of urgency, and Ginia . . . sometimes would close the shutters so as to darken the room and feel more cut off.

Or behind the curtain of her painter friend:

Behind there too she could smell Amelia's perfume, and she thought it must be pleasant to sleep alone tucked away in that corner. . . . She could hear both their voices at her back; in that corner it was like being in an empty house surrounded by a great peace in which to collect her thoughts.

But soon we discover that, in solitude as well as in happiness, Ginia has a need of love which must soon find an outlet, a direction: "She imagined herself alone in the unmade bed in that corner of the studio, listening to Guido moving about on the other side of the curtain, living with him, kissing him and cooking for him."

In fact, Ginia does fall in love with the painter Guido, but the story of her love will be one of sorrowful failure, of progressive and unrelenting degradation. Ginia's destiny is contained in one significant sentence when she is thinking about Guido's first embrace, which she had repulsed:

But the more she thought about it, the more she knew she would go back. . . . The whole evening in the darkness of the cinema, she thought with a heavy heart that whatever she might decide now, she would end by going back there. She knew that this longing to see him again and to ask his forgiveness and tell him she had been a fool would drive her mad.

Subtly linked to the story of Ginia's love for Guido there is the undercurrent of her relationship with Amelia, the model who "looked rather heavy round the hips in her bathing costume, and her features were faintly horsey," a "poor blighter" with her "crudely made-up mouth" that roused Ginia's pity but was also a confused and powerful attraction for her, an echo of sin. It is in fact Amelia who introduces Ginia to the gay, corrupt world of painters in Turin, and, what is more important, to her own inclinations to vice. Amelia is attracted to Ginia, who is unaware of it and talks to her about Guido, but then Amelia reveals her unnatural feeling when she kisses her "swiftly on the lips." Ginia's reaction is to give "a frightened smile under Amelia's stares." And when she listens to Amelia's explicit confession, made in a husky voice and combined with the announcement that she is ill with syphilis, Ginia does not believe her friend and yet feels disgust at being near her:

Ginia was puzzled what to answer because she herself did not know what she should have done. But she did not mind Amelia's criticism, because she now knew what nudes and poses were and understood her jargon. She allowed Amelia to go on talking excitedly, but at the same time she was conscious of a nausea like that she had felt as a child when she was having a bath and was undressing on a chair close to the stove.

Whatever the relationship is between the two girls, it is not so much one of friendship as of subordination and attraction, unconscious on the part of Ginia, who is still an adolescent and inexperienced in comparison with Amelia, who is already an adult with a little too much experience: a relationship that

we have already seen in other Pavese characters and that is
here described in a passage revealing the mediation resulting
from the dialectic of master and slave:

Reluctantly and in defense against her boredom, Ginia tried to
pick up with her former friends again. After all, by the following
summer she would be seventeen and she felt she knew her way
around as much as Amelia, the more so now she was out of touch
with her. During the evenings, already becoming cold, she tried
to put on an Amelia-act with Rosa. She often laughed openly at
her and took her for long, chatty walks.

Remember in this connection Amelia's words about models:
"The cleverest models are the ones who drive the artists fran-
tic. If you don't move every now and again, they forget
you're a model and treat you as if you were a servant. Behave
like a sheep and the wolf will eat you." The master-slave
dialectic as seen by Pavese in the microcosm of love begins
now to extend to other human relationships; the same dialectic
will be found later in the macrocosm of history, with a sad
combination of results: impotence and failure on both
levels.

But meanwhile, to return to the *poétique du regard*, we
notice the increase in Ginia's self-knowledge: at the beginning, when she watches her reflection in the store window and
compares it with her friend Rosa:

The only things Ginia and Rosa had in common were that short
stretch of street and the star of small pearls in their hair. But once
when they were walking past a shopwindow Rosa said, "We look
like sisters," and Ginia saw that the star looked cheap and realized
that she ought to wear a hat if she didn't want to be taken for a
factory girl.

Then, under the looks of her painter friends, and because of
them, Ginia becomes increasingly more self-conscious, in-

creasingly *pour soi;* at first she reacts with ill-concealed em-
barassment, as if paralyzed:

Ginia climbed the last stair, reluctantly, feeling the grey inquisi-
tive eyes fixed on her. She could not decide whether they were
the eyes of an old man or a cunning old devil. . . . Amelia went
and sat down on a chair under the shadow of the curtain, and
Ginia found herself standing for what appeared an endless time
not knowing how to respond to the glances she received from the
two of them, who stared at each other and then at her.

Ginia turned over several sheets; at the fourth or fifth, she was
in a cold sweat. She did not dare to say anything, feeling the grey
eyes of the man behind her. Amelia, too, was looking at her
expectantly. . . .

Those grey eyes and that lead pencil had fixed, measured and
scrutinized her more shamelessly than a mirror and put an end to
her gaiety and chatter.

In the second phase Ginia reacts with a certain self-assurance: "When she came out, she noticed they were looking at
her inquisitively. Ginia had removed her hat by this time,
[raised her head] and picked up a large plate by the window,
all daubed with colors like a palette." Her love for Guido is
also marked by looks and glances; at their first meeting, he
shook hands with Ginia, "looking her over with an impudent
smile on his face"; then later,

as she wept, she thought, "supposing Guido were to cry, too," and
a burning sensation ran through her whole body as if she was
going to faint. Suddenly the support was removed; she realized
that Guido was getting up and she opened her eyes. Guido was
standing there looking at her, puzzled. She stopped crying then
because she felt as if she were crying in public. As he looked at
her, Ginia, who could hardly see, felt more tears welling into her
eyes.

Or again:

She had embarked on her real life as a lover because she and Guido had now seen each other naked and everything seemed different. She felt as if they were married; even when she was alone, she had only to recall the expression in his eyes and her loneliness vanished.

When she is alone, however, Ginia feels all the strange and morbid fascination that surrounds artists' models, and, just as she had looked at herself in the store window, she now gazes at herself in the mirror, in a scene in which the delicacy of her no longer virginal, yet still innocent love equals the subtlety with which the cunning corruption of an evil example is at work:

That evening when Ginia had arrived home, she locked the door and then got undressed in front of the mirror and looked at herself, absorbed, comparing her skin with the color of Guido's neck. [Now all the pain was over] and it seemed strange to her that there were no marks left on her. She imagined herself posing before Guido, and she sat down on a chair in the way Amelia had done that day in Barbetta's studio. Heaven knew how many girls Guido had seen. The only one he had not really seen was herself, and Ginia's heart beat fast at the mere thought. How lovely it would be to become dark, slim, devil-may-care like Amelia all of a sudden. But she could not let herself be seen naked by Guido; they must get married first. . . .

Ginia felt chilly there before the mirror and flung her coat over her bare thighs; it gave her goose flesh. "Look, that's how it would be if I posed," she said, and envied Amelia who had ceased to have any sense of shame.

Eventually Ginia poses in the nude for Guido, in order not to lose him; and loses him, precisely then, because of her clumsiness:

While they were all laughing and trying to cheer her up, she ran barefoot to the curtain and desperately flung on her clothes.

Nobody followed her. Ginia tore the waistband of her knickers in her hurry. Then she stood there in the semidarkness; the sheets of the unmade bed nauseated her. They were all quiet outside.

Ginia becomes a woman more through her own reflection in the mirror than through the actual act of carnal love: the self sees itself as another before it even has an awareness of itself:

Seeing her reflection in the shopwindows, reeling as if she was drunk, she felt she bore no relation to that vague image that was moving past like a shadow. . . .

As soon as Severino had gone out, Ginia closed the door and undressed in front of the mirror. She found herself unchanged; she could not believe it. She ran her hand over her skin as if it was something separate from her body, which still gave a few final shudders. But she was otherwise no different; she was as white and pale as ever. "Guido should see me if he were here," she thought hastily. "I would let him look at me. I would tell him that I really am a woman now."

The secret distress Ginia experienced the first times she watched Amelia posing in the nude expressed her discovery of the community of the human condition, a discovery which went beyond the eye-catching appearances, "something barbaric and exotic"[11] about women in the city similar to the Babylonians or to the Alexandrians, to the exploration of a deeper reality, to the search for the essence of life:

It was the sort of foolish excitement she would have felt if they had been alone, the excitement at the discovery that they were both made in the same mould and whoever had seen Amelia naked was really seeing *her*. She began to feel terribly ill at ease. . . .

Surely a woman offered a better subject dressed? If painters wanted to do them in the nude, they must have ulterior motives. Why did they not draw from male models? Even Amelia when disgracing herself in that way became a different person; Ginia was almost in tears.

Or again: " 'But why have we to be nude?' she thought despairingly."

Nevertheless, on to Ginia's feeling of outraged spiritual virginity is grafted the hope that love can soothe, console, and protect; but these moments are brief, because Ginia's truly existential nudity is more often a recognition not so much of a common human condition, but of something more than that, of the insuppressible solitude of individuals:

Then she became conscious that Guido was asleep and felt they could not go sleeping like this, locked in each others' arms, and she disengaged herself gently and found a cool spot; then she felt uncomfortable, naked, and alone. Again she was overcome with a kind of nausea, as when they bathed her as a child.

These are almost the same words as Pavese uses in the story "Nudism": "the isolation and sadness of when I was a child and took my clothes off to wash myself."[12] (Note that a similar state of mind brings out the theme of childhood memories.) Ginia's weeping at the end of the novel will seal the failure of her love; she will be truly naked and alone: " 'We did not even say goodbye to each other,' she murmured and dashed into bed so as not to burst out crying in her naked state."

It should be noticed that the original title of the novel— *The Curtain*—had its own precise significance in relation to what I call the *poétique du regard:* the dark, heavy curtain that divides Guido's studio in half is the theatrical backcloth, a stage curtain, for the looks that hover, meet, and turn away. This truly theatrical function is emphasized even by Ginia's thoughts: "How pleasant it would be to be snugly ensconced there, spying on someone who thought he was alone in the room." The final title, *The Beautiful Summer*, seems instead to give bitter emphasis to the girl's lively, joyous hopes as she discovers herself and the world, and the terrible final disillusionment, projected into the cycle of the seasons. Summer opens the novel:

It was so hot that year that they needed to go out every evening, and Ginia felt she had never known before what summer was, so pleasant was it to stroll along the avenues every night. Sometimes she thought the summer would never end and they must make haste to enjoy it together, because when the season changed something was bound to happen.

Summer is also the typical country season, and as such provides a *leit motif* that underscores by contrast the painter's lack of love: "Then Guido pressed her arm. 'You're not the summer. You don't know what it is to paint a picture. I ought to fall in love with you to teach you all about it. Then I should be wasting time.' "

But above all summer is the symbol of Ginia's now wasted innocence and youth:

Sometimes Ginia would stop in the streets as she suddenly became aware of the smells of summer, its sounds and colors and the shadows of the plane trees. She thought of them while she was still surrounded by mud and snow; she would stop at the street corners, desire catching at her throat. "It *must* come, the seasons never change," but it somehow seemed improbable now that she was all alone. "I'm an old woman, that's what it is. All the good days are over."

Thus, the novel about the "beautiful summer" ends in the saddest winter: "When she was alone in the snow, she still felt naked. All the streets were deserted; she did not know where to go." Ginia's maturity has been a fallen fruit, a short season that has already passed and cannot be repeated. From now on, she will follow Amelia's road, as the last line of the novel indicates, full of a desolate abandonment: " 'We can go where you like,' said Ginia, 'you lead the way.' "

In *The Beautiful Summer* Pavese continued and intensified his efforts to take hold of and understand reality, to strip it of its more obvious and contingent aspects in order to get at the marrow, the essence; to achieve his aim, he has used a dialogue that precludes and limits lyrical outbursts, a dialogue that he himself called his "real muse in prose."[13] It enabled him to present his characters with their existential problematic in the context of a style that is itself significant for its apparent poverty and aridity: there has been a transition from Stefano's elegiac and contemplative evocation of solitude in *The Political Prisoner*, through Berto's interior monologue in *The Harvesters*, to the concrete and active dialogue of Ginia's attempts at love: Ginia by nature is ingenuous and a dreamer, but she wants to become a woman; she wants, in other words, to live, not just to be present in life; she wants to mature and not remain an adolescent; she wants to love, i.e., to communicate, not to remain alone. But her attempt fails, and its failure will be reflected later in the analogue of Silvia and Giovanni, the two characters of *A Great Fire*, a tense and violent novel in which converge the motifs of *The Political Prisoner*, *The Harvesters*, and the poetry of *Earth and Death*. For example:

I realized that with Silvia there was no other way of loving her—without a kiss, [which] meant nothing [anyway]—without a word, without a gesture of love-making. I remembered my clothes on the floor and reflected that it was just like at the [whorehouse]. You got undressed, dressed again and went off. It did not even last the night through.

Then I set on her in a frenzy. She murmured my name; I said

nothing; in the end I bit her blindly in the neck. Somehow I [wanted to] hear her cry out.[14]

Or, a passage which has a lot in common with similar and contemporary passages from the mythological stories of *Dialogues with Leucò*:

Because ever since my boyhood days I had always known that I would find a Silvia and weep and scrap with her too. At the present time it seemed impossible that I had ever believed in any other look, any other pair of lips; but already in the blazing days of that summer I realized that the person who had preceded her had merely announced her. Now that sudden and savage disharmony had arisen continually between us, that fierce tenderness which is the [return] of the country turned city. And with my new conquest of physical love, now that I had ceased to be the slave of her blood or of anyone else's, I rediscovered my childhood memories, over beyond the roads and the houses; fantastic, light-hearted memories like a person dreaming of a destiny or a horizon which is no longer bounded by the hills or the clouds, but by blood, by the woman of whom the clouds and the hills are merely a symbol. And the Silvia [I had pushed away from myself and suppressed inside myself] was, for all her sophisticated appearance, a wild creature of blood and sex.[15]

However, it is not necessary to analyze *A Great Fire* in detail: the very way in which this novel is put together (alternate chapters written by Pavese and Bianca Garufi) and the fact that it was published incomplete would seem to indicate the impossibility of communication and comprehension between the self and the other: it is in itself structured incommunicability.[16]

Giovanni remains, in fact, fundamentally a stranger for Silvia, nor is he any more successful at identifying with her childhood memories. Thus, there would seem to be a connection between the childhood memories and the failure of love, as we see in the fragment "Years," which should have been the beginning of the novel:

Now nothing remains of what I was then: I was barely an adult and at the same time a boy still. I had known it for sometime, but everything happened at the end of the winter, one evening and one morning. . . . All the time I had spent with Silvia in that room seemed no more than a day and a night, and it was coming to an end now with morning. Now I understood that she would never go out into the cool fog with me again.

The images of winter in this fragment are linked with the end of *The Beautiful Summer*, whereas the morning is analogous to that beautiful and heart-rending morning that appears in the poems of *Death Will Come and Its Eyes Will Be Yours* (and the fog adds a delicate touch of city landscape—of Turin, of Gozzano).

But it is only in *Among Women Only* that the ultimate results of the failure of love to give meaning to life will become fully apparent: Clelia (a grown-up Ginia) will tell the unhappy story of the inability to communicate that ends in the suicide of Rosetta (a Ginia who refuses to accept compromises).

Meanwhile Pavese, perhaps as an understandable reaction, focuses his search in a different direction than that of *The Beautiful Summer*, but one that has, nevertheless, already been mentioned or anticipated on some occasions in that novel: the mythical, childhood world of *August Holiday*.

5

The Honey of a Problematic Mind

"In studying very young souls one would clearly perceive in them the seeds of virtues and vices."
VITTORIO ALFIERI

"It is perhaps childhood that comes closest to real life."
MARCEL RAYMOND

Childhood, since Rousseau, has become one of the most characteristic and significant themes of contemporary literature, perhaps because, as Salinari says, in it is catalyzed

a *real* trait of the psychology and condition of modern man: the longing for a place that is free of the chaos and contradictions of contemporary society, for an oasis of original innocence that cannot be reached by echoes of the violence and ugliness of our life, in which conflict and struggle disappear, in which our problems vanish. A longing that is born of a natural desire to avoid man's slavery to things, the frenzy of industrial society, the inevitability of wars, the rule of money. A desire that virile man represses, considering it purely as a dangerous illusion, and throws himself, instead, into the daily struggles: it nevertheless remains in his mind as one of the terms of the dialectic of his personality and occasionally fascinates him and makes his struggle more dramatic and his "engagement" more human and more difficult. The symbols of this conception in decadent literature are childhood and the country, compared more or less explicitly with adult man and the city.[1]

Pavese fits such conditions perfectly, not only by the manner in which he seeks refuge in childhood, escaping from the world's violence and the ugliness that is linked with the failure of love (as I have tried to show in the preceding chapters), but particularly for the dialectical framework he gives from the outset to his existential search in the direction of childhood: its main aspects—the consolation and the problematic, the escape and the "engagement"—are woven subtly into the short stories and essays, marking the difference between Pavese's conception and the similar conception of others, such as Leopardi or Pascoli.

In his contrast of city and country, Pavese reveals his decadent roots; if we remember the ambiguity of the two extremes of the dichotomy, it would be worth noting that Pavese, in contrast to Pirandello, rediscovers in the country not only that nature is a refuge, an escape, the ideal of childhood, but also and above all that nature is the source of adult problems concerning art, history, and man's destiny. *August Holiday* contains to a greater degree than any other of his books all the different shades and variations of Pavese's childhood themes.[2]

The main inspiration of *August Holiday* is directly linked to "Festival Night" and "First Love," but its roots go much farther back, as for example in "Land of Exile":

And when I reflect how intensely I longed for the skies and streets of Piedmont—where I am living so restlessly now—I can only conclude we are made that way. Only when a thing has passed, or changed, or vanished, can we really see what it is like.

The nucleus of these stories is therefore the search for the real in the past: the probing of childhood and adolescence when all the characteristics of adulthood are prefigured and therefore the shape of present reality. For Pavese, in fact, as already for Alfieri with his echoes of Rousseau, the boy contains *in nuce* all the salient characteristics of the mature man. Such a concept or variations of it is repeated on numerous occasions.[3] It is sufficient here to quote two passages from "The Family":

If everybody knew what I know now—this morning I wept with rage—what it means to be the prisoner of one's own identity, a victim of predestination! In a child of six are already engraved all the impulses, the capabilities, the [value] he will have as a man of thirty. If only people understood that, no one would dare to think of the past. Instead, they would invent a detergent to wash the memory clean. . . .

Experience serves to teach us, not what we ought to do, but what we inevitably shall do. A man, no matter how bright, is like a bridge that can carry a certain weight and no more.

In his search for the boy, Pavese really examines the man; in his search for the past, he explores primarily the present. Before asking ourselves what is the point of such a search, it would be worth examining the way in which he carries it out. The short stories represent the boy's world, either seen directly or re-evoked by an adult, or else the world of adults seen through a boy's eyes. Gradually the relationship of adult and boy is developed along lines that show more and more a rational reflection in their essay-like form, as we shall see presently, thus revealing the direct intrusion of the author, whose characters alone do not suffice to articulate a world vision. The results of the search are extremely important and decisive; they are at the heart of Pavese's work and therefore of his life: his search for the real, in fact, evolves and ends in the poetic of myth, and later, of destiny.

In the fragment "The Beggars," Pavese sketches the sentimental education and instinctive aversion to adults of a boy, Geri, who looks on the beggars primarily as grown-ups and fears or resents them.[4] The only ones who appeal to him are those who excite his childish imagination, the picturesque and decent vagabonds found in the poems of *Work Is Wearying*:

On the other hand, the poor he felt really sorry for, and even envied a little, were ragged street urchins, old men with the tearful look of drunkards, women carrying a baby that looked like a dirty bundle of clothes, but especially buskers [street musicians] who played and played on street corners, never saying a word or looking around them, the poor who never asked for anything and looked at the ground if anyone stopped by them.

One remembers also "An Old Trade," which describes the "fascinating" life and freedom of wandering carters, already mentioned in a poem.

Later, Geri with his friend Achille explores the strangest aspects of the city:

One day he went into a café frequented by prostitutes; another time it was to hang around outside the prison, eating monkey nuts, on the off chance that some prisoner might be brought along in handcuffs; another time he would wait about outside a large tailoring shop until the seamstresses came out, in the hope of picking up something worth while.

Compare the preceding description with the key attitude, so important for the understanding of Pavese's mind, of the narrator of "Evocation" (the title in itself seems to be a confession or manifesto):

"I've always been a bad lot, but more important than that, a boy. Some nights I didn't want to go to bed, because it seemed such a waste of time. I'd have liked to be awake all the time, out breathing the air and looking around. Looking, always looking. That would have been enough for me. It thrilled me just to go out of doors and look at the weather, the people going by; to get the smell of the street. It was fun to think it over afterwards, too. There are humiliations, too, but one must have patience.". . .

Hence I am a great frequenter of cafés and taverns, and like to sit in a dark corner with my back to the window.

The narrator of "Awakening" also ends up in "a tiny dark tavern"; it is not worth mentioning again all the similar characters and images that have already been quoted in the preceding chapters. But to return to the fragment we are examining, the conclusion gives an invaluable indication of Geri's (and Pavese's) character: "If only Achille wouldn't keep murmuring, whenever he passed a pretty girl: 'How I'd like to kiss you when you're naked.' Geri found it distasteful. There shouldn't be any need to say things like that to prove oneself a man." There is another character like Geri in "End of August" who explains the boy's attitude very well, in a passage that continues the themes of *The Beautiful Summer:*

That gale in the night had, as sometimes happens, unexpectedly brought back to me, under my skin and in my nostrils, a joy from the past, one of those bare secret memories, like our body, which have been ingrained in us, one would say, since childhood. . . . A boy—was it me?—was standing by night on the seashore, under the music and artificial lights of the café, and was sniffing the wind—not the usual sea smell but an unexpected gust of flowers scorched by the sun, exotic and palpable. That boy could exist without me; in fact, he did exist without me, and he didn't know that his joy would after so many years flower again, incredibly, in another, in a man. But a man presupposes a woman, *the* woman.

The fact is that the man and the boy in turn exclude each other, and it is precisely the woman who is the cause of the break, the seal as it were of the time between the two ages:

The man and the boy are unknown to each other and seek each other; they live together and don't know it, and when they find each other they need to be alone. Clara, poor thing, loved me that night as she always did. . . . But from then on I couldn't forgive her for being a woman, the one who transforms the remote smell of the wind into the taste of flesh.

These words reveal, clearly, poetically, piercingly, the point at which Pavese's search for reality fails. The smell of the wind, the illusions and dreams of childhood, are transformed into the taste of flesh, in an adult and concrete reality. But Pavese, although he recognizes this reality, does not know how, or cannot, or does not want to accept it. Woman therefore represents for him his crisis in the face of reality: the childhood-maturity dichotomy is not resolved, the fallen angel remains desperately lonely. (We are reminded of such stories as "Wedding Trip" and "Suicides.")

But meanwhile we see what riches are enclosed in the world of childhood; one of its aspects, the countryside, is sketched in "The Name" and resumed on broader lines in other stories: hunts for snakes among stumps and stones, constantly interrupted and disturbed by the echoing yells of Pale's mother, a singsong complaining yell that acquires almost magical powers. In the figure of Pale, as in Biscione, there is *in nuce* something of Cinto in *The Moon and the Bonfires:*

The one I called Pale was very tall and thin, with a face like a horse. Whenever his father gave him a thrashing he would run away from home for two or three days. When he came back his father was always looking out for him with his belt handy, ready to whip the skin off his back, so he would run away again. Then his mother would start yelling for him at the top of her voice, cursing him as she leaned out of a dirty upstairs window that overlooked the fields and the reed beds by the river, down towards the mouth of the valley.

The whole short story is pervaded with the atmosphere of magic created by the name being yelled in the wind. (Though it may be pure coincidence, Pale, as well as being the diminutive of Pasquale, is also the name of a mythological divinity of the fields):

That damned old woman kept on calling him. . . . Pale held me by the wrist for a minute or two, then he said: "Come on then! Let's run!"

We ran as far as the level ground, pretending we weren't afraid by shouting every minute or two: "Look! There's a viper! After it!" But our real fear—mine, at least—was something more complex, a feeling that, for all I knew, we had offended the powerful spirits of the air and the rocks.

The motif, on the other hand, of a boy's admiration for a man, gradually shaken and destroyed by the intrusion of a woman, is brilliantly described in "The Leather Jacket," set in a restaurant-marina on the Po. Its proprietor, Ceresa, is gradually attracted by Nora and diverted from the exclusive relationship he had had with the boy. This is how the two adults are presented, and the boy's reaction to the situation (resentment for the woman, and affection for the man as for a father):

Ceresa always wore the leather jacket. . . . Once, I remember, when we were out in a boat and a storm blew up, he took it off and told me to wrap it round myself. Under it he was always bare to the waist, and he used to tell me that if I spent my life on the Po I'd have muscles as strong as his when I was a man. He had little moustaches and he was out in the sun so much his hair was almost blond. . . .

Nora would stand leaning against the door, cupping her elbow in one hand, wearing a red dress and staring at everybody without saying a word. . . . But if she was now keeping Ceresa company, it meant there was something quite extraordinary about her, and this worried me because I didn't understand what it could be.

Again: "It made me furious that Nora, who never went out in the sun and must have been as pale as the belly of a fish, should treat him as an equal and walk arm in arm with him. I would have given a good deal to [be able to talk like them]." There is almost a shiver of disgust and fear in that "pale as the belly of a fish"; the paleness does in fact reappear at the end, emphasizing the tragic epiphany: Nora is unfaithful to Ceresa and he strangles her and throws her into the Po; again, it is the boy who describes the events, abridging in his sensitivity:

I was seized with fear or shame, which, I don't know. I was still thinking of Nora's white skin. It seemed to me that [everything was crying aloud and that I heard myself being called]. Then the window opened. Ceresa leaned out and said: "Pino, slip along home, now." Then shut it quickly.

A boy's admiration for a man is the theme of "The Hermit" too, and of "Mr. Pietro," in which the whole counterpoint of exotic images should be emphasized—sea, ports, ships' sirens —apparently echoes from Melville. Since they reflect the fundamental nature of the narrator, they will reappear frequently in another group of stories. In "The Hermit" a widower father recounts the experiences of his son Nino:

The mornings he spent chasing through the fields behind the house, or wandering around the noisy market among the women and the men from the country, eager particularly to meet peddlars and charlatans who had come from far away, from places over the hill, beyond the river terraces: people who talked in a lively way and wore large red sashes round their hips and who would sometimes brag about being in exotic lands.

Fascinated as he is by the exotic, Nino does not hesitate to follow a good-for-nothing tramp into a cave on the hill, but is immediately brought back home:

It was mid-day and I was returning worn out in the rain, when there appeared in the square a blond hairy giant enveloped in a faded military cloak. When he reached the doorstep he opened the cloak and there was Nino, head and legs dangling like a kid, who stood up shamefacedly.

"This boy has been in a scrape," he said in a cheerful harsh voice. Drops were trickling from his blond beard, and his coat gave off a stench of wet dogs. Nino gazed at him enchanted, although traces of recent tears could be seen on his cheeks.

This is enough for the father to concede an atom of trust to the hermit, who actually is a laborer:

Pietro was not from the country like the others. He had even been in some seaport and chewed over in his dialect exotic words which captivated Nino. Now that he had substituted the smell of the cave-dweller with the smell of whitewash I understood that his real smell was one of health, of the open air, of a wise animal. I felt older with him than with my son.

Obviously the hermit also fascinates the father, and he describes the delight of that season (summer as always) almost as rapturously as a young boy: "August was drawing to a close and the imminence of the first harvest began to disturb the calm of the long mornings. The carts creaked; one heard talk of festival and balls in the near-by towns." And again: "If not one day then another, Pietro and Nino would go off together: there was always some farm or field from which echoes of accordions and songs would be carried on the wind. . . ." Finally, after a festival night, Nino's education is complete, the infatuation over: "The memory of that night when we returned is in my heart like Nino's childhood. The songs, the exhaustion, the excitement under the moon had an unreal, sad effect on me. I almost love that Pietro; one would think *I* was the child." The tone of the passages quoted is certainly that of the father's (the adult's) nostalgia for his own boyhood, a subtle but explicit nostalgia that faintly permeates the whole narration.

With "Mr. Pietro," on the other hand, we return to a direct childhood memory, and its importance lies in the many themes which express the boy's admiration for Mr. Pietro (a similar character to the cousin in "Southern Seas"). Briefly, the boy is an oprhan, a fact that has more existential than biographical importance for Pavese:

My father died when I was six, and I was twenty before I had any idea of how a man behaved in a house. . . . My mother tried to bring me up tough like a man, and she made it a rule that we should not kiss each other or go in for superfluous words, or even know what a family could be.

His only real memory of the time when he had a father is re-evoked with pensive and distressing tenderness:

When we sat down to the table, [mother and Mr. Pietro] had already remembered so many brave deeds from my childhood that I seemed to be in the house again where we used to spend summer and to be reliving those summer evenings, when he and my father would arrive together, shouting and laughing on the porch steps, and I would be waiting to run to meet him and fish in Dad's pockets, while mother appeared on the garden balcony, and they would greet each other and chat from a distance, and I would pull on his arm not to go home but come and eat with us.

But the father is most present in the child's imagination, rather than in his memory, in the sea images, which acquire a quite considerable psychological depth:

Around the corner of the last house, in the clear sky or the red glow of evening, the sea would appear, a sea I had never seen, huge with smoky ports, beaches, noises. In my mind, in fact, this image was confused with the vanished memory of my father, and I had always been extremely eager for news of him, for anecdotes, for details about him . . . so that I could identify my nature with his at the very roots, simply because I felt my own destiny was prefigured in him.

It is easy to imagine the attraction of Mr. Pietro, "one of those men who have achieved such a state of solid equilibrium that they would always stay unchanged," the living incarnation of so many fantasies and dreams: he is, in fact, living in the hotel surrounded by "many-colored cases, studded with labels," nonchalantly receiving letters with exotic stamps. Thus, the boy dares to ask of him what his father was never able to give him:

I asked Mr. Pietro directly if he did not have a sailor's job for me, a steward on some ship. I told him he must free me from that life or I would end up like my father. I spoke heatedly, and I remember I didn't dare stop for fear of the inevitable answer.

Mr. Pietro promises to help and makes the boy happy, for the thought of the sea represents the perfect escape from his everyday life, almost an echo of Leopardi's poetry, in which pleasure is only to be found in memory and longing, never in reality and the present: "I didn't go home that night. Instead I went into a café at the station to enjoy by myself the thoughts of the future and to taste my new freedom. I was drunk but not from wine. . . ."

Longing to escape is at the heart of another story, "Insomnia," and is shown in its origins, against the background of a night in which the stillness of the moonlight, of the shadows, and of the figure of the father seems to underline the restlessness of the vagabond son in a pure lyrical image:

When I returned to the threshing floor before dawn (home from the celebrations, arguments, and adventures) I knew my father was there, under the dark shadow of the walnut tree, standing motionless for goodness knows how long, gazing into the trees, his eyes flashing, always about to go out under the stars. . . . The walnut tree half filled the sky, but a big part of the threshing floor was not covered and gleamed white: I moved onto that white and the night was so clear that I saw my own shadow under my feet.

The desire to escape is explicit:

Outside were the countryside and the empty streets; next day in the sun it would all be different; but right now the frenzy to be done with it, to take a train and go off to the city and lead more of a man's life wouldn't let me sleep.

"Insomnia," therefore, concentrates on the pole of departure without which the poetic current of the return could never be developed. The long story "The Sea" elaborates on the idea of departure as escape and together with a group of short stories constitutes an extremely important prelude to *The Moon and the Bonfires.* "The Sea" begins:

Sometimes I think that if I'd had the courage to climb to the top of the hill I wouldn't have run away from home later. It must have been just after San Giovanni, because we had already several times been along the valley road and climbed as far as the walnut trees looking for the beds of the bonfires. We knew there were some at the top as big as a field. But one day Gosto bragged that as a boy his grandfather had run away from home and going through the valley had climbed so high that from up there he could see the sea.

The idea of the sea from the very beginning is at the back of this whole childish world of vineyards, hills and "groups with sunshades," "scattered voices of drunkards and dogs," bonfires in the night, boys for whom going barefoot is a badge of merit, strains of music and echoes in the wind—a world that seems "unreal" because it is filtered through the poetic imagination of the narrator, who transforms the reality of childhood places into myths: "Gosto doesn't know what it is to stand in front of a house and stare at it until it doesn't seem like a house any longer."

The two boys never actually made the decision to set out to see the sea; they acted, out of the blue, one night when they were all excited from the burning of some farm during a wedding, amid the confusion of joy and tears caused by two such different events. In the story the magical or mythical element is blended with realistic notations:

I had sat down on the wood box, and from there I could feel the fire and smell the meat cooking and hear the noise of the board where they were making pasta. The hill could be seen from the door and a little of the sky, and at that moment there was nothing better than the thought that I was with Candido and had spoken with my people and no one knew that the sea was down there. The hill looked like a cloud. Just close one's eyes and all that was left was that trunk of vines.

Or there is another example where we are left with a momentary image of the men, dirty and in their shirt-sleeves, who during the fire "were slapping their necks with their hands to kill the flies." But here we have the two boys' flight:

"Don't yell," I said to him. "They might hear us." We strained our ears to hear whether the singing was over, but that time we were alone with the crickets. Even Gosto stopped acting like a drunk and understood that yelling caused fear.

The "powerful spirits of the air" in "The Name" are present here too, as they are in *The Beach* and *The Devil in the Hills*, when the animal bellowing of Doro and Pieretto is understood as a challenge to restrictions. Perhaps the powerful spirits in the story we are examining are the same as provoked the fire, and it is to them that the huge bonfires on the festival nights are dedicated, and the music and songs; on to it is grafted the motif of Candido the street-player, who picks up again the theme of the poem "Smoking Cheap Cigarettes" and is rather more than a prefiguration of Nuto in *The Moon and the Bonfires*. He is in fact a complete and independent character:

Candido went and stood in the middle with his clarinet, and every time he stretches his lips and begins to play I like him more and more because he becomes more serious. The voice of the clarinet is the most beautiful and leads the others. Candido stretches his tongue under his moustaches and stares at the ground, but it is he who leads, commands with his eyes. The whole time they were playing not a word was heard and the music filled the courtyard. Then suddenly Candido shook his head, raised the mouth of the clarinet to the sky, and they stopped.

But he dominates the final pages of the story in a different, more intimate and touching sense: the runaway boy is looking for a father in Candido (he is the orphan of "Mr. Pietro" and will be the bastard in *The Moon and the Bonfires*), a father who is at the same time his link with the earth:

That evening we ate like newlyweds, with me sitting close to Candido, and a lady asked him in a loud voice whether I was his son. But everyone knew that Candido was young and that all he liked to do was play, and they laughed . . . I gazed at the dark hill where there was no more bonfire, and it seemed as if I had been born in that courtyard, and that I had always been up there with Candido.

All the motifs in "The Sea" are, moreover, taken up again in another very lovely story, "Intimate History," but this time in a more elegiac and perhaps more decadent vein, as we see from the breadth of the beginning, in which the figure of the father is deliberately given mythical proportions:

This was the road my father would take. He would do it at night because he wanted to arrive early. He climbed the hill on foot, walked the whole valley and then the other hills until the sun struck his face as he reached the top of the last crest. The road climbed into the clouds, which broke in the sun over the smoke of the valley. I have seen those clouds: they still glistened like gold. . . .

The background is always one of imagined rather than real escape (seeming to emphasize the echo of D'Annunzio's "the soft archipelagoes of clouds"):

I would imagine myself on distant coasts and long journeys: we would pass by gateways and all the many hidden flowers became confused in my thoughts with the sea. . . . As we climbed higher —but we didn't go up there very often and never alone—we could see the plain; the tiny flecks lost in the depths were houses or villages, they looked like sails, archipelagoes, surf.

But the escape, despite its vague outlines, becomes precise in the city:

In the chill of dawn I watched carefully to see where the main road ended and the apartment buildings began, and there was always this sort of gilded, cloudy haze that seemed like some other air, and one gradually entered it; once inside, it seemed impossible there could still be towns and hills. Far away, who knows where, there was the sea.

Or again, this passage, which has more depth:

I said nothing and gazed again at the city in the fog. That wasn't what I wanted from him. Women had made him my father, but there was something more ancient than this, more ancient and buried forever. A boy, is what I want to say. Just like me, my father had gone to the city, not to shut himself up in school but to make a fortune. He had gone there wild and hadn't changed. I wondered what had pushed him down there, what rage, what instinct, this man who nevertheless had been born in a field. . . . Maybe he too was looking for something wild and unknown in the city.

In trying to trace his dead father's life, the narrator, relying a great deal on sensory perceptions such as "I saw once more the women with veils on their heads and the Stations of the Cross; I smelt the incense and the freshly dug earth," is really looking for himself; in this search we find that escape-rootage dialectic that is the fulcrum of the motifs and images in *August Holiday* and is found in the background of all Pavese's work and life: city and country, sea and village:

I thought my father now existed as something wild, and he didn't have to wander night and day to make it clear to me. The church, as is only right, had swallowed him up, but even the church goes no farther than the horizon and my father, though under the ground, hadn't changed. From his body and blood roots were made, one of the thousands of roots that when the plant is cut are lost in the earth.

To become roots, to become the sap and juice of the earth, signifies a return to nature, discovering one's own metaphysical being rather than family origin; here we find one of Pavese's profound and recurrent needs, which can also be seen in the short story "Nudism." (In the following quotation the added italics draw attention to the wholly human awareness of death.)[5]

Every time I stretch my long legs out on the grass and turn my head, I know that the sun is looking at me and rummaging around in me from head to foot to see what I am; and I am no different from a stone, or a trunk, or a variegated snake, except for the *agitation* that I feel in showing myself. Now the water and sun have done me to a turn and bronzed me and even in this I get the idea that nature will not tolerate a naked human being and tries with everything at its disposal, like it does with *corpses*, to absorb it into itself.

In "Intimate History" this need to discover a more personal and yet more universal reality is something profound and touching, which founders in time even before space; it is a need felt with a primitive, gentle strength. Even the somewhat enigmatic figure of Sandiana, the woman whom his father loved, has a powerful attraction for the narrator-son, an attraction that consists of the mysterious strength of the nature she incarnates and interprets for the boy:

Then I sniffed the damp air and finally smelt the lightning: a new smell, like a flower I'd never seen, squeezed between the clouds and the water. . . . Now I understand why so many strange things are said about the woods, why there are so many unseen plants and flowers, and noises of animals who hide in the bushes. Perhaps the lightning becomes a stone, a lizard, a species of little flowers, and must be smelt. There was a smell of scorched earth, but scorched earth doesn't have that fragrance of the water. Sandiana's answer was no. . . . "Of course not," Sandiana said, "everything born comes from the earth; water and roots are in earth; in the grain you eat and the wine from the grapes there is all the goodness of the earth.

The style, in which the use of analogies can be traced back to D'Annunzio and Pascoli, is an accurate reflection of the narrator's character—"It wasn't what I was doing that I enjoyed but what I heard from others"—and reveals his fundamental lyricism, his essential basis of memories:

Then I thought about the things, animals, flavors, the clouds which Sandiana had known when she was in the woods, and I realized that everything wasn't lost, and that there are things which one just has to know are there to be able to enjoy them. Even the sloes, Sandiana said, one didn't eat more than two or three at a time. But it's a pleasure to know they can be found everywhere.

The basis of dreams and fantasies may be seen in an image which seems to have been taken literally from Leopardi's "The Infinite":

A hedge of blackberries shut off the horizon, and the horizon is clouds, distant things, streets, and it's enough to know they are there.

Thus, there is a poetic transition from the feeling of temporal search to that of spatial search, which takes the form of return to one's own home, to one's own land. "The Langhe Hills" exemplifies such a return in the most direct and explicit way and is a prelude to Anguilla's return in *The Moon and the Bonfires*, for in the short story that return is made a part of the dialectic of escape and rootage without which it is incomprehensible, and the profound need of totality that underlies it would not be apparent:

I didn't get married. I understood immediately that if I were to take one of those girls back to the city, even the smartest of them, I would have my village in my house and I wouldn't be able to remember it anymore the way I had just enjoyed doing. Each one of them, each one of those peasants and landowners, was merely a part of my village, and represented a villa, or a farm, or a hillside only. And I instead had it all in my memory; I myself was my village. All I had to do was close my eyes . . . to feel that my blood, my bones, my breath were all made of that substance and apart from me and that earth nothing existed.

Only solitude and distance make it possible for the narrator to be a narrator, to understand within himself all his little world and to make of it the subject of a story; between contemplation and action, essence and existence, perhaps between art and life, his choice has been made: he does in fact continue to travel around the world, carrying enclosed in his body and in his consciousness "everything in that land that mattered." His attitude and feelings could be described in Nicolò Tucci's words as "the exile of exile": "Some days I gazed at the outline of the hill more carefully than usual; then I would close my eyes and pretend I had already gone out into the world and was remembering every detail of that familiar scene."

This attitude is willed not endured, and it acquires a more

positive character in a story such as "A Certainty," where it leads to the discovery of one's own nature; for this reason, in the following quotation, the presence of psychoanalytic images, such as the cellar and the closed room, is very important. (They are particularly noticeable as a *leit motif* in *Earth and Death*.)

Just when I think I see something, I realize that it is only the reflection of a moment of my boyhood and I didn't even know what I would become. With all that I have done, seen, and known in the world, still the things which most belong to me are a heap of stones where I used to sit in those days, a cellar-grating at which I used to stare, a closed room I was never able to enter.

To rediscover oneself in a place or an object is to rediscover one's own past and one's own present at the same time; in this way the normal course of time becomes modified. In the story "Time" memory becomes a "discovery," a "reawakening" of the awareness of self, which thus sees itself in its own *durée*, in its own identity, in its own reality amid the things around it:

Things left unsaid appeared in the depths of the moment like a familiar object at the bottom of a pond, and all that was needed was a little courage to plunge in one's hand, to touch the distant elusive apparition. This happened particularly at the turn of the seasons, when the air is filled with shivers of the past that, fresh and unexpected, bring back old certainties. This feeling of the past, these shivers, gave me a kind of increase of life, a sort of feeling that beneath the ephemeral moment had accumulated a treasure that was already mine, that I only had to take notice of it.

This recognition is sealed by a mythical image:

One evening the moon was rising over the rim of the hill. The shrubs in the distance were black; the moon, enormous, mature.

We stopped. I said: "Every year, in September, the moon is the same, yet I never remember it. Did you know it was yellow?"

My friend looked at the moon and thought about it. It really seemed to me I had never seen it like this, but at the same time I seemed to have the taste of it in my mouth, to recognize in it something ancient, something from childhood, so I said: "It's a vineyard moon. As a child I used to think that the moon made and ripened the bunches of grapes."

While the search for reality and the self is being located in space (in the mythical places: the field of grain, the vineyard, the hill), it is simultaneously becoming oriented in time, or rather is escaping temporal dimension; in "Intimate History" we come across sentences such as the following, which give an unexpected glimpse of the Pavesian summer, season of maturity, admittedly, but also, and even more so, season of childhood—a closed cycle: "Time scarcely passed at all any more in our house. Every year summer was as if I never went away, a single summer that went on for ever."

We see too with what inventive and stylistic brilliance the summer is made to appear as a barefoot girl with a "harsh smile that could be heard in her voice like the blight of the sun," coming between the adult and the boy in "Dialogue by the River." In "The Field of Grain," on the other hand, timelessness is achieved in a moment of ecstasy: "That time then came to a halt I know, because I still find it intact today by the field of grain. . . . I know I have a certitude in front of me; I touched the bottom of a lake that was waiting for me, unchanged eternally." Enclosed magically in atemporal immobility are both the real and the mythical, all the sensations and images dear to Pavese:

Now, in the distance, the night bonfires on the hills and the growing dark between the faintly seen stalks in the field have merged into one. There was comfort in one thought only, that it is the boy who threw himself down on the ground to hide, and that hanging from the stalks were huge ears of corn which the peasants would come and pick tomorrow. And tomorrow there won't be a boy there anymore. . . . That furtive glance I gave is enough for me, and the empty sky is peopled with hills and apparitions.

There is really something magical about the adult and the boy meeting, about the place where this meeting happens. In "The Vineyard," Pavese probes and examines the mechanism of feeling and memory that makes such a meeting possible and gives the magic quality to this place: the anticipation of an event that has not yet happened. The anticipation of a moment, perhaps "composed of nothing" but which the boy lives without knowing he should remember, is "expanded beyond time" in the anxious desire to "grasp and know it thoroughly":

A simple and profound nothing, never remembered because it wasn't worth the effort, spread out through the days and then lost, crops up again in front of the path, in the vineyard, and appears childish, from beyond things and time, as it was in the days when time didn't exist for the boy. Then something really did happen. It happened a moment back; it is the moment itself: the man and the boy meet and recognize and tell each other that time has vanished. . . . In front of the path that climbs to the horizon, the man does not return to the boy: he is boy. For a moment, in which every memory is silenced, he finds beneath his gaze the still vineyard, instinctive, immutable, which he always knew he had in his heart. And nothing happens, because nothing can happen that is greater than this presence.

But if nothing happens and nothing can happen, what is the point of the search for the self? If the "immemorial ecstasies" by their very nature cannot last, to what do they lead? Pavese himself gives the real answer when he writes, almost incidentally:

There are skies and plants, and seasons and returns, meetings and tenderness, but all this is only the past, which life remolds like a play of clouds. The vineyard is made this, too, a honey of the mind, and something from its horizon opens up plausible views of nostalgia and hope.

"A honey of the mind," "nostalgia" and "hope," perhaps these phrases, even if they are not sufficient in themselves to explain the long search, can at least pinpoint the secret leavening which inspires it on the psychological and sentimental level and illuminate with gentleness and serenity, apart from the author's own intention, the ephemeral victory over time.[6]

Actually the world of childhood is something more than a honey of the mind. It is the vital nucleus, the origin and point of development of the whole of Pavese's adult, poetic world.[7]

Perhaps the best evidence of childhood as the matrix of the future is not in the short stories but in two letters Pavese wrote to Fernanda Pivano from Santo Stefano Belbo on June 25 and 27, 1942:

And so this morning I go out into the roads of my childhood and gaze cautiously at the huge hills—all of them, the enormous, succulent one which looks like a big breast, the rocky and sharp one where they used to make the big bonfires, the jagged hills which look as if they are towering over the sea—instead underneath was the road, the road which wanders around my old vineyards and disappears suddenly, with a leap into nowhere. . . . That was my Paradise, my Southern Seas, my Prairie, the coral reefs, Ophir, the white elephant, etc. And then this morning, I who am no longer a boy, I who have taken in the village in a flash, I took this road and walked to that leap and glimpsed the distant hills and took up my childhood at the point at which it had been interrupted. My valley was hazy and cloudy; the distant horizon, spotted with sun and cornfields, was what the body of the loved one must be like when she is blond.

Rediscovering myself before and amid these hills of mine would always move me deeply, and this time more than ever. You have to remember what primordial images, such as the tree, the house, the vines, the path, evening, bread, fruit, etc., are locked up for me in these places, indeed in this place . . . and therefore to see these trees, houses, vines, paths, etc., gives me a feeling of extraordinary, fantastic power, as if there were being born within me, now, the absolute image of these things, as if I were a child, but a child who brings to this discovery of his a wealth of echoes, states, words, returns, imagination in other words, which is really measureless. Now, this state of dawning virginity that I taste has the effect of making me suffer, because I know my task is to transform everything into "poetry.". . . Myths are needed, universal fantasies, to express completely and unforgettably this experience that is my position in the world.[8]

The text we have quoted contains the whole crucial development of *August Holiday:* Pavese never abandons himself entirely to the emotion of *temps retrouvé* but remains, though moved, nonetheless in a problematic state. If the melancholy sweetness of memory characterizes the poetic and human tone of so many of Pavese's stories, it also constitutes for him the foundation for a more rational search for transcendence, for the awareness of self: as we have seen partially at the beginning of this chapter, on the one hand he discovers the determinism of his own life, and on the other he can gather and formulate his scattered intuitions into a poetry of myth and destiny.

A similar search by Pavese is found, as Jesi has shown, not only in the ethnological texts but also, and more profoundly, in the ideas conceived and elaborated "under the influence of

German poetry of the end of the last century";[9] George and
Rilke, therefore, are the basis of a whole development that
leads up to Thomas Mann and the expressionists, and finally to
the ethnologists such as Frobenius and Kerényi, a development that has for its constant the religion of death, sacred
death, as an index of now inaccessible myths:

In Pavese the need to trace every new experience to mythical,
childish prototypes appears, in the perspective outlined by us, a
constantly renewed act of devotion to death, which stands precisely on the threshold of childhood experiences . . . permeating
all of them through its primordial symbols.[10]

Thus, Pavese rationalizes the discovery of self in stories
such as "Adolescence" and "Job-sickness"; he criticizes
Proust's sensation without thought as an incomplete method
of remembering and asserts that, in order to rediscover the
true, instinctive state of childhood,

more than mnemonic force is needed; one has to probe present
reality and lay bare one's own essence. Without having a clear
idea of our own depths we cannot go into what we were as boys.
At this point in the search, time disappears. Our boyhood, the
spring of all our bewilderment, is not what we were but what we
have always been. Duration does not affect interior moments:
otherwise the jump for joy that greets us in absolute memory
would turn out to be inexplicable. Here to remember is not to
move in time but to come out of time and know who we are.[11]

Here timelessness has a precise meaning: Bergson's *durée* does
not affect interior moments; the sphere of the absolute wanes
in the contingent moment; what really counts is essence not
existence.

Even what Pavese calls "the effort to become a god through
the beast," which has already been shown in the short stories
and is picked up again in *The Devil in the Hills*, is subjected

to a careful and rational analysis that brings to light the obstacle against which the search for self is shattered:

Because we really were something else in childhood, little unconscious brutes, reality received us the way it receives seeds and stones. There was no danger then that we would admire it and want to dive into its abyss. We were the abyss itself. But the intimate story of everyone's childhood is made up precisely of the starts and wrenches that tore us from the real, whereby—today a shape, tomorrow a color—by means of language we compared ourselves with things and learned to value and contemplate them. . . . The temptation to go back and enfold in an unnatural embrace the childhood universe of things, is the mistake.

Perhaps this is the point at which Pavese's poetic (childhood *reality*) diverges abruptly from Leopardi's (childhood *illusions*). However, what Pavese wrote for the cover of the first edition of *August Holiday*, that "only when one is a man does one know how to be a boy," is not wholly true, because there is always a distinct separation between knowing and doing, between the brink and the abyss, between childhood reality and adult illusion. (We are also reminded of the richly poetic results of such a conception of the real in the work of Elsa Morante, which concentrates precisely on the world of childhood in contrast to that of the adult.)

At this point the transition from reality to myth takes place, and we enter the second phase of Pavese's search: for Pavese childhood reality is indeed a *mythical* reality: "Not even in our childhood memory are field, wood, and beach just so many real objects, but rather *the* field and *the* beach as they were revealed in the absolute and gave shape to our imagination." Inasmuch as childhood reality is mythical, it is also timeless:

Myth after all is a norm, the schema of an event that happened once and for all and derives its value from this absolute uniqueness that raises it beyond time and endows it with the quality of revelation. For this reason it always springs from the source, as in childhood: it is out of time. We know within ourselves that the unexpected image had no beginning: therefore the choice took place beyond our consciousness, beyond our daily life and ideas; it is repeated each time, on the plane of being, by means of grace or inspiration, in other words through ecstasies. . . . Here the moment equals the eternal, the absolute.[12]

The uniqueness, the universality of the objects, of the acts, therefore, signify that they are symbolic, to be interpreted *ex novo* as in a religious rite:

Μυστέριον and *sacramentum* also [used to] signify "symbol." This is how we get the idea of the symbol as being magically or charismatically effective. This is the root common to poetry and religion.[13]

Here we have an undoubtedly religious core. Life is filled and enriched with unrivalled events, which, precisely because they occurred once and for all and are above the laws of the sublunary world, can be considered the supreme forms of reality, its content, its meaning, and its marrow. . . .

As far as style is concerned, it is plain that myth corresponds to the image-story:

These touches when, without pausing in your story, you seize an opportunity of using memories to deepen the total experience, are more symbolic than descriptive. Although they may be imaginative, in the sense that they recur at moments when it seems natural to clarify an inner reality, they play the same part in your story as the recognized attributes of a god or a hero do in a myth (the white bodies of the Oceanids, the murderous hands of Achilles, the belt of Aphrodite), stories within the story, alluding to the hidden reality of the character.[14]

But it is important to draw attention to the fact that mythical reality is, for Pavese, above all a personal reality:

Each of us possesses a personal mythology (a feeble echo of some other one) that gives a value, an absolute value, to his most remote world, endowing the slightest little thing of the past with an ambiguous and seductive splendor in which, as in a symbol, the meaning of his whole life seems to be summed up.

Moreover, this mythical reality contains within itself the germ of poetry, which, since it is invention, immediately takes root in the imaginative substratum of childhood experience: the difference is that poetry can invent, whereas myth lives on faith. The relationship between poetry and myth is a delicate and important one: "The life of every artist and every man is like that of peoples, a constant effort to reduce his myths to clarity."

The consequence of such a relationship is that the poet has to discover in his own personal myth the point of contact with other men, a universal element that can be understood by others; in every imaginative creation, therefore, there are "essential symbols" common to everyone: to try and understand them

will be a descent into the fertile darkness of the source where one finds universal man, and the effort to illuminate an incarnation of him will not lack its own peculiar, tiring sweetness. It is a question of grasping the ecstasies, the eternal quality of another spirit. It is a question of breathing briefly its rarefied and vital atmosphere and getting comfort from the magnificent certainty that nothing differentiates it from that which lies stagnant in our own soul or that of the most humble peasant.[15]

In the preceding passage Pavese was trying, and trying very hard, to reconcile the demands of his own contemplative nature with those of his rational and social consciousness; it remains to be seen how far, in his work and in his life, he was successful in his aim. Thus, on the metaphysical plane we shall have the "dizzying" symbols of *Dialogues with Leucò* as an effort at universalization of the self, a return to the origins of humanity; then, on the intersubjective plane, *The Moon and the Bonfires*, in which reality and present are myth and past, and vice versa, in a totality in which history, the individual, and the absolute exist in a dialectic relationship with one another. In these two books Pavese realizes the development and completion of his poetic of the myth into the "poetic of destiny" and finally into *ripeness*. So we must pass from the plane of literature to that of life and examine and try to understand their relationship and tension. In tracing this development, we shall find other works, which will be worth examining now in order to add to the ultimate results: the works in question are those in which Pavese's characters express the difficulty they have in their relationships with others, and in their role in society and in history; "political" works in the broadest interpretation of the word, and "individualistic" works placed almost in contrast to the former, in an unresolved tension between participation and incommunicability.

The Hubbub of Actions

"Manca ancora il silenzio nella mia vita."
EUGENIO MONTALE

"In the end, everyone is alone and there is no
fellowship in the presence of destiny."
GYÖRGY LUKÀCS

In examining the inability to communicate, we are dealing
with the central theme not only of Cesare Pavese's work but,
unfortunately, of his life. The theme reveals the failure of the
dialectical relationship between self and others, the self's de-
nial of the world. It originates in existential solitude; some of
the poems of *Work Is Wearying*, and especially the novel
The Political Prisoner, show the first sure signs of it. It is the
theme that, in Pavese's life, ended in an act through which the
author joined the absolute that he had sought in vain for so
many years.

By inability to communicate, then, one understands solitude
in the context of a social group. It is a spiritual condition,
difficult and tragic, which can lead to the sterility and atrophy
of feelings, states of mind, and unexpressed emotions. It makes
human relations incomprehensible and creates a tense and evasive atmosphere, a rarefied air.

Many of Pavese's characters move in this atmosphere,

breathe this air; their acts and their words and most of all the things they leave unsaid, the refined feelings on the brink of consciousness, the states of mind composed of fragile shadows, combine to form what Marcel Raymond called *"une métapsychologie,"*[1] linked to a whole cultural climate derived from the later Freud: civilized society, to be fully established and developed, should "repress" the violent sexual instincts of the individual. It is worth noting that such a climate, nourished by Marx (man thus "repressed" ultimately becomes "reified"), has been brought to its ultimate conclusions (relative to the industrial civilization of the mass) by such philosophers and sociologists as Erich Fromm, David Riesman, Vance Packard, C. Wright Mills, Herbert Marcuse; from the "lonely crowd" to the "one-dimensional man," this alienation has invaded almost all aspects of human life, work, recreation, and even consciousness.

Obviously Pavese does not treat the problem of inability to communicate from a philosophical or sociological point of view; he describes it, rather, with vibrating subtlety, in individual relationships, in the atmosphere around him, in his own surroundings. He senses it and bears witness of it first in a society dominated by the fear and repressions of a dictatorship (inability to communicate in this sense could be interpreted as a poetic metaphor for a precise historical-political condition, that of Italy under fascism). Subsequently he describes it in a society that, once liberated, immediately is "afraid of liberty," for it brings new and grievous problems (in this sense inability to communicate is presented concretely as one of those social and individual problems). In both cases the "metapsychology" of an alert and sensitive Pavese corresponds exactly with the sociological "metapsychology" of his characters and real models.

Three novels, in particular, give evidence of the extraordinary importance this inability to communicate holds for Pavese: *The Beach, The Devil in the Hills,* and *Among Women Only*. Written at different times, they are three novels of bourgeois life, a bourgeoisie pictured primarily in their leisure moments, on holiday or enjoying themselves, rather than at work, which rouses in Pavese, the peasant from the Langhe hills, a confused but unequivocal sense of attraction-repulsion.

Even in his short stories, however, we see some typical situations of "metapsychology," of inability to communicate, as for example in "Every Day at the Swimming Pool":

The nakedness of the sky draws attention to our own. It is difficult to hide one's thoughts in this unusual nakedness. The slightest start and one feels as visible as pebbles at the bottom of the water. Our solitude is a vacuum, an immobility of thoughts. Only like this, something of our own remains in our hearts. Sometimes we forget about it, and we say something unexpected in a loud voice that immediately sounds superfluous, something the others already knew. . . . We are all uneasy, those of us who are sitting and those of us who are stretched out, some hunched up, and inside us there is a vacuum, a sense of waiting that makes the bare skin tingle.[2]

Or else we think of the short story "The Villa on the Hill": a tense, impalpable atmosphere that seems about to be shattered at any moment is dispelled by the announcement that Ginia, the woman whom the timid and mysterious young man silently adores, is pregnant—a theme that recurs in *The Beach* and, with its intimate sensations of the husband and wife relationship, in *The Devil in the Hills;* the end of the short story, in particular, really sums up the whole of its tone: "The dark outline of the trees was lost in the gloom. The deep awareness of earth and night reigned alone under the stars. I walked unheedingly, barely replying to the conversation, longing for the moment when I should be alone again."

The fragment "House by the Sea" (perhaps the first sketch for *The Beach*) also indicates very clearly the marital "metapsychology" that interests Pavese and ends in inability to communicate; the wife is speaking about her husband, who seems almost "an intruder" at her side on the beach:

If there is some damp in the air Andrea wakes up before dawn and can't stay in bed. They say it's nerves, but I think it's the need to be alone that is in everyone's blood . . . I am convinced he has been done with the frenzy of "loving me" constantly; we all feel the need of a secret distraction to help us gather our thoughts and think about things without lieing. Now his jealousy has turned into what I really wanted: the affectionate interest of one who is discreetly anxious and leaves one alone.[3]

The Beach develops these points with a rigor and lucidity unusual for such a slim topic.[4] But the fact is that this topic is only apparently slim: it is not really dealing with the life of the upper middle class on vacation at a beach in Liguria, with "desultory husbands," idlers, gossips, and flirts; the essence of the affair consists in the subtle and tormented analysis of a marriage in which there is seemingly no real love. The adolescent Berti and the narrator, both in love with the married woman, both happy with their negative sort of possession, seem to represent the last attenuated gleam of that love in the western world theorized by Denis De Rougemont, a love that is no longer passionate and tragic, but silent and renunciatory, a hint of which had been seen in Stefano's attitude towards Concia and Elena in *The Political Prisoner*. There enters into it, too, the personality of the narrator, a professor who is contemplative and solitary like other characters in so many of the preceding stories and like the narrator of *The Devil in the Hills*:

When I got back at night I used to stand at my window smoking. One imagines that smoking is conducive to meditation, whereas the truth is that it merely disperses one's thoughts like so many clouds; at best one ends up in a reverie, which is a very different thing from cogent thought. . . .

"I'm here for a rest cure," I explained. "My outlet is to be alone."

The visible sign of the narrator's contemplation and solitude is the "large gnarled olive tree" that he sees from the window: "It gave me a sense of being in the country, an unfamiliar country, and I often caught a tang of salt in the air." This is also the symbol of his silent fondness for Clelia, the married woman, a fondness that is its own contentment and brings more happiness than possession would, but for that very reason is sterile as if isolated "under a glass bell":

The night was so clear that the white edge of foam was visible below the promenade railing. I said that I really did not believe in all this water and that the sea made me feel that I was living under a glass bell. I described my olive tree as some lunar plant even when there was no moon shining. Clelia, turning round between me and Doro exclaimed, "[How] lovely! Let's go and see it.". . .

In the meantime we came to our narrow street; the sight of the olive tree irritated me. I was beginning to realize that nowhere is more uninhabitable than a place where you have been happy.

Clelia is truly delightful: presented first as a tomboy and then immediately as a married woman whose hand is to be kissed, she gradually acquires a personality as a voluble and capricious sort of woman who sometimes has an "evasive but irrepressible smile," at other times is pouting, at others vague or sometimes confiding. Clelia's confidences, which consist mainly of her childhood memories, describe her character; for example, the following words, which curiously re-echo those used by Mario Praz to describe a painting by Delacroix:[5]

Clelia said that in those years she was a continual prey to fears. Her first love had dawned when she stood before a picture of

Saint Sebastian, a naked youth smeared with blood, and the paint flaking off; his body was pierced with arrows. She felt a sense of shame as she looked at the saint's sad, enamoured [eyes], and for her this scene came to represent love.

Or, as an echo from the narrator himself:

"I [used to believe in] all the things they [told] me. I did not dare put my face between the bars of the gate in case someone should go past and poke out my eyes. But from the gate you could see the sea, and I had no other amusements because they always kept me shut up, and I used to sit on the garden seat, stare at the passers-by, and listen to the noises. Whenever a siren sounded in the harbor I felt happy."

Even Clelia's decision always to swim alone in the sea is part of her character: "The company of the sea is enough for me. I don't want any other. I have nothing that is just mine in life. At least leave me the sea." Clelia's decision is confirmed and explained by the observation, reminiscent of Montale, of another character, according to whom "this preoccupation . . . represented Clelia's pet vice, her secret, her disloyalty to us all," whereas one gets an idea of the narrator's feeling from a phrase taken directly from Pavese's diary (note the sexual, psychoanalytic image of the water): "Why be jealous? He doesn't see in her what I saw myself. In all probability he sees nothing. One might as well be jealous of a dog or the water in a swimming pool. In any case, water is more all-pervading than any lover."[6]

But the center of the short novel is all in the search for the relationship that husband and wife, Doro and Clelia, hide under urbane appearances; the narrator carries on the search pig-headedly, questioning the couple explicitly and with eyes ready to grasp the slightest act, the least indication, any shadow that might reveal who knows what contrasts, either quarrels or incompatibility, but finding only how difficult it is for two people to live close to each other and always understand each other, love each other always, bear with each other always. Thus, there is a current of tension that underlies the whole narrative, at first inadvertent, but later accentuated and obvious, not only in the dialogues, but even in some of the descriptions:

Daytime on the beach was a different matter. You talk with odd constraint when you're half naked. Words seem to sound different. Sometimes there are silences, and these silences in themselves appear to speak ambiguous words. Clelia would luxuriate in the sun; she extended her body on the rock, and as she lay full length under the sky, a whisper, a slight twitch of her knee or movement of her elbow would be her sole response to the occasional remarks the company made to her. I soon realized that when she lay stretched out like this she was not really listening at all. Doro was aware of this and never addressed any of his remarks to her. He sat there on his towel, hugging his knees, gloomy and worried. He never lay back like Clelia. If on occasion he seemed about to do so, within a few minutes he would be wriggling on to his stomach or sitting up again.

Words such as "twitch," "gloomy," "worried," "wriggling" seem to continue the tone of "Every Day at the Swimming Pool" ("uneasy," "hunched up," "tingle"), assuming psychological values that transcend the description itself and frame it successfully in the atmosphere of the novel, in connection with which F. Scott Fitzgerald's name has been mentioned.[7] The reference seems apt, especially if the American writer is considered as a representative of that late European decadentism to which Pavese on so many counts belongs. (*Tender Is The Night* actually begins, one remembers, on the beach.)

In two chapters at the beginning of *The Beach* Doro goes

with his friend the narrator to see the hills where he was born "under a cool summer moon." Just as his wife wants to be alone with the sea, he needs to be alone with his hills, with his childhood memories: the presence of a friend does not diminish the solitude, because a friend is a mirror of the self: "We were at the age when one listens to a friend speak as if we ourselves were speaking, when one shares a life in common the way I still believe, bachelor though I am, some married couples contrive to do." The hills on a tender moonlit night, therefore, represent Doro's infidelity to his wife, his fidelity to himself: "They talked at random, and the rough dialect suddenly gave back to Doro the authentic flavor of his old life, the wine of happiness in which he was born."

At the same time the nocturnal scene has magical and ritual overtones (note the importance of the "mask" in the following passage), which place it on the plane of unreality:

We left the inn to have a stroll, and the moon illuminated the road for us. Under its light we all looked like the bricklayer's mate to whom the white plaster stains gave an air of [a mask]. . . . The moon bathed everything as far as the high distant hills in a transparent mist which covered up every memory of the day.

Even Doro's shriek, before the revolver shot fired by the jealous policeman brings us back to reality, from years that are now gone and can't be lived again, even this shriek is immersed in the magical atmosphere of the night on the hill: "Finally Doro interrupted every quiet interval with a terrifying yell, the kind drunken country yokels let out when they get to singing. It sent a shudder through the moonlit silence. Dogs barked furiously from the distant farmyards."

A shriek similar to Doro's and an echo of the yells of Pale's mother in "The Name" will assume exceptional emblematic force in *The Devil in the Hills:* a challenge to the "powerful

spirits of the air and stones," a reckless and somewhat blasphe-
mous determination to break the limits, the norm.

The novel *The Devil in the Hills* is one of the most complex
and varied Pavese wrote; inability to communicate is a constant condition of this novel, dominating and underlying the
many themes. In fact the only real relationship among the
characters is that of the three friends; women are excluded
from it, "the sort who separate" people;[8] but we must consider
that the narrator, Pieretto, and Oreste are, as it were, reflections of one another: the narrator is contemplative, Pieretto
sarcastic and rational, Oreste simple and impulsive, but they
are all three different aspects of the one self that does not
communicate with others except at a distance. In fact, the
relationships of these three with Poli and Gabriella remain on
a level of superficial contact that consists sometimes of attraction and sometimes of repulsion; and the same may be said of
their reactions to the hard-working peasants in Oreste's village
(especially his family and two cousins). Besides, at the center
of the novel there is always the couple, Poli and Gabriella,
who remain in isolation at Greppo: certainly not a happy
marriage, in which metapsychology acquires a much more
extreme significance than in *The Beach.*

Inability to communicate, therefore, is the uncertainty of
the relationship between the various characters and their surroundings, and the recurrent need or feeling of solitude that
results from it.[9] But most of all this inability to communicate is
noticeable in the rarefication of the narrative atmosphere
achieved by alternating a brilliant dialogue with magical descriptions, each contributing nuances to the other. It is, therefore, necessary to examine how the various themes of the novel
stem from this inability to communicate or reflect it more or
less directly.

After describing the "defenseless" faces of the parents when confronted with the peculiarity of their sons, the narrator states: "What did they know about our nocturnal manias? Or perhaps they were right: it's always a matter of boredom and then of an initial vice, and everything is born from that." From this existential boredom comes, above all, that taste for night life, wandering, hours spent in cafés and taverns, with which the novel opens ("We were very young. I believe I never slept that year") and which resumes an analogous motif to so many other Pavesian characters, continuing then in the form of a discreet refrain for the rest of the story.[10] One extremely important significance that can be attributed to this taste, this attitude, consists in the lack of participation in the life of others which it implies: to use words taken from Pavese's diary:

This gentle benevolent feeling of love for humanity that comes over you on a cold day—when you are spending a few moments in a café and notice one man's thin sad face, another's twisted mouth, the kind, sorrowful voice of a third—and you give yourself up to a sentimental, luxurious surge of pity and grief at so much daily suffering, that is not real love for your neighbor, but complacent, expansive introversion. At such moments we would not lift a finger for anyone: we are, in fact, blissfully happy in our own tranquil futility when faced with life.[11]

If we compare the bitter sense of futility in this reflection with a sentence of Albert Béguin's quoted by Pavese in the diary,[12] on the necessity of looking on life as a "game" if one is not to be overwhelmed by it, we shall understand the great importance of amusement, holidays, and festivals, in contrast to work and the daily effort, in Pavese's work. (Whereas in Hemingway life *is* a game, complete with rules to be adhered to carefully and coherently.) Even the country-city dichotomy to which we have so often drawn attention, fades into the background in the presence of the play-work dichotomy, *homo ludens* and *homo laborans,* which is plain from the beginning. (For the boy "work is a pleasure" in the country, but soon he begins to have doubts and agrees instead that "work is wearying.")

Seated on the thwarts of that boat, I developed a taste for the open air and came to understand that the pleasure we get from water and earth is something that continues from the far side of infancy, from the far side of a vegetable garden and an orchard. Those mornings I used to think that all life is like a game beneath the sun.

But the sanddiggers who stood in the water up to their thighs were not playing any game; they hoisted shovelfuls of sludge and emptied them into the barge, breathing hard.

Naturally, play is connected with the other fundamental aspect of so many of Pavese's characters: introspection, the fondness for daydreams, and fantasies that are obviously futile in actual life and in which the noncommunicative self is exhausted. But the dramatic quality and awareness of such an attitude are clear.

A second less obvious significance of the taste for night life and wandering is seen in a sentence of Pieretto's: "And he explained that people have need of experience and of danger and that your limits are imposed by the environment you live in." Going out at night while the rest of humanity is sleeping is an act that exceeds a limit imposed by one's own environment; shouting by night also goes beyond the norm, which demands silence and respect.

"Let's see if he replies," Oreste said, and he gave a shout. Lacerating, bestial, it began like a roar and filled the earth and sky, the bellow of a bull which then faded out in a drunken laugh. Oreste jumped out of the way of my kick. We all kept our ears cocked. The dog barked again, the crickets went silent, terrified.

Nothing. Oreste opened his mouth to give the cry again and Pieretto said, "All together now."

This time we bellowed in unison, for a long time, with strident returns and responses. My skin crawled, and I thought that, like the ray of a headlight in the night, the sound reached everywhere —the slopes, the bottom of the paths, the clots of shadow, entered the dens and penetrated roots, making everything vibrate.

Note the almost morbid insistence with which the shouting is described, the sadistic quality it acquires in the eyes, or rather the ears, of the narrator and will have again when Pieretto lets out a yell at his friend Oreste when he is strolling with Gabriella;[13] it is really and truly an act of profanation; "bestial" is precisely the description. Moreover, this yell, which "reached everywhere . . . the clots of shadow, entered the dens and penetrated roots," is a psychoanalytical image connected with many other analogous images in Pavese's work. For Poli the yelling has a subtler and more personal significance:

"I should like you all to know that these days are very important for me. Yesterday I understood many things. That cry the other night has waked me up. It was like the shout that wakens a sleepwalker. . . . It's beautiful to wake up and have no more illusions," he continued, smiling. "You feel yourself free but responsible. There is a tremendous power within us, freedom. You can reach innocence. You become disposed to suffer."

Another way to exceed the limit is nudism: we have already seen in the preceding chapter that nudism has significance as a search for one's real, more intimate self, which is a part of nature; it has the same significance in the novel, but now nudism is primarily looked on as a breaking of the rules. For the narrator "a naked body is not beautiful in the open air. The idea bothered me; it offended those places"; and his two friends play at desecrating the countryside: they spend hours in a pond, almost the "slime" of D'Annunzio, "as naked as snakes, sun-bathing between the walls of cracked earth."

Under the broiling heat in the bed of the stream, I saw a sky colorless from so much light, and I felt the earth tremble and hum. I thought of Pieretto's remark that the red-hot countryside under the August sun makes one think of death. He wasn't wrong. The thrill we got out of lying there naked and knowing it, out of hiding ourselves from everyone's sight and browning ourselves like tree trunks, had a touch of the sinister about it: it was more bestial than human. On the high wall of the fissure, I could see the out-croppings of roots and filaments like black tentacles: the earth's internal secret life.

There is an effort to make one's own body a mysterious natural object in order, as it were, to remove the body itself from consciousness. But the effort is futile; consciousness remains active even at the height of "bestialization": in that "touch of the sinister," in the "black tentacles," there is in fact a feeling of the forbidden, of temptation, which will not become explicit until later: " 'I feel as though I'm committing a sin,' I admitted. 'Perhaps that's why it's pleasant.' "[14]

However, to talk of nudism simply as a breaking of the rules is not enough, for it would be too gratuitous; nudism is indeed linked with the obscure "mythical" forces of nature: "In the clear sky over the reeds, the white sickle of the moon gave a magic, emblematic quality to the day. Why is there a relationship between naked bodies, the moon, and the earth? Even Oreste's father had joked about it with us." What is this relationship between naked bodies, the moon, and the earth? Perhaps it is the relationship that exists between the life of the individual and his destiny, between man and a god? We are reminded of an entry in the diary where Pavese speaks of blasphemy as "the best testimony we can give of human dignity";[15] but if nudism is blasphemy, it is also a manifestation of love: man beats his head against the mystery (of life, of the self) and cannot break it or solve it, so he denies it—like a despairing embrace.

In this sense, Poli's words seem enlightening: "Everyone uses drugs of some sort, from wine to sleeping powders, from nudism to the cruelty of the hunt." But spilling blood is a way of exceeding the limit, of understanding the mystery, which in itself is too mysterious for man to give himself up to it as easily as he can take a drug:

The moon disappeared behind the pine needles. We were then talking about hunting and the poor animals: Poli said that shedding blood was to him the least comprehensible of all drugs; Rosalba had taught him that blood has something diabolic in it.

And Pieretto, who sarcastically teases a bourgeois girl, telling her, "a taste for the intact and untamed was basically a taste for shedding blood," since "you make love in order to wound, to shed blood," is the one who puts the seal to the mystery by denying its sacral character, just as we saw in *The Harvesters*:

He fastened on me savagely. "If someone happened to have his throat cut in the woods," he declared in his peremptory tone, "do you really believe that it would be like something out of a legend? That the crickets would fall silent around the corpse? That the puddle of blood would matter more than some spittle?"

In this connection the following reflection in the diary seems noteworthy:

Poetry, *now*, is the effort to grasp superstition—the savage, the unspeakable—and give it a name, understand it, make it harmless. Hence, true art is tragic—it is an effort. Poetry participates in everything that conscience forbids—[lust, love, passion, sin, but it saves everything with its] need for contemplation, that is, for knowledge.[16]

What Praz wrote about Baudelaire can easily be applied to Pavese:

It was precisely in this "savoir" which Baudelaire emphasizes that his own personal tragedy lay: ferment of the brain, *exacerbatio cerebri*, this was Baudelaire's form of sensuality, the desire for the forbidden fruit because forbidden, in order to "know"—in which theologians see the supreme sin against the Holy Ghost.[17]

We can trace to this same need to know, and therefore to possess, the narrator's tendency to perceive all of reality with heightened senses. He is alert to sense "the smell of the earth," to notice the voice of the water, of the crickets, of the hill; if we remember that "our voices and the smell of our bodies change less than anything else about us,"[18] it is easy to understand the significance as discovery and possession of similar sensory observations for Pavese; as he wrote in his diary, quoting *Corinne:* " 'Listening to pure and agreeable sounds, it seems we are ready to penetrate the secret of the Creator and seize the mystery of life.' "[19] The same wish to discover is affirmed in the same expressions, but in a more general context, in another entry in the diary:

I explained to M. L., in front of the beautiful hill, that I was angry at not being able to do anything about it. I could only admire it. That was all. I could not even express the idea of wanting to possess it, to drink its secret, to make it part of my flesh.[20]

Such a subtle and total search for reality has for counterpoint both the narrator's contemplative nature and his "students' discussions" with his friends. His ability to take part in life around him is completely intimate and dreamy, as for example where women are concerned: "Often I would notice some woman at her window, bored and absorbed as only women know how to be, and I would raise my head in passing, catch sight of an interior, a room, a sliver of mirror; and I would carry that delight away with me." The same may be said for the objects around him:

I liked confined places, which thereby had form and meaning—inlets, narrow streets, terraces, olive yards. At times, flat on a rock, I would scrutinize a piece of stone a few inches from my eyes and no bigger than my fist; against the sky it would resemble a huge mountain.

We are reminded of the boy in "The Sea," who would stare at a house until it no longer looked like a house. The narrator enjoys most of all watching the spectacle of life, particularly the landscapes:

I crossed the parched stubble and met them on the crest. It was like being in the sky. At our feet, diminished by distance, we could see the village square and a jungle of roofs, ladders, haystacks. You felt you wanted to jump from hill to hill, to embrace everything in a single glance. . . . The great light was entrapped down there, in the hollow between the hillsides, and the horizon wavered. I had to half-close my eyes, but I made out only haze.[21]

The Greppo hill is, for him, "an island in the sky" on which you really do smell a sort of sea fragrance: "That indefinable odor of August, of brackish earth, was stronger there than anywhere else." In the diary the "briny of the countryside" is the "foamy smell of maceration,"[22] i.e., of decay; death in these images is indissolubly linked with the idea of summer, of maturity, and will appear again in the novel. Furthermore, the capacity for sensory associations, typical of the decadents, is constantly found in the narrator: "Alone, I went to sit on the brow of the hill and look at the plain, the wild slopes. Large white clouds moved slowly in a mild sky, and there was an odor of fruit in the air."

It is worth noticing that Oreste shares much of the narrator's nature, with his dreamy exoticism, which could be linked with Pavese's earliest translations from Melville:

Oreste had said that the low hills through which we were now driving had seemed to him from the time that he was a child a marine horizon, a mysterious sea of islands and distances into which he had in his imagination dived from the heights of the terrace. "God, how I wanted to be on the go, take a train, see things and do things."[23]

The narrator's exoticism is contrasted with and completed by his attitude towards Oreste's and Poli's village: "I thought of how many places in the world belong to other people in the same way, places that they have in their blood and that no one else knows." A similar attitude can be placed within the framework of the poetic "myth of return" in the short stories, which will culminate in *The Moon and the Bonfires*. Then there are other images that recur in Pavese's poetic themes and stress the narrator's contemplativity: such as "the carriage with parasols open," the "house with pots of geraniums on the window sills," or Gabriella's terrace, from which "you couldn't see anything but the sky and the geraniums." To the same type of stylistic refrain belong those narrative forms through which reality acquires a magic, ritual tone, as for example the dancers at the night club fascinated by the music as if it were a spell, or the Greppo hill ["overgrown, solitary amidst the humming of bees, like a mountain from another time"], which after the horde of friends from Milan has passed seems desecrated, "no longer virgin."[24]

As for the "students' discussions," these turn on their experiences in the world and its significance: life, death, destiny, nature—all themes that had already appeared in Pavese's previous works and are now rendered more explicit and more lively by the dialogue form. For example:

"What!" Pieretto cried into the wind. "Don't you know that what happens to you once, goes on happening to you? Or that if you act a certain way once, you always act that way. It's no fluke when you find yourself in a mess. And you go on finding yourself in the same mess over and over again. It's called destiny."

Or:

"Religion," Pieretto said, stopping, "is understanding how things go. Holy water is no use. You have to speak with people, understand them, know what each of them wants. They all want something out of life, they want to do something, exactly what, they're never sure of. Well, it is in this intent that they all find God. It is enough to understand, and to help others to understand."

Most of the discussions, however, are centered on the countryside:

One day in the vineyard . . . I asked Oreste if there was any cranny, bank, or uncultivated spot in the country where no one had ever set foot, where, from the beginning of time, the rain, the sun, and the seasons succeeded one another without the knowledge of man. Oreste said no, that there was not the remotest spot or center of a wood that man's hand or eye had not disturbed. Hunters at least—and in other times bandits—have been everywhere.

"But the peasants, the peasants," I said. Hunters didn't count. The hunter lives on his game. I wanted to know if the peasant as such had penetrated every spot, if everywhere the earth had been touched. Or, better still, violated.

An exact contrast with this discussion is offered by the description of the sudden summer storm, which seems to concentrate the interior images of *The Harvesters* and the exterior images of "Intimate History":

A storm, fortunately without hail, came and beat the countryside and eroded the paths and roads. . . . The crackling vine faggots in the fireplace threw fantastic reflections on the scalloped shelf-linings of colored paper, the battery of copper pans, the colored lithographs of the Madonna, and the olive branch hung on the wall. An odor of garlic and basil rose from the pieces of rabbit on the bloody trencher. . . . You could hear the mass of water, almost solid, fall and rumble. I imagined the smoking and flooded fields, the boiling cleft, the uncovered roots, and the most private spots of the earth now penetrated and violated.

It ended as it had begun, suddenly. . . . A frothy wind blew up from the valley, and the clouds rushed along. The sea of nearly black hills speckled with whitish clay seemed nearer than usual. But I was not surprised by the clouds or the horizon. A heavy odor, a mixture of wetness, bracken, and crushed flowers—a sharp, almost salty odor of lightning and rootstocks—assailed me. Pieretto said: "How delightful!" Even Oreste inhaled and laughed.

Pavese achieves in this description a wonderful fusion of tones; he combines a minute interest in realistic details with the mythical and lyrical transfiguration of reality. The central image—"the most private spots of the earth now penetrated and violated"—is obviously sexual, obsessive, echoing similar images that we have already examined in this chapter (for example Doro's and Pieretto's yells, which reach everywhere, even to entering "the dens and penetrating the roots"); more-over, it seems to go right back to the earlier story "Summer Storm," with all the tension expressed in it between the at-traction and repulsion of violence; but here the tension is transferred from the immediate plane of the weak-willed im-agination of the earlier Pavese, the "ferryman," to the indirect plane of the tranquil Pavese, the "professor," who has trans-formed the frustrations of the man into natural images preg-nant with mythological echoes (the rain from Olympus that fertilizes the earth). We also notice that the reaction of the three friends to the smell of the lightning and the earth is the same, emphasizing their basic identity.

But the countryside is not merely the jealous wild earth that is violated; it also signifies work,[25] because "only if you cultivate your own land are you worthy to live on it." Oreste's family and his two solid cousins are described with a strength and serenity that we shall only find again later in Nuto of *The Moon and the Bonfires;* in fact, here emphasis is laid on the wild, uncultivated aspect of the countryside, rather than the orderly and measured aspect of work. Perhaps this emphasis is the most decadent part of the whole novel. To so immerse oneself in nature to the point that "it was pleasant . . . to go back into the thicket like an insect or a bird. You seemed to [have *your paws*] in that perfume and sun," (italics added) is to turn into an animal, but it is also an *exacerbatio cerebri* through which the countryside is invested with a latent sensuality, which in turn develops into a sense of death:

"Nothing," [Pieretto] continued, "has the smell of death about it as much as the sun in summer, the strong light, exuberant nature. You sniff the air and you smell the woods, and you realize that the plants and animals don't give a damn about you. Everything lives and consumes itself. Nature is death. . . ."

Later: " 'Let's be sincere. In August the country is indecent. What about all those seed pods? There is a musty odor of coitus and death. And the flowers, the animals in heat, the fruit that drops?' "

It is apparent from the passages quoted thus far that there exists a profound link between the solitude of the individual and his temporality, his merging with the cycle of the seasons; however difficult it is to communicate with others and with nature, it is nevertheless impossible to escape from the natural cycle, from time. Let us look at the following passage in this connection:

> Yes, it was hard not to see Gabriella, not to hear her talk, not to be in Oreste's place. . . . The thought that she could go willingly through the wood with one of us, even into the kiosk, and that together in the light of day. . . . I recalled the Po, I recalled the cleft. Where was the summer's odor of death now? And where all our chattering, all our conversations? . . . We would have to leave some time or other. And they would have to leave too. What was this villa like on winter evenings? A sudden pain, a discomfort, seized me at the thought that summer on the Greppo, Oreste's love, all our talks and all our silences, and we ourselves would all be over in a short time, finished and done with.

There are few other passages in Pavese where one finds such elegiac, subdued abandon, which at the same time is so controlled.

The preceding observations were intended to analyze and sift many of the familiar Pavesian themes in the light of inability to communicate; now it remains to examine how this inability to communicate finds its focal point of expression in the couple Poli and Gabriella, around whom the whole novel revolves.

The figure of Gabriella is one of the most evasive (and therefore fascinating) of all Pavese's women characters. She is presented in shorts, like James Cain's Cora, and she says, about herself and her husband: "We're here to be bored. I keep him company and act as his nurse a little," which is a very personal and nonchalant way of expressing herself, typical of the *blasé* upper bourgeoisie. Very young, with an "unpredictable, tanned and sly face," and with "her constant air of just having stepped onto a beach," a sign of her inclination to treat everything as a game, Gabriella is a most desirable, unobtainable woman, whose outline we have already seen in the figure of Clelia in *The Beach*. Both of them preserve the secret of their small world intact, remaining *en soi*, out of reach of every real contact, either on the part of their respective husbands (Poli and Doro) or of their respective admirers (Berti, Oreste, and the two narrators); both fit the pattern of conjugal love that De Rougemont opposes to love *tout court* (which really appears to be a form of narcissism); one can apply to both of them that inability to communicate that Pavese describes so bitterly in his diary: "What is there, really, in my fixed idea that everything lies in the secret, loving 'inner self' that every creature offers to anyone who knows how to reach it? Nothing, for never have I been able to attain that loving communion of spirit."[26] In fact, Pavese's female figures are characterized from the outside; they are seen by a narrator who has not attained with them "that loving communion of spirit."

However, there is much more to Poli as a character than there is to Doro. He reminds us of J. D. Salinger's Seymour Glass, who can be traced back to Scott Fitzgerald, who influenced Pavese. (Even "Zen" would seem to be prefigured in the allusion to Poli's possible "Buddhism.") "Already a libertine before he was a man," tired of a pitiful mistress named Rosalba who, when abandoned by him, tried first to kill him and then committed suicide, Poli is also a cocaine addict and tubercular. However, without being aware of it, Poli "ought to be a hermit. He was born to live in a cell, but he doesn't know it"; he feels death and life's difficulty weighing on him and believes in the "unconscious innocence that is in us" and says, "It seems to me I've always been a boy. It is the oldest habit that we have. . . ." Vice and innocence coexist in him; he is seeking the reason for things, for life, and he strives to find a philosophical-mystical solution to his existence. Pieretto says of him "He is more ingenuous than they. He does these things seriously, you know. You'll see him become a Buddhist, if he doesn't die first." In a way there is more of Pavese in Poli than in the narrator himself; the following passage from the diary can explain the importance of what I have called the dichotomy between *homo ludens* and *homo laborans:*

The active life is a feminine virtue; the contemplative, masculine. One significance for my presence in this century could be the mission to explode the theory of Leopardi and Nietzsche that the active life is superior to the contemplative; to show that the dignity of the truly great man lies in *not* giving himself up to toil, social life, the mere *trivia* that pad out existence. Without, of course, ceasing to follow Dostoievsky's advice on the way to live. Whatever passions may come. But not forgetting that one counts for what *one is*, and not for what *one does*.[27]

Poli, more than any other of Pavese's characters, is the incarnation of alienated contemporary man who strives, often uselessly, to go beyond the surface of things, to exceed the relative, to give significance and certainty to actions and words, to attain the absolute:[28]

Then Poli began to complain and to accuse us all, Gabriella, everyone, of remaining on the surface of things, of reducing life to a futile drama, to a senseless series of motions and manners. . . . Now, looking at us out of the corner of his eyes, Poli had begun to say that if God was within us, there was no sense looking for Him in the world, in action, in works. "Then if we resemble Him," he murmured, "it must be our inner selves, the internal man that is made in His image. . . . For me, God is absolute liberty and certainty. I don't wonder whether God exists: all I want is to be free, certain and happy, as He is. And to reach that point, to be God, a man has only to touch the depths, to know himself completely."

As can be seen, this religious feeling is the more direct result of an individualism driven to the extreme by contemplation; it is the ultimate result of that inability to communicate between self and others, between self and things, which no drug can truly cure. In fact, the relationships of Poli and Gabriella, both in the tension and the ambiguity of their fragile "metapsychology," are basically of reciprocal alienation: " 'Let me talk,' Gabriella cried. 'When two people live together, they speak so little, and each knows what the other will reply. When two people live together, it's like being alone.' " The same is true of the connection between them and their environment:

The abandonment and solitude of the Greppo was a symbol of her and Poli's mistaken life. They did nothing for their hill, and the hill did nothing for them. The savage waste of so much land and so much life could bear no other fruit than discontent and futility.

Thus, Poli and Gabriella are the nucleus on which the main themes of the novel converge: futility and work, city and country, contemplation and action, mystery and revelation, individualism and incommunicability. But Poli and Gabriella are a nucleus that has not yet been disentangled, and Pavese will try and free it in *Among Women Only*, which will resume and develop *The Beautiful Summer* and *The Beach*.[29]

Even though thoughts of suicide are found frequently in Pavese's letters and diary,[30] none of his characters has as yet committed suicide, except for Carlotta in one of his early short stories and Rosalba in *The Devil in the Hills*, and her action remains secondary and off-stage. It is only with Rosetta Mola, in *Among Women Only*, that suicide acquires a decisive importance, underlying the whole novel and providing its inevitable conclusion. The road Pavese takes to this conclusion is indirect but rigorous; we no longer find a luxurious abundance of themes as in *The Devil in the Hills*. *Among Women Only* is more compact, less lavish, and more essential.

The initial theme is the antithesis between futility and work. Clelia Oitana, the first-person narrator, returns to her native Turin to open a branch of a big Roman store. She arrives during carnival, "just like a juggler or a nougat peddlar":[31]

None of those show windows and signs was humble and familiar, as I remembered them, nor the cafés, nor the cashiers, nor the faces. Only the sun slanting down and the moist air had not changed.

And no one strolled along; everybody seemed to be busy. The streets weren't for living in, but only to escape by. To think that when I used to pass those central avenues with my big box on my arm they seemed to me a kingdom of carefree people on holiday, in a way in which I then pictured seaside resorts. When one wants a thing one sees it everywhere.

In this way the antithesis of futility and work is embedded in the passing of time; memories flood back to Clelia on her return and they take her (and the reader) back to the age and surroundings of Ginia in *The Beautiful Summer:*

While I smoked, my hand dangling above the surface of the water, I contrasted the protracted bathing that now lulled me with the exciting days I had seen, with the tumult of countless words, with my impatient desires, with the projects which I had always realized: this evening they all had come down to that tub and that pleasant warmth. . . . Perhaps twenty years before, when I was still a little girl playing in the streets and waiting with beating heart for the season of confetti, booths, and masks, perhaps then I might have been able to relax. But in those years the carnival meant only merry-go-rounds, nougat, and cardboard noses. Later there was the desire to go out, to see Turin, to run through it; there were the first escapades in the alleys with Carlotta and other girls when, hearts beating, we felt ourselves being followed for the first time: all this innocence had come to an end.

But apart the echoes of characters and situations already familiar, there is always an element of stylistic continuity in Pavese's work, and especially in this novel, through the constant and careful use of background details (for example, the arcades and store windows of Gozzano's Turin,[32] or the current clothes fashions, or the leather armband of Becuccio, the sympathetic construction-chief who is another Bruno of "First Love"). There are also sensory images: time and time again Clelia's various states of mind are emphasized by different smells: the smell of lime in the new branch of the store, of the walls "under the narrow slits of sky above the alleys," of "incense and dead flowers" in the church after a funeral, of the grass and leather in the open car in the sun at Superga, "of piss, carbide and frying" in the tavern near the house where she was born.

Here is Clelia once more in the poor area where she was born, in the old and well-loved via della Basilica. But there is no real satisfaction in the pilgrimage, nor can there be; like Verga's 'Ntoni, Clelia is a stranger in her own town:

This was all my past, intolerable and yet so different, so dead. I had told myself many times in those years—and later, too, as I thought it over—that the aim of my life was really to be a success, to become somebody and one day return to those alleys where I had been a child and enjoy the warmth, the amazement, the admiration of those familiar faces, of those little people. And I had been a success and I had returned; and the faces, the little people, had all disappeared. . . . Maurizio always says that you get what you want, but only after you have no more need for it.[33]

What is hard is that Clelia feels like "an intruder" even in the vain, empty world of *haute* Turin,[34] to which she always wanted to belong, and now that she has arrived it seems unreal to her, it is so foreign:

I'm used to hearing all the scandals and gossip of Rome in our shop, but this bickering between friends because a third one didn't succeed in killing herself struck me. I was on the point of believing that the acting had already begun and that everything going on was make-believe, as in a theatre, as Loris wanted. Having arrived in Turin I had entered the scene and now I too had a part to play.

And later, in an almost grotesque context:

She didn't talk teasingly but with a child's voice as if she were acting. Before, when the lights went out, it had seemed to me a scene on the stage. Again the notion came to me that there had been absolutely no one on the stretcher that evening.

It seems more obviously and cruelly grotesque if the passage we have quoted is compared with the scene in the studio of the painter Loris, whose face resembles his "mess of violet and blackish colors" and who has organized a party on a funereal theme to celebrate the death of his second period: "Mariella came over and asked if I was having a good time. She told me to look at the coffin—how theatrical, how surrealist it was—and she started off again on her acting." Clelia is not the only one to feel disgust for such a world; Momina feels it too, but since she was born and lives in that world, she cannot see it with Clelia's detachment, and so disgust is broadened to include the whole of life and the whole of humanity in a general nihilism:

Momina was telling me how at times she herself was seized, not by the momentary nausea you get from this or that person, or from an evening or a season—but by an utter and complete disgust with living, with everything and everyone, with time itself, which goes so fast and yet never seems to pass. She lit a cigarette and sounded the klaxon.

Momina's loathing is somewhat the negative side of the "initial boredom" of the three friends in *The Devil in the Hills* and remains like it, imbuing a whole world. Faced with this, Clelia begins to feel a bitter sense of frustration:

I wondered if it was worth the effort to work and get where I had got and then find I was no longer me and even worse than Momina, who at least lived among her own kind. Other times when I thought these things I always consoled myself by saying that it wasn't the things I had obtained or the place I had carved out for myself but the act of carving it out and obtaining them that made my life worth while. This, too, is a destiny, I said to myself, and nobody made it but me. But my hands were shaking and I couldn't calm down.

Clelia's destiny, which she has shaped for herself, is her ambitious character, inherited from her mother, which she takes with her into a world where ambition doesn't exist because no one works, and so the amusements of the others seem undeserved to her; as her friend Morelli says: " 'You hate other people's pleasures, Clelia, and that's a fact. It's wrong. You hate yourself. And to think you were born with such talents! Be happy, forget that grudge of yours. Other people's pleasure is yours too.' " These words are very important, because they explain on the one hand the futility of action, in general; and on the other Clelia's preference for being alone, which is carried to the point of "a real vice." To be alone means to exclude others, to have no need of them, not to communicate: " 'We are the others, the outsiders,' I said, looking at Rosetta. 'If you can manage to do without them, to keep them at a distance, then even living becomes possible.' "

Clelia, in other words, has achieved her autonomy like Helen Tindaridis in *Dialogues with Leucò* and like the woman Clementina in this novel: "No man can say he had her in hand."

But there may be in Clelia, beneath the proud exclusion of others, beneath her hard-won autonomy, which does not make her happy, a profound and unavowed weakness, an inability to live and accept certain responsibilities of life—like other characters of Pavese's, especially Corrado in "The Family" and *The House on the Hill:*

Momina had taken off her shoes and curled up in the armchair, smoking; we talked a lot of foolishness. She examined me with her dissatisfied air, catlike, listening; I talked but inside I really felt bad. I had never thought about things the way Momina had talked about them. I knew they were just words—"we're here to enjoy ourselves"—but anyhow it was nevertheless true that not to have children meant that you were afraid of living.

Therefore, Clelia's solution turns out to be basically precarious and insufficient, but at least it is a solution that lets her live. Whereas Rosetta, who goes through the novel wearing her dress of blue tulle, on which the author's pity seems focused as on a luminous spot, does not succeed in finding even a partial solution, and her destiny is marked from the first moment she appears on the scene, lying on a stretcher, "with a swollen face and disordered hair," in a hotel corridor where she had tried to kill herself.

"When they try once, they try again," and "If you can't save yourself, nobody can."[35] The whole of Rosetta's tragedy seems to be concentrated in those two sentences; her internal suffering, her *"vizio assurdo,"* and the terrible egotism of those around her who do nothing to help her. An example of this tragic situation can be found in the following dialogue:

"If you really wanted to do it," Momina said, "shooting yourself would have been better. It didn't come off right with you."

Rosetta looked at me out of her deep eyes, intimidated—at that moment she seemed to be somebody else—and she whispered: "Afterwards you feel worse than you did at first. That's what's frightening."

And later, when Rosetta says in answer to her friends that when she tried to kill herself she had not looked at herself in the mirror:

"I knew a cashier in Rome," I said, "who went crazy from seeing herself all the time in the mirror behind the bar. . . . She got to thinking she was somebody else."

Momina said: "One should look at oneself in the mirror. . . . You've never had the courage, Rosetta."

We talked on like that, abour mirrors and the eyes of a person killing himself. When the waiter came with another tray, we lit the lights. Rosetta's face was calm and hard.[36]

Rosetta herself explains her attempted suicide and links it with the life around her and her own loneliness; she speaks wearily, painfully, in words that echo such poems as "The Star" and "Deola's Return," especially when she speaks of the disgust felt at night and the futility of the morning:

Rosetta, surprised, told me that she had no idea herself why she had gone to the hotel that morning. In fact, when she entered, she was happy. She was feeling relieved after the dance. For a long time nights made her shudder; the idea of having got through another day, of being alone with all her disgusts, of waiting for morning stretched out in bed—all became unbearable. That particular night, anyhow, she had already got through. But then precisely because she hadn't slept but paced back and forth in the room thinking of night, thinking of all the stupid things that had happened to her in the night, and now she was again alone and couldn't do anything, little by little she became desperate, and finding the veronal in her bag. . . .

"Wasn't Momina at the dance?"

No, Momina wasn't, but at the hotel she, Rosetta, stretched out in bed, had thought a lot about her, had thought about many things Momina had said, their conversations, Momina's courage —Momina, who was even more disgusted with life but who laughed and said: "I'll wait till the weather's better before killing myself; I don't want to be buried in the rain."

Rosetta said: "But I didn't have the patience to wait any longer. . . ."

Notice Momina's tremendous influence over Rosetta, something like Amelia's over Ginia in *The Beautiful Summer* and typical, as we saw earlier, of the relationship between adult and child. Rosetta, with her need of purity, of beauty and of the absolute, typical of youth, can never succeed in accepting what is dirty, ugly, or relative (nor does Momina's cold intellectual nihilism provide her with an alternative):

"And when you're not in love anymore," she said calmly, as if everything were settled right, "and you know who you are, what do you do with this knowledge?"

"Life is long," I said. "Lovers didn't make the world. Every morning is another day."

"Momina says the same. But it's sad that it should be so." She looked at me as a dog looks at one.

Clelia understands this absence of motives for Rosetta's suicide:

Rosetta Mola was ingenuous, yes; but in any case she had taken things seriously. At bottom it was true she had no motive for killing herself; certainly not because of that stupid story of her first love for Momina or for some other mess. She wanted to be alone, wanted to isolate herself from the ruckus, and you can't be alone or do anything alone in her world, unless you take yourself out of it completely.[37]

What actions and etiquette were for Poli in *The Devil in the Hills,* uproar is for Rosetta: different names for the same world. Poli's refusal takes the form of drugs and apathy in death; Rosetta is more impatient, tears herself from its midst, and seems "sulky" in death as she seemed so often when alive:

The curious thing was she had rented an artist's studio and had had an armchair brought there, nothing else, and she had died in front of the window which looked out on Superga. A cat had given her away—he was in the room with her, and the next day he miaowed and scratched so at the door that someone came and opened it.

"It's beautiful up here," Rosetta had once said when she had climbed with her friends up to the sanctuary of Superga, far away from the daily futile world of her life in Turin, far from the uproar. Superga is the sanctuary, the mythical place for Rosetta, the symbol of that life of silence, of the absolute, which she couldn't find in the world nor within herself.

In this way Rosetta's destiny gradually appears as the subtle catalyst for all the other destinies in the novel. And not only in the novel. Although it is easy, *a posteriori,* to talk of Rosetta's destiny as an unconscious warning or prefiguration of Pavese's own destiny, yet in the many entries in the diary Pavese thinks of *Among Women Only* as Clelia's story, not Rosetta's.[38] It is difficult, however, to reconcile Clelia and Rosetta, the "necessity" of living courageously for one girl and the "necessity" of dying uselessly for the other, with the life and death of Pavese. In reality, Clelia and Rosetta are dialectic poles in Pavese's personality: there is the author who, like Clelia, forges tenaciously his destiny on the faith of his profession; and there is the man who, like Rosetta, cannot find any value in life (despite the many books he wrote, as opposed to his character's sterility). There are two Paveses: one the responsible adult who knows how to accept life, like Clelia; the other the young Pavese, eager for the absolute, who refuses any compromise whatsoever, like Rosetta. We must therefore go back to Pavese's youth to understand fully the interior resonance, the significance revealed for us by the figure of Rosetta. The parallel between the justifications she gives of her own attempted suicide and a letter written by Pavese in his youth is terrifying, especially when we remember how "young" (in Rosetta's sense) Pavese always remained:

After so many experiences of failure, the memory of which can only make one suffer, one has the desire to close one's eyes and mouth, and be silent, disappear. Have you never felt in the evening shame and horror of having spoken, laughed, and *existed* in the world that day? I am beginning to think it's my mania since never a night goes by without my suffering this torment. And yet I am cheerful, I go around, I know people, I talk, work, live in other words.[39]

There are all the premises of suicide in this letter, and in almost the same words as Rosetta's. When Pavese's faith in his profession diminishes, only emptiness will remain; then will come the tragic end to that tension between the relative and the absolute, between uproar and silence, between action and essence, between life and death, which in the letter still remains suspended by the question mark, as in a passage from the diary written when he was drafting the novel:

No one charms you any more. If you had no faith in what you are doing, in your work, the material you are creating, the pages you write, what a horror, what a desert, what a void life would be! The dead escape this fate. They keep themselves intact. . . . Fundamentally, you write to be as dead, to speak outside of time, to make yourself remembered by all. This for others, but what for yourself? Will a memory, many memories of yourself, suffice you?[40]

7

The Others

"Man is a two-faced god: with one face he smiles at society and accepts it as the environment for his own development, and with the other he mistrusts society and seeks his inspiration and development within himself, in that dark and lonely world which can become either a heavenly refuge or an infernal prison, but where in any case even the most dearly loved may never enter."

JOHN CLARKE ADAMS

In contrast to the tragic inability to communicate examined in the last chapter, we also find in Pavese's work an attempt at participation in the life of others, at acting within the framework of political and family society, at intersubjectivity. This attempt is an effort to break the circle of one's own solitude, to break away from contemplation, to assume responsibilities, to overcome the narcissistic solipsism of one's own nature with a rational decision, deliberately willed and binding. Early in this attempt there are several short stories that apparently have nothing to do with it; in fact, they echo the themes that are intimately bound to solitude, as for example "Loyalty," which indicates from the very bitterness of the title the failure of a human relationship—woman's betrayal—a theme that first appeared in "Land of Exile."

The protagonist of "Loyalty" is a certain Garofolo (the name originally given to Stefano in *The Political Prisoner*)

who, when his friend Amelio is paralyzed in the legs by an
accident, visits him frequently, but gradually takes away his
girl, Natalina, sensual, alive, whose most marked visible characteristic is her smile (immediately marking her as a first
sketch for Linda in *The Comrade*, which uses the theme of
this short story as the basis for a much broader development):
"Natalina looked up at him through her hair and gave him her
usual half-smile."[1] Even the setting of "Loyalty" is a prelude
to *The Comrade*, as for example the fog of Turin seen from
poor Amelio's kitchen: "It was a chilly morning, with a little
light mist. The window was full of sunshine, bright but
cold."[2] But meanwhile the theme of feminine infidelity is
alluded to again in "Vespa": another sick man isolated in his
room, a protagonist who visits him (and who this time is
called Corradino, as in "The Family" and *The House on the
Hill*), a girl who is unfaithful to him. In fact, in "Vespa" the
solitude and wandering of so many of Pavese's characters is
portrayed very clearly:

Besides, every so often Corradino gave up going to Sangone, and
in the hours that the late season left him free, he would wander
idly around the city, along out-of-the-way alleys. If Vespa had
asked him why he came up to visit, Corradino would have answered it was because it made him feel more lonely, and he
wouldn't have understood, but Vespa wasn't the man to ask
questions. . . .[3]

"The Castle" also is connected with infidelity, that of
Carmela (who appears typically at the window behind
geraniums) to Ciccotto:

When Carmela didn't come back to the Castle and it was known
she had run off with another man, Ciccotto was the only one who
didn't seem surprised, and he told me he'd known for some time
that it would come to this. He spat several times into his handker-

chief and didn't move from where he was sitting hunched over the table. I seemed to see Carmela still sitting beside him on the edge of the table, with her legs crossed, and I couldn't believe that she had really gone off and left him like this.

There is another short story in which politics evolves from love and infidelity, even though as yet its appearance is very vague, unconvincing, and ingenuous. "Why do you want to get mixed up in politics, it isn't your job?" the mysterious elderly conspirator nicknamed the Captain, in the story of that name, asks the young narrator who goes to look for him.[4] The young man's reaction confirms the old man's words:

I said with some weariness that I wanted to listen precisely to get an idea. But he didn't go on with the discussion and that night, when he said good-bye to me, he didn't tell me to come back. . . . As a result, the next day I quarreled with the girl who wanted to know why I was so absorbed in my thoughts, and of course I couldn't tell her that decision: thus I spent some pretty miserable moments, when it seemed I wasn't fit to do anything.

Only later, when he thinks he has learned from the Captain how to stand alone, how to do without company as if he had just come out of prison into a world that "becomes a sort of prison," will the narrator acquire some confidence in his own ability—though the confidence seems somewhat illusory from his jaunty tone:

That night I thought of nothing else; I was enjoying the memory and anticipating with pleasure the fervor of many other similar discussions in the future, because I seemed capable of undertaking and doing everything, that timeless March night. I was young.

Thus we find the infidelity of a woman and political "engagement" are organically fused in *The Comrade*,[5] a novel which was supposed to be "proletarian" and "didactic," but which only partially fulfills the author's intentions. All the first half, in fact, is centered on the by no means proletarian theme of the carefree night life of cafés, taverns, music, and conversation, described with pleasure and sincere enjoyment.[6] The narrator realizes right from the beginning that he is tired of such a life and therefore devotes himself to political activity in order to discover a purpose: and it is in this sense, therefore, that we can talk about it as being "didactic." The whole development of the novel is summed up in the first paragraph:

They called me Pablo because I played the guitar. The night when Amelio broke his back on the Avigliana road I had gone with three or four others for supper in the hills—not far away, you could see the bridge—and we had been drinking and joking under a September moon until finally, stimulated by the cold air, we broke into song. Then the girls started dancing. I played my guitar—first one then the other would shout for me—but I was not happy; I have always preferred to play to an audience that has some notion of music, whereas the only thing these people wanted to do was to kick up a noise. I strummed again on the way home, and somebody sang. [My hand was wet in the fog.] I was fed up with that kind of life.

The Spanish name, night life, music, mist, and discontent are all motifs and images that recur in the novel and indicate the conversion of the narrator, Pablo, to political activity. There is the same instructive purpose in the episode where the protagonist passes in front of the prison in Turin and like the boy Geri in "The Beggars" stops out of curiosity:

As I cut by the *Nuove* prison, I remember glancing at those grim walls and thinking "I wonder if the cells are heated?" Then I noticed a van in front of the iron gate and some men opening it. I was tempted to stop; I had never seen anyone go in. So many things happen in this world. "So they put them in as early as this."

And on the way home I wondered if they ever got milk to drink in prison.

Pablo's attitude comes from an egocentric curiosity; in the second half of the novel he will see prison in quite a different light and will even enter it with a calm awareness. Similarly, his outlook on the poor also changes; it is more humane after he has seen Amelio's paralyzed legs:

And then it occurred to me that the beggars, all those who stand at street corners and are lame and blind and [have scabs on their skin], were once young men like Amelio. I wondered if the same thought had occurred to Linda. [It made me angry that she was] coming that morning.

But Pablo's weariness for the life he is leading turns into disgust and remorse for having betrayed his friend Amelio, into a growing feeling of solitude and uselessness: "I was like a baby that is left naked on the table abandoned by mother and sisters alike. I hid my head and was troubled." This attitude is delicately emphasized by the few notes concerning the environment, especially the descriptions of the Turin fog that provide the poetic background of the whole of the first half of the novel.[7]

Only Linda is able to overcome Pablo's weariness with his useless life: from the moment she appears on the scene ("One morning the girl . . . strode in boldly and asked with a laugh . . .") to her exit ("She lifted her hand, opened the door and was gone. The last thing I noticed was the bracelet.") she seems one of those incomprehensible and elusive figures whose very presence is refreshing and enlivening. Pablo gradually falls for her and betrays his friend Amelio, for whom he really has great admiration:

As we danced that evening I tried to discover what scent Linda used. I would like to have been by the sea, in the sun with her, woken up with her next to me, taken the train, to have been working and going round with her. I would like to have known everything about her, everything she had been to Amelio, what she had been like as a child; I would like to have known every detail of her life.[8]

It is noticeable that Pablo is dependent on Amelio: the weak man in comparison to the strong, or the young man compared to the adult, quite apart from any real difference in age, as is clear from the episode of the boy Martino, a perfect example of mediation:

They listened for a few moments, then said what they thought about it. Only young Martino stood against the window and listened intently. . . . I raised my eyes and my glass and smiled at him as Amelio does to me. He acknowledged it with a glance.

It is obvious that Linda understands Pablo's weakness, his contemplative nature: for example, she tells him that one "ought to be calm and not depend on other people," and later: "Don't you understand that everybody is a law to himself and that what I do concerns me alone?" whilst Pablo is content with the thought of her (and the parallel between himself and his model, Amelio):

We stayed together all night. The next day it was an understood thing that I was going off with Milo, and knowing that Linda would be waiting for me was better than sleeping with her. It was the kind of life Amelio had led. I was happy as I strolled across the piazza in the dark.[9]

Pablo's weakness then becomes more apparent when Linda leaves him: "Perhaps Amelio had realized what I was now beginning to understand. And everything was decided from that day when she had come into the shop and called me Pablo. And once again I felt [scratched in my blood, because] she had used me as a catspaw." Pablo's weakness is also partly egotism; with vivid feminine clarity Linda remarks, "He doesn't need anyone's help but you all run round him in circles." However it is a weakness that reduces him to the point of real masochism when it becomes a "pleasure to get close to the ground, to be as it were downtrodden and yet stick it"; it drives Pablo to think of suicide (touched on lightly much later when he is remembering in the prison in Rome).

It is from his weakness when disappointed in love, and from nothing else, that Pablo's first impulse comes to leave Turin and the places where he had been happy, and his consequent involvement in politics introduces him to new surroundings and people: but we are not deceived by Pablo's apparently decisive and self-assured aspect in the second half of the novel (the less successful half), an aspect vaguely reminiscent of Berto's in *The Harvesters*.[10] In the beginning, politics is only the chance for Pablo to forget his bad luck in love, and his political convictions acquire strength extremely slowly. The first allusion to politics is made during one of Pablo's trips in the truck; the war in Spain is mentioned briefly, without significance, and is dropped immediately: " 'I was in Spain once,' said the mechanic. 'What a lot they are! All the petrol there was used up setting houses on fire.' Then Milo winked. 'There are some of our people too on the other side.' " But later the idea of the war in Spain acquires more precise outlines:

Milo's mechanic called at midday, bought his cigar, and talked politics.
   "He's got this talk from Amelio," I thought. ["It comes from their job."] He attacked those who consumed the people's money and expected to govern without arousing protests. "But this time the fat's in the fire," he said. "They realize that in Spain. Do I make myself clear?"

Pablo remains cold and skeptical during these discussions; but nevertheless, the need to take part, the need for political actions becomes increasingly clear in the conversations of the people around him: "[Carletto] said that I was partly to blame; I was one of the many who were content to be spectators. How had the Fascists got where they were? They had fought, taken Rome, and done battle. We needed to band together and put up resistance." Finally even Pablo, who from the very first remembered his own ignorance during the discussions that Amelio would begin and never finish, and felt some human sympathy for "those poor misguided wretches in prison," as well as a sudden angry wish to "get away from that face on all the walls, tear all those posters down," even he begins to get worked up, to make up arguments of his own, to act freely, proclaim a political cause and a cultural engagement:

What did the gentlemen and students want? To put themselves in the Fascists' place. If only they could! We chaps, the workmen, market porters, Luciano and Giulianella, the families that had to crowd ten in a room, didn't count. There were always others climbing on to the bandwagon. . . .

Next time we met I let Carletto have it straight. "You yourself need to study before you can have confidence in others who do. Have you ever been able to understand when they talked whose side they were on?"

I talked at him partly for the sake of talking and to shut him up. But I have been given some thought to this business of studying. You couldn't understand things without doing so. Not the rubbish they taught us at school, but how to read a newspaper, what a profession is, who gives orders in this world. You've got to study to be able to dispense with those who study now. So you don't get cheated.

Pablo's political comprehension grows with his education:

One day I put my hand on the famous book parcel. . . . There were books in French and other languages; I dropped them in the river by the bridge next day. But I kept the books in Italian. They were accounts of the 1915 War and the Fascist march on Rome. Socialists, peasants, workers, action groups, all were involved. The Fascists had imprisoned them and beaten them up, murdered the most active of them, and burned down the working-class houses. "You see," I said, "read the papers—they never mention the Italian working-class people." [It was always the rich people who paid the Fascists, and the rich people's sons who were the Fascist *squadristi*.] It made you mad to read how many working-class people had been cheated by one boss after another.[11]

And so Pablo now sees his whole life in a different light and can give his own destiny some significance: "[But I realized that whereas once I used to put up with things, now I knew for whom I was working.]" The last words of Gino Scarpa, the important and mysterious comrade whom Pablo associates with his memories of his "guide and master" Amelio, put the final seal on his new purpose:

"If you didn't understand the situation, you wouldn't be a 'comrade,' " he explained. "But it's one thing to know about it, another how to control it. We're all [bourgeois] when we're frightened. Shutting one's eyes in order not to see is middle-class panic. Isn't the whole principle of Marxism seeing how things are and anticipating them?"

And later, after concluding that "We've got to [save ourselves] or die along with the others": " 'Don't forget our comrades in Spain,' he said as he left." Thus, the Spanish Civil War is the fine thread linking or explaining in part the stages in Pablo's political evolution, "the little bourgeois upset when faced with certain facts": in the beginning Pablo was carefree and happy; he was nicknamed Pablo because he played the guitar. In the end Pablo is mature and aware, engaged and determined, active and hopeful, and his nickname points to the significance of a historical and personal experience. This significance is all the more important if one remembers Pablo's true nature, which is just the opposite of a man of action and, despite the external resemblance to Berto, reminds one much more of Stefano in *The Political Prisoner* in his intimate inner motives. This is most apparent in his relationship with Gina, who reminds us of Elena in *The Political Prisoner*, even though she is treated less clearly:

That's how women are, I thought; she has already understood that she doesn't matter to me. A [remote] anger [returned] inside me as if she was someone different and as if I did not enjoy being with her. . . . I felt I must go home and be alone. Was I going to have her dogging my steps all day and all night?[12]

Pablo's love life is substantially a less intensive version of Stefano's situation in *The Political Prisoner*. Stefano's passion is unrequited, Pablo's disillusioned; Stefano gives in reluctantly to a simple, servile woman, Pablo to a simple but strong woman: just as Elena cannot compete with the idea of the wild Concia, so Gina cannot cancel the memory of Linda, even though Pablo as he leaves for Turin tells her, Gina, that she is worth more and that he will see her again.

So Pablo's contemplative nature is evident in every page and contradicts his every action: what he feels as opposed to what he wants. Among the many possible examples we will mention three; the first is the smell of the sea, which brings back to Pablo memories of a happy time—just as many other smells in the novel emphasize his state of mind:[13]

There was a wind blowing that fairly cracked your lips, and you could smell the sea. It was dark and the lamps swung to and fro in the narrow streets. The smell of the sea reminded me of Turin when it has been snowing in the mountains and [the sky is clear].

I bit into this smell like a dog and looked for the terrace where I had been with Linda and the inn we had called at. Linda was in my blood, but [I saw] the sea from another terrace.

Another example is Pablo's memory of the Po and of Turin when he is in Rome, crossing the Milvio Bridge on a moonlit evening. Finally there is his departure from Rome, which is already sensed in the colors and smells of a future memory:

I was already a different man, self-contained and happy. I looked at the taverns, the dark trees, the vast buildings, the ancient stones and the new ones—and it was borne upon me that you didn't see a sunset like that [twice]. And they sell so much fruit in Rome—green, red, yellow fruit lay there on the counters; they were the colour of the sun. I thought that in Turin [too I would eat fruit and thus I would taste the flavor of Rome].

Moreover, the use of so much slang and dialect syntax in the dialogues (e.g. "*gli*" instead of "*le*") is corrected and moderated by the use of a first-person narrative so that even at the level of style Pavese's "proletarian" needs meet (even collide) with the lyrical ones.

The more intimate nature of the narrator is seen in several passages from the diary and from Pavese's essays, in which the more spontaneous and true nature of the author becomes apparent fairly directly:

The proof of your own lack of interest in politics is that, believing in liberalism (i.e., the possibility of ignoring political life), you would like to enforce it autocratically. You are conscious of political life only at times of totalitarian crises, and then you grow heated and run counter to your own liberalism in the hope of quickly bringing about the liberal conditions in which you can live without bothering about politics.[14]

Or, less obviously, in impersonal terms:

Whoever has experience of the masses . . . knows that they accept an intellectual's culture that is alive and his competent and industrious solicitude as well, as at one time their ancestors would have greeted the presence of a priest. And the intellectual is *frightened* and flies from the embrace of such trustful cordiality, which sounds to him like a *terrible* liability.[15]

Or again, in an almost dramatic tone:

It is up to the intellectual, and especially to the narrator, to break the isolation, to take part in active life and deal with reality. But this is a theory. It is a duty that is imposed "by historical necessity." And no one makes love by theory or out of duty. . . . The disaster begins when this obsession with the escape from self becomes the actual argument of the story, and the message that the narrator has to communicate to the others, to the person closest to him, to his comrade, is reduced to this weak auscultation of his own perplexity and foolish aspirations. To reach the heart of things by theory or duty is impossible. One can argue and wear oneself out with it, certainly. To accept oneself is difficult.[16]

Similar passages can be found in Pavese's more "engaged" essays, those in which, echoing Pablo's discussion and thoughts in a systematic and rational way, he tries to get at man "beyond all the solitudes of pride and the senses."[17] His human approach is linked with the necessity of collaborating with others,[18] and with the definition of the intellectual's role in society: culture must be compassion and comprehension,[19] freedom must be historical certainty,[20] writing must be above all communicating.[21]

It is particularly worth looking at a passage from the essay "Communism and the Intellectuals," which better than anything else would seem to explain in what sense one can speak of Pavese as a "Communist":

Is it possible for someone to go along with communism out of love of freedom? It has happened to some of us. For a writer, for a "workman of fantasy," who ten times a day runs the risk of believing the whole of life is books, his books, it is necessary to have a constant cure of violent shocks, of people, and of concrete reality. . . . Nothing of any value can come from the pen and from the hands if not the result of collision with things and men. He alone is free who becomes a part of reality and transforms it, and not someone who lives in the clouds. Besides not even the swallows can fly in an absolute void.[22]

In these essays, as in *The Political Prisoner*, we have on the one hand all Pavese's conscious and determined effort toward a social and political engagement, which he accepted and lived with a clear historical understanding (think of his own early antifascism and his later "marxism"); and on the other we see the limits in Pavese's nature that such an engagement encounters—his incurable solipsism, at which he himself lashes with an irony that is even more ferocious because it is unconscious, in the question: "Is it possible that the narrator can be allowed to chatter on only about himself?"[23]

Confirmation of the limits inherent in the social and human approach, in the intersubjectivity of Pavese's characters, is found in the short story "The Family" and in the novel *The House on the Hill*.[24] In these two works the problem of responsibility to others is expressed from two different angles: that of the family and that of war and society.

The first person narrative voice in "The Family" does not deceive anyone and is only a means of treating more objectively the actions and behavior of the real protagonist, Corradino, "a man of thirty,"[25] whose name, lengthened by the diminutive suffix *-ino* (only Cate called him Corrado) seems to indicate the persistence of a childish attitude, a refusal of the responsibilities of adult life imposed by being a grown man with a full name. One can say of him, as Svevo wrote of Emilio Brentani, "He thought he was still in the period of preparation." What could be more childish and useless, in this sense, than becoming tanned in the sun of Sangone in order to "become a different man" unconsciously, like an animal changing its skin: to become a different man signifies to mature, to become an adult, and instead he remains, right up to the end—Corrad*ino*, "little Corrado." This is how he is introduced to us:

In [everyday life], as we all knew, Corradino hated being alone. He lived in a furnished room, but was always in and out of our homes and dreaded nothing more than being left to spend an evening on his own. To the last minute he always hoped someone would ring or drop in to see him.[26]

His loneliness is a fundamental clue, for it provides the element of dialectical attraction-repulsion in relation to responsibility, clearly seen in the typical Pavesian situation and now familiar to us. The character (Stefano, Pablo) again is divided between two women: Ernesta is the woman here who "would look meekly up at him . . . like a dog being petted," and Corradino broke away from her with a leave-taking that "like so many other irritating things in the past, had strengthened his old longing for solitude."[27] Cate, on the other hand, the girl who was once abandoned by Corradino, is different now, a woman, strong and self-possessed, a mother, and she looks at him with "a grave, solicitous look as though she were comforting a child" and she replies "blushing and proud" to her friend's question about the son. For Corradino it is not worth the effort of coming out of his own solitude for Ernesta; with Cate it would be worth it, but he does not have the courage,[28] just as he has never had the courage to bind himself to anyone.[29] Even when Cate, "a smile of pain in her eyes," reveals to him that Dino is his son "not to worry him or to trick him into anything. Her tone was hesitant, almost forced, as if she knew she was hurting him and wanted to make light of it, to spare him"—still Corradino cannot act like a man and hides behind tortuous arguments that scarcely conceal his *mauvaise foi*:

[Ever since], said Corradino, he understood that Cate [did not want him]. Hence the calm, the hope that sustained him. But I know that Corradino likes to run himself down, and I tried to convince him that if, among his wild thoughts of that night, that sense of futility he had felt in other crises no longer intruded, this stemmed primarily from the fact that this time he was [being tackled by] the crisis like a man. He was now facing, not imaginary nonsense, but reality, aspects of human life, a problem of human behavior that would snatch him out of his isolation. But Corradino shook his head and told me the truth was very different: he did not feel a scrap of love for Cate—rather he disliked her, as he did everyone else who [was stubborn].

Corradino's *mauvaise foi* is even more obvious when he stands aside and encourages as far as he can a possible union between Cate and someone else, a certain Pippo:

His lack of any love for Cate, his very resentment towards her, seemed to him a sacrifice he was making for the boy's sake. It was in this state of mind that he telephoned an influential man he knew in the theatrical world and recommended Pippo to him as a capable, reliable performer. He felt he was being generous.

Consequently, even his relationship with young Dino is weak and superficial:

Corradino had seized him by the wrists and tried to detain him, but the boy had resented the restraining arm and had broken away with the energy of a young puppy. His shrill voice as he wrenched himself free struck Corradino to the heart. He had never thought of the gulf that lies between grown-ups and young children, a perpetual distrust; or that children, all unaware of it, live in a different world.

Since he is a stranger to his son, Corradino is reduced to spying on him—again he is watching life instead of living it:

He peered through the trees, hiding himself behind a clump of bushes. He didn't want, or didn't dare, to let Cate catch sight of him; perhaps it was the romantic idea of concealing himself to spy on his son. His eyes followed a little boy he had seen before; along came another, then another. The third was Dino.

Failure in family life is then developed to correspond to failure in the field of political responsibility; the transition comes in the fragment "The Fugitive." It is set in the Piedmontese hills during the time of the Resistance, and it is a prelude to some of the pages of *The House on the Hill* (in which family and politics are truly fused) and also of *The Moon and the Bonfires*, especially with its poetic motif of the fire.[30]

In *The House on the Hill* the theme of responsibility is developed in a paratactic dialectic between family and politics and reaches the dimensions of love and history. The novel resumes the basic situation of the story "The Family": the protagonist Corrado (who narrates in the first person) is desired in vain by one woman and himself desires another woman, equally in vain, whom he once abandoned and who had a child by him without his knowledge; confronted with the revelation that he is a father, he is unable to behave like a man, in exactly the same way as (and from this stems the political theme) he is unable to bear the necessary consequences of war and the Resistance. Like Svevo's Zeno, in fact,

Corrado could exclaim: "War has caught up with me!" But unlike what happens to Zeno, nothing is changed or resolved in Corrado's character; rather it accentuates his inclination to solipsism:

The war had made it legitimate to turn in on oneself and live from day to day without regretting lost opportunities. It was as if I had been waiting for the war a long time and had been counting on it, a war so vast and unprecedented that one could easily go home to the hills, crouch down, and let it rage in the skies above the cities. Things were happening now that justified a mere keeping alive without complaining. That species of dull rancor that hemmed in my youth found a refuge and a horizon in the war.[31]

The war, as it is, cannot change Corrado's nature; the verbs in the following passage, taken from the last pages of the novel, are all in the future: "It [the war] will end by forcing the rest of us to fight as well, extorting our active consent. A day will come when nobody is outside the war—not the cowards, or the melancholy or the solitary."

Corrado is condemned to solitude by his nature, but he is also conditioned by his failure to participate in the life of the city—he being from the country—and dominate it through the love of the rich and bourgeois Anna Maria, a figure who is only faintly sketched but quite important: "This [love affair with her] went on for three years and brought me almost to suicide." If Anna Maria is a burning memory, Elvira and Cate are two living realities. Elvira is "a forty-year-old spinster . . . buttoned-up, bony," who grew flowers in her garden that were "scarlet, fleshy, and obscene" like "evil night thoughts" and has "an assured tone," thinks anxiously of Corrado, and gives him "her faithful-dog, patient-sister, victimized look": a grey figure meek and resigned. Cate on the other hand dominates two thirds of the novel with her presence, and the thought of her is always there. Just as in the short story, she appears for the first time in the mirror; here her voice is heard first, "a somewhat hoarse, abrupt, and challenging voice." She is no longer the girl she used to be, "a thin, indolent, mocking girl, a bit awkward and violent," with whom Corrado behaved boorishly even when he was apparently being kind.[32] Now Cate, rediscovered on the hill, is truly a woman fully aware of her duties as a mother, decisive and self-possessed, sweet and understanding, yet terribly feminine and young: "Cate was coming down in the sunshine, colorfully dressed, skipping." Moreover, she has reached a political maturity—as shown by her involvement in the antifascist struggle in Turin—which Corrado is far from achieving.

In this novel, in fact, there are more numerous aspects of the political-social reality, which the author gathers along the way, than in any other of Pavese's works (such as for example "Friends," "Work Is a Pleasure," *The Comrade*): in it are described the events of July 25 and September 8, 1943, the Allied air-raids, the German occupation, the broadcasts from Radio London, the Resistance; there are also descriptions of little-known aspects of Italian society during the period of the air-raids:

A whole class of people, the lucky, the top drawer, were going, or had gone, to their villas in the mountains or by the sea. There they lived pretty much as usual. It was left to their servants, their doormen, the poor, to take care of their mansions in town, to pull their chestnuts out of the fire. Left to the porters, the soldiers, and the mechanics.

Most important of all is the explanation of the historical and social conditions of an epoch and an environment, such as the beginning of the Resistance:

The war raged far away, methodical and futile. We had fallen, this time with no escape, into the hands of our old masters, now more expert and blood-stained. The jolly bosses of yesterday became ferocious in defense of their skins and their last hopes. Our escape was only in disorder, in the very collapse of every law. To be captured and identified was death. Peace, any kind of peace, at least imaginable during the summer, now seemed a joke. We had to see our fate through to the end.[33]

Nevertheless, the political and social interests of the narrator are substantially limited and even subordinate to his personality and to the story of his "protracted illusion" of being able to remain a boy amid so many events so much bigger than he.[34] Linda's sentence to Pablo in *The Comrade* is repeated here in different words, but with the same truth and efficacy, by Cate to Corrado: " 'We're all children to you,' she said. 'We're like your dog.' " This sentence reflects accurately Corrado's egoism and weakness, his way of reducing all relationships with others to the plane of superficiality and inauthenticity, just like Svevo's Emilio Brentani when he does *not* say to Angiolina at the beginning of *As a Man Grows Older:* "I like you very much, but in my life you could never be anything more important than a toy." Cate shows she even understands the reasons for Corrado's behavior, when she says to him:

"You're like a boy, a conceited boy. One of those boys in whose lives something has gone wrong but they don't want anyone to know about it, to know they are suffering. That's why you bother me. When you talk to the others you are always resentful, malicious. You're afraid, Corrado."

Even Corrado understands, when he thinks of himself as a young man, a "rash young man who ran away from things thinking they might still happen" or when he suddenly hears the siren:

The ground as well, the hill and its skin must have shuddered. All at once I saw how foolish this indulgence of mine in the woods had become, that pride in the woods I didn't forget even with Dino. Under a summer sky turned to stone by the howling of sirens I saw that I had been playing like an irresponsible child. What was I for Cate but a baby like Dino? What for Fonso, the others, myself?

In fact, like a boy, Corrado does not know how to assume responsibility toward Cate and Dino, yet he realizes that he is still "futile [and even wicked], half-lost, half-humiliated":

We were alone among the houses, waiting for the trolley. On the Via Nizza only a few wrecked houses stood out. I took her hand.

"No," she said. "There's no need for you to pretend. We're not the same. What does it matter to you if Dino is your son? If he were, you'd want to marry me. But one doesn't marry for that. Also you would want to marry me to free yourself from something. Forget about it." She pulled my lapels, caressing me. She smiled at me. "I've said so before. He's not your son. Are you content?"

Corrado's fear is more obvious, *a fortiori*, in the public sphere: confronted with the war that is imminent, he feels like "a scared rabbit"; he reacts contemptibly to the capture of Cate and the other antifascists and yet with agonizing sincerity: "Of Cate, Nando, and the others I hadn't dared think, almost as if to give myself a testimonial of innocence. At one point I shuddered, sick of myself. I pissed against a tree for the third time."[35]

Thus Corrado is condemned to nonparticipation in the world around him. He shuts himself off from family life; his relations with his son Dino, who resembles him in his "stubborn witholding," are somewhat difficult, and they find their best moments in a common feeling of exclusion from women, which is further evidence of Corrado's immaturity and is expressed in nature images, (which reoccur typically in *Dialogues with Leucò*):

But one thing we had in common: for us the idea of woman, of sex, that burning mystery, didn't belong in the woods. Too disturbing. For all that the ravines, roots, embankments reminded me each time of the bloodshed and ferocity of life, I never succeeded in conjuring up, in deep woods, that other savage thing, a woman's embrace.

There is another fine moment when Corrado listens to his son talking and seems to see, beyond the boy of the present, the birth of a boyish epic of the Resistance, such as really happens with Calvino's Pin:[36]

He already knew the first stories of weird ambushes, spies being shot. If Elvira came in, he clammed up. With each new revelation I saw what an enormous legend was being built up in those days and how only a boy who was astounded by everything could live with it and not lose his head. It was a mere accident that I wasn't a boy like Dino.

For Corrado the best thing still is to contemplate his familiar world, and that is all:

My relief was the daytime, Le Fontane—Cate and Dino. I didn't even need to appear in the yard: it was enough to stroll the usual paths and know that Dino was there. A few times I managed to keep Belbo crouched down while I peered unseen over the hedge. . . . It seemed an abandoned, lifeless place, a part of the woods. And what is true of woods also: one could only spy on it, sniff around it, not live there or really possess it.

But Corrado's nonparticipation in the political field is even more obvious and decisive than in the domestic field: "*I can't*," he says, after preaching the necessity of an armed fight; and Cate confirms this, seriously: " 'You know so much, Corrado, but you do nothing to help us.' " This is how Corrado is able to preserve his "strange immunity" but not without being uncomfortable and ashamed:

Why I should have been saved and not Gallo, or Tono, or Cate, I don't know. Perhaps because I'm supposed to suffer for others? Because I'm the most useless and don't deserve anything, not even punishment? Because I went into a church that time? . . . At times, after having listened to the useless radio and looked through the window at the empty vineyards, I think that living by accident is not living, and I wonder if I have really escaped.

The "topsy-turvy world" about him bears signs of grief and violence against which he struggles and rebels, but uselessly, as when he looks for peace in a little chapel or when he tries to understand the bloodshed, the grief, and violence, reducing them to current phenomena, to ritual sacrifices, unquestionably cyclical, liturgical, and already to be seen in the pages of the breviary:

One read of festivals, of saints; each day had its own. I deciphered horrible stories of sufferings and martyrdoms. There was one about forty Christians thrown naked to die on the ice of a pond, but first the executioner had broken their legs; the one about women beaten and burned alive, of tongues torn out, of intestines wrenched away. It was astounding that the antique Latin of those yellowed pages, those baroque phrases as worn as the wooden pews, should contain so much convulsive life, should virtually drip with so much atrocious bloodshed [that was so present]. . . .

"As far as prayers are concerned," Father Felice said, "novelty doesn't count. One might as well deny that the day is made up of hours. Life is summed up in the changes of the year. The country is monotonous, seasons always return. The Catholic liturgy follows the year and reflects the work of the fields."

Nevertheless it is difficult to understand and accept:

I thought of the echoing explosions, the sniping. How much blood, I thought, has already soaked these lands and vineyards. It had been blood like mine, of men and boys who grew up in this air, this sun, speaking my dialect and having my own stubborn look. It was unbelievable that such people who lived in my veins and memory should have suffered the war, they too; the tornado, the world's terror. I couldn't take in the fact that fire, politics, and death had overwhelmed my own past. I wanted to find everything the same as before, like a room that has been shut up. That was why—not merely from an empty prudence—I hadn't given the name of my village for two days; I trembled for fear of hearing anyone say: "It was burned down. The war passed by."

The psychoanalytic image of the closed room (resumed from the story "The Langhe Hills" and typical of many of the poems of *Earth and Death*) expresses all his desire, his temptation to reject the adult world of history and responsibility and take refuge in the maternal womb; yet this image in the context is nevertheless given a concrete historical reality that provides an opening for intersubjectivity. In fact, when confronted with the evidence of destruction, of enemies killed in an ambush, of conflagrations or bonfires, Corrado undergoes an experience that frees him from his solipsism and links him to the others in a painful need of understanding, of solidarity, of pity, in "an austere and fraternal consciousness of the grief of all, of the vanity of all:"[37]

But I have seen the unknown dead, those little men of the Republic. It was they who woke me up. If a stranger, an enemy, becomes a thing like that when he dies, if one stops short and is afraid to walk over him, it means that even beaten our enemy is someone, that after having shed his blood, one must placate it, give this blood a voice, justify the man who shed it. Looking at certain dead is humiliating. They are no longer other people's affairs: one doesn't seem to have happened there by chance. One has the impression that the same fate that threw these bodies to the ground holds us nailed to the spot to see them, to fill our eyes with the sight. It's not fear, not our usual cowardice. One feels humiliated because one understands—touching it with one's eyes —that we might be in their place ourselves: there would be no difference, and if we live we owe it to this dirtied corpse. That is why every war is a civil war; every fallen man resembles one who remains and calls him to account.

It is the same feeling with which Corrado looks at the people around him, in his desire to embrace all of mortal time, from Gregory, old "like the earth or trees," to Dino, "the dark seed of a closed future"; it is the same feeling that rises above time, away from the absurd, toward a motionless and absolute region ("of perennial certitude, far from carcasses and blood," Tomasi di Lampedusa would have said), where everything finds its explanation, finds peace, in a mysterious destiny:

A moment before, I had gone out to the yard with Dino while he crouched down in the dark; I lost myself a moment in the starlit emptiness. The same boyhood stars, now also glistening over the cities and trenches, on the dead and the living. Was there somewhere in those hills a corner, a peaceful courtyard, where at least for that night one could watch the stars without terror? From the door we heard the noises of the dinner [and I thought that we had death under our feet].

Perhaps we can find in this desire for total comprehension at least a partial reason for Corrado's contemplativity, his way of cherishing things as if he were a boy, in one long illusion which not even the dead, with their tragic, unsolved mystery, can dispel:

I see now that throughout this year and earlier too, even during the season of my meager follies, of Anna Maria, Gallo, Cate, when we were still young and the war a distant cloud—I see that I have lived a long isolation, a useless holiday, like a boy who creeps into a bush to hide, likes it there, looks at the sky from under the leaves and forgets to come out, ever.[38]

This is why the hill has such importance here as in Pavese's other works: because it is, as it were, "the sea or the wood, . . . not just another place but [an aspect of things], a way of life," a whole world revealed to the eyes of the boy. The hill with its wild and brackish smell, with its hidden, steaming slopes "like fresh dung" in the distance, is his childhood world, which, being nearer to the absolute, does not accept the responsibilities, the compromises, and struggles of adult, civic life; a childhood that, however, implies a sense of atrocious impotence in the face of love and history.

It is therefore the refusal of the others that leads Pavese to the absolute: in the self-others dialectic, the final term corresponds to that derived from inability to communicate, from rejection of the world.[39] In both cases only by retreating into isolation can the self find the absolute in comparison with which human destiny in essence seems like inexplicable futility. For this reason Pavese can look on both Rosetta's death in *Among Women Only* and the death of Fascists in *The House on the Hill* with the same grief and awareness; he can cover them both with the same veil of austere and brotherly pity, as he himself wrote to Rino Dal Sasso, March 1, 1950:

As for the young girl who commits suicide and the Fascists who are killed . . . either we are writing tragedy or we are not. If we are, then we must be prepared to allow the *villain* (or victim, according to the context) the fullness of his suffering, the positive quality of it, and especially not to forget that, as the *Iliad* teaches us, war is a sad thing, also and above all because one has to kill the enemy. This must not weaken our arm, it is true, but on the whole the best fighters are precisely those who are aware of the tragic necessity. Apart from the fact, of course, that the character of Corrado, aside from his cowardice in the face of action, represents also the extreme problem of every action—anguish in the face of mystery.[40]

8

The Smile of the Gods

"The first men, the children, as it were, of the human race,
not being able to form intelligible class concepts of things,
had a natural need to create poetic characters; that is,
imaginative class concepts or universals, to which, as to
certain models or ideal portraits, to reduce all the particular species which resembled them."

GIAMBATTISTA VICO

"La Deità di Venere adorai."

UGO FOSCOLO

The unresolved question of human destiny, with which
both *Among Women Only* and *The House on the Hill* end, is
the point of departure of *Dialogues with Leucò,* in which
Pavese contemplates human destiny and imagines it in its mysterious origins and mythic manifestations. But it must be emphasized from the beginning that the mythological figures of
the dialogues are also different aspects of Pavese himself, revealing his own metaphysical and Jungian drives as exemplary
of psychoanalytical man.

Before dealing with these mythological figures, it would
perhaps be well to return to an analysis of Pavese's search for
maturity, a search that, starting from childhood and adolescence, arrives at myth (especially in the prose of *August
Holiday*), and from myth develops into a poetics of destiny

—of "ripeness" to be exact. To transform myth into destiny: such is the concern of a whole phase of Pavese's search. The essay "The Wood" marks the fundamental passage from myth to man, from symbol to destiny—the indispensable prerequisite for the human universalization of the mythical dialogues: "The wild that interests us is not nature, the sea, the woods, but the unforeseen in the hearts of our fellow men," Pavese writes at the beginning of this essay, and continues:

At the beginning there is only nature: the city is a landscape, rocks, heights, sky, sudden clearings; woman is a beast, flesh, an embrace. Then nature becomes words, the natural was only a symbol, we know the true *wild*, and we feel a need to scream. . . . If it were possible to destroy symbols, all symbols, we would be destroying only ourselves. We can discover richer, subtler, truer symbols. We can make substitutes for them, but we cannot deny the will underlying them, the adverse will, the wood. It is in our blood, our breath, our hunger. One cannot escape the wood. It, too, is a symbol. . . . We must accept symbols—everybody's mystery—with the calm conviction with which we accept natural things . . . and love all this, with desperate caution.[1]

Thus, Pavese establishes the *human*, rather than the poetic, value of symbols, reaching a fruitful and compelling conclusion: fellowship and acceptance in the face of a common destiny.

Dialogues with Leucò is the finest result of the "return to man" theorized in "The Wood," but above all it represents the fusion of Pavese's own suffering, anxieties, and longings with the sufferings, anxieties, and longings of all mankind. It is his most complex nocturnal and solar song, at once both intimate and universal.[2] Pavese's childhood really becomes here the childhood of the world, caught in its most famous and most obscure myths as told by Herodotus and Homer, by Virgil and Vico, interpreted in the light of ethnology and psychoanalysis, even expressed in a fashionable terminology,[3] but above all permeated with Pavese's own suffering and love. That is why in the dialogues there is more human fellowship, more political participation, than in *The Comrade:* in Mediterranean mythology Pavese seems to have found himself *and* the world without a loss of stability and without tensions. By going to the origins of mystery, which being irrational "raises us to kinship with the Universe, the [Whole],"[4] Pavese has found the link connecting himself and others, yet without completely overcoming his own solipsism, without conquering the difficulties inherent in intersubjectivity, which remained problematic for him. His solipsism remains, though sublimated and universalized. In turning to the origins of mystery, Pavese did not succeed in understanding and dominating the reality of contemporary history, which is so complex and perplexing in its various political, social, and sentimental aspects. He found a refuge in the irrational, a salvation that can be a refuge and salvation for any other self. Thus, with a multiplication of solipsisms, with the universalization of solipsism, at best one step is taken toward an intersubjectivity not yet reached or realized.[5]

This univeralization, this metaphysical viewpoint, this experience of Being, however, are perhaps the prerequisites for dominating the sublunary world, for really understanding the total movement of history in which the relationship of self to others finds its true meaning. In fact, *Dialogues with Leucò,* written at the same time as *The Comrade,* chronologically precedes *Among Women Only* and *The House on the Hill,* the novels that in turn lead to *The Moon and the Bonfires.* In the foreword to the dialogues, Pavese writes:

A true revelation, I am convinced, can only emerge from stubborn concentration on a single problem. I have nothing in common with experimentalists, adventurers, with those who travel in strange regions. The surest, and the quickest, way for us to arouse the sense of wonder is to stare, unafraid, at a single object. Suddenly—miraculously—it will look like something we have never seen before.[6]

It is the same boy of the short story "The Sea," who said: "Gosto doesn't know what it is to stand in front of a house and stare at it until it doesn't look like a house any longer." But here the object being stared at is a myth, which is unveiled, even if partially, to the astonished spectator. The great questions of mankind, irrational in that they cannot be answered sufficiently to explain the mystery of life, are discussed by mythological characters into whom Pavese has put himself. By naming the mysteries of sex and love, life and death, chaos and light, Pavese has, as it were, liberated himself; in a certain sense he has overcome and possessed them—for himself as well as for other men.

The anxious contemplation of the birth of the human world from shapeless, monstrous chaos is the core of the first two groups of dialogues. It is a slow and confused birth, but necessary and definitive; with awareness of self man also acquires the sense of the other-than-self, of material reality, of destiny and death. In particular, sex is seen as an irreducible aspect of reality, one in which life and death meet, sealed by mystery. For instance, in the dialogue "The Blind," Tiresias says:

Nothing is vile, except to the gods. There are irritations, feelings of disgust, and illusions which, when they reach the rock, vanish. Here the rock was the force of sex, its ubiquity and omnipresence under all forms and changes. . . . Above sex there is no god. It is the rock, I tell you. Many gods are beasts, but the snake is the oldest of all the gods. When a snake sinks down into the ground—there you have the image of sex. Life and death are in it. What god can incarnate and include so much? . . .

We all pray to some god, but what happens has no name. The boy who drowns on a summer morning—what does he know of the gods? What does it help him to pray? There is a great snake in every day of life, and it sinks down and watches us.

Tiresias is echoed by the centaur Chiron in the dialogue "The Mares," when he underscores the destiny of Asclepius with words reminiscent of Melville:

Your father is cruel, blinding light, and you must live in a world of bloodless, anguished shadow, a world of festering flesh, of fever and sighs: all this comes to you from the Bright One. The same light that made you will lay bare the world before you, implacably; everywhere it will expose sadness, wounds, the vileness of things. Snakes will watch over you.

Further on he says, referring to Olympus:

That mountain is death. That's what I mean. The new masters live there. They're not like the masters in the old days, Cronos or the Ancient One. They're not like us as we used to be, when [our happiness had no boundaries and] we bounded among things like the things we were. In those days wild beast and swamp brought gods and men together. We were mountain and horse, plant and cloud and running water; we were everything then, everything on earth. Who could die in those days?

There is in these words an effective description of the beginning of self-awareness, and therefore of death. Secondarily there is an explanation of Pavese's theme of nudism (in the remote swamps in stories such as *August Holiday* and *The Devil in the Hills*), which was felt as "an effort to become god through the beast." In the third place there are an eroticism and a pantheism that become explicit only later, in the dialogue "The Mystery," where Demeter, Mother Earth, almost repeating a line from *Earth and Death*, says: "For them [the men] I am a fierce mountain, bristling with forest; I am cloud and cave. . . ." This brings to mind the passage from *A Great Fire* (already quoted in Chapter 4) the meaning of which is so explicit it would seem to require no comment: "I found again my childhood memories, as of someone who dreams of a destiny and a horizon which is not hill or cloud but blood, woman of whom clouds and hills are only a sign."

At this point it is perhaps necessary to note that even a writer like Pirandello, who is very different from Pavese in so many ways, uses similar images, evoking similar feelings, in his "Conversation with His Dead Mother":

The tall young acacia trees in my garden, with their thick foliage, are blown indolently by the wind that ruffles them and would seem inevitably to break them. But like a woman they enjoy feeling so opened and divided in their leaves, and they follow the wind with a resilient flexibility. It is the movement of a wave or a cloud, and it does not wake them from the dream they close within themselves.

In commenting upon the preceding passage, typical of a certain cultural and spiritual climate in our century, Gaspare Giudice remarks:

It is an abandonment to the unconscious, where Pirandello's love for his dead mother comes to the surface in the primal forms of an immediate eroticism, which is one with the symbols of the wind, the sea, the wave and the cloud, the eternal movement and the pantheistic dispersion of birth. Pirandello's pantheism . . . clings to him physically like a lost nostalgia for a profound and primordial experience, with scarcely any intellectual involvement.[7]

We cannot but note the perfect relevance of Giudice's words to Pavese's poetical images and symbols. Indeed, they express an "abandonment to the unconscious" that is fully revealed in another dialogue, significantly entitled "The Mother": "In every man's flesh and blood, his mother rages" —words that by themselves might remain unexplained, were it not for the preceding considerations, whereby they acquire a meaning and a value that underlie much of Pavese's work: nudism, mythology, the countryside, the despairing love lyrics are thus all interconnected aspects of a *vision du monde* whose roots go deep into the irrational, into the dark forces of sex and the psyche as explored by Freud and Jung. *Dialogues with Leucò* is a precious aid in discovering these roots.

In the dialogue we are examining, "The Mares," Hermes introduces a symbolic image that will recur throughout the book: the smile of the gods—which is both perfection and death, the longing and the tragedy of Pavese:

The new gods of Olympus are always smiling, but there's one thing at which they do not smile. Believe me, I've seen destiny. Whenever chaos spills over into the light, into their light, then they must strike down and destroy and remake. That is why Coronis died.

Chiron replies: "But they can't remake Coronis. I was right when I told you that Olympus is death." But at least Coronis, the beautiful woman who "walked through the vineyards and . . . played with the Bright One till he killed her and burnt her body, . . . found herself as she died"—a mythical prefiguration of Santa in *The Moon and the Bonfires*. Man, born of chaos, always longs for the light and order imposed by Olympus. Perfection destroys, true, but it is worth being destroyed in order to achieve it: "In order to be born, a thing must die: even men know that," says Thanatos in the dialogue "The Flower," speaking of Hyacinth transformed into a flower by Apollo.[8] The same motif of love-perfection-death is taken up again, with poignant intensity, in "The Lady of

Beasts," where Pavese's personal experience is transfigured and transfused into a universal myth, probably to a greater extent than in any other dialogue.[9] Endymion speaks to a Stranger, who is already on the move at dawn because he likes "to be awake when things are just coming out of the dark, still untouched," and tells him about his nocturnal adventures on the sacred mountain Latmos—about his immense love for an unspeakable creature:

Friend, you're a man; you know the shiver of terror you have at night when suddenly a kind of clearing opens before you in the forest? No, you don't. Or how at night you remember the clearing you passed through during the day: you saw a flower there, or a kind of berry swaying in the wind—and this flower, this berry, became something wild, something untouchable, mortal, there among all the wild things? Do you know what I mean? A flower like a wild beast? . . . Have you ever known someone who was many things in one, who brought them with her, so that everything she did, every thought of her seems to contain the whole infinity of things of which your countryside, your sky consists, and [words,] memories and days gone by you'll never know, and days to come, and certainties, another countryside, another sky forever alien—have you ever known such a person, stranger?

One notices the Freudian sexuality of the natural images in the first part of the quotation; and in the second part, the decadent spiritualization of sexuality, which follows a literary pattern that can be traced back to D'Annunzio's *The Pleasure:*

Andrea [Sperelli] felt an exotic air involving her person, felt that from her a strange seduction, an enchantment came to him—the vague ghosts of faraway things she had seen, the views she still preserved in her eyes, the memories that filled her soul. It was an unspeakable, undefinable enchantment. It was as if, within her person, she brought a trace of the light in which she had immersed herself, of the scents she had breathed, of the languages she had heard; it was as if she bore within her all the confused, vanished, vague magical qualities of those lands of the Sun.

The substantial similarity of the attitude of Pavese-Endymion and D'Annunzio-Sperelli toward women in the above two passages is obvious. In Pavese, however, the subtlety and exoticism are tempered by a painful, desperate, psychoanalytical sincerity lacking in D'Annunzio.

This is confirmed by several of the poems that we partially examined in Chapter 1, in which are to be found the tender and erotic image of the cloud (see too the observations on Pirandello above); for instance "Nocturne," which closes *Work Is Wearying*: "You are like a cloud / glimpsed between branches. There shines in your eyes / the strangeness of a sky that is not yours"; or "You Have a Blood, a Breath," one of the first poems in *Death Will Come and Its Eyes Will Be Yours*: ". . . as a little girl you played / under a different sky, / you have the silence of it in your eyes, / a cloud. . . ."

Between these two poems there is the collection *Earth and Death*, in which almost every line shows Pavese's sorrow, the poignant desperation of being rejected by the "wood," by the adverse will of the "other," the impotence in the face of the wild mystery of sex and especially in the face of the other's lack of recognition—an impotence that D'Annunzio did not feel and that Pavese expresses in tormented, psychoanalytical images, comparable perhaps to those in Pascoli's poem "Nocturnal Jasmin": "sure / like the earth, dark / like the earth, mill / of seasons and dreams"; "you are dark"; "you are a closed cellar"; "you are the dark room"; "you are closed, like the earth" and "unknown and wild thing."

One understands how, in the mythological texture of the

dialogues, Pavese has sublimated and universalized his personal *datum*, which is so overwhelming in the lyrics. But at the same time he has preserved it in poetical images that never before seemed to be so significant: the hill, the cloud, the different sky, the glance, the wave, the blood, the wild, and the smile.

Some of these images, in fact, are to be found in Endymion's story, when he tells of his encounter with Artemis, the virgin and proud goddess, "a slight, awkward girl":

The moon was shining when I woke. In my dream I felt a shiver of dread at the thought of being there, in the clearing, in the moonlight.

Then I saw her. I saw her looking at me, looking at me with that sidelong glance of hers. But her eyes were steady, clear, with great deeps in them. I didn't know it then, nor even the next day, but I was already hers, utterly hers, caught with the circle of her eyes, in the space she filled, the clearing and the hill. She smiled at me, timidly. "Lady," I said to her, and she frowned, like a girl, like a shy, wild thing. . . . Then she spoke my name and stood beside me—her tunic barely reached her knees—and stretched out her hand and touched my hair. There was something hesitant in the way she touched me, and she smiled, an incredible, mortal smile. . . . I [was] like a small boy. "You must never wake again," she said. "Don't try to follow me. I'll come to you again." And she went off through the clearing.

Endymion goes on to say that he walked all over Latmos, following the moon, listening, and all he could hear was her voice, "like the sound of sea water, a hoarse voice, cold and maternal"; at dawn, he says, "I knew that my home was no longer among men. I was no longer one of them. I was waiting for night." Then he speaks again of the goddess, above all of her glance:

And those great transparent eyes have seen other things. They see them yet. They *are* those things. Wild berry and wild beast are in her eyes, and the howling, the death, the cruelty of flesh turned stone. The shed blood, the savaged flesh, the ravenous earth, the wilderness—all this I know. For her, the Wild One, this is wilderness, and loneliness.

After all that has been said there is no need to point out how many of Pavese's motifs are included and relived in Endymion's story—from Concia in *The Political Prisoner* to the poems of *Death Will Come and Its Eyes Will Be Yours*. It might be more worth while recalling that the myth of Endymion was a poetical subject for Baudelaire and D'Annunzio, two poets dear to Pavese; this myth is placed by Mario Praz within the framework of the romantic-decadent conception of the *belle dame sans merci*, of the *femme fatale:*

In accordance with this conception of the Fatal Woman, the lover is usually a youth, and maintains a passive attitude; he is obscure, and inferior either in condition or in physical exuberance to the woman, who stands in the same relation to him as do the female spider, the praying mantis, &c., to their respective males: sexual cannibalism is her monopoly. Towards the end of the [nineteenth] century the perfect incarnation of this type of woman is Herodias. But she is not the only one: Helen, the Helen of Moreau, of Samain, of Pascoli (*Anticlo*), closely resembles her. The ancient myths, such as that of the Sphinx, of Venus and Adonis, of Diana and Endymion, were called in to illustrate this type of relationship, which was to be so insistently repeated in the second half of the century. The following point must be emphasized: the function of the flame which attracts and burns is exercised, in the first half of the century, by the Fatal Man (the Byronic hero), in the second half by the Fatal Woman; the moth destined for sacrifice is in the first case the woman, in the second the man. It is not simply a case of convention and literary fashion: literature, even in its most artificial forms, reflects to some extent aspects of contemporary life. It is curious to follow the parabola of the sexes during the nineteenth century: the obsession for the

androgyne type towards the end of the century is a clear indication of a turbid confusion of function and ideal. The male, who at
first tends towards sadism, inclines, at the end of the century,
towards masochism.[10]

There is no doubt that Praz's observations can be equally well
applied to Pavese, who belongs historically to the late European decadentism in his style of writing and of living (the
passive and masochistic young man; the basic lyricism, beyond
the lesson of *verismo;* the mastery of the "analogical" word;
symbolism; extreme sensitivity, "metapsychology," and psychoanalysis).

But to return to the dialogue, after Endymion's story the
Stranger, who has lived "always alone" and knows that the
"immortals know how to live alone," manifests himself as a
god. Endymion prays to him, "O wanderer god, her sweetness
is like dawn, or like earth and heaven revealed." The god
concedes that he may see her again, and while leaving exhorts
him:

Everyone has his own kind of sleep, Endymion. Your sleep is
infinite with the cries and the voices of things; it is full of earth
and sky and day following day. Sleep your sleep bravely, you
have nothing better. The loneliness, the wild places of earth are
yours. Love them as she loves them. And now, Endymion, I must
leave you. You will see her tonight. . . . Farewell. But you must
never wake again, remember that.

Artemis' smile that destroys is really the symbol of a perfection sought in vain, achieved only through death. In fact,
Artemis is also "the cruel virgin who walks on the mountain"
and who presides over the bloody story of the house of Atreus
in the dialogue "In the Family." The Atreidae, just like many
Pavesian characters, "wouldn't know what to do with a tame,
submissive woman. They need a woman with cold, killer's

eyes, eyes without shame, eyes like arrow slits," eyes which hide at least a reflection of Artemis' brief smile.

The same smile reappears in the dialogue "Sea Foam" as an attribute of Aphrodite, "the tormented, restless one who smiles to herself," and seems intended to symbolize, to sublimate, the unattainable love of Helen Tindaridis, who "lied to no one, smiled at no one."[11] Britomart the nymph explains admirably what smiling means: "Smiling means living like a wave, like a leaf, accepting your fate. It means dying in one form and being reborn in another. It means accepting—accepting oneself, accepting fate."[12] But for Sappho it is difficult to accept:

I didn't know it was like this. I thought everything ended with that final jump. I thought the longing and the restlessness and the tumult would all be done with. The sea swallows, the sea annuls, I thought. . . . I knew how to run away too, when I was alive. My way was to look into things, into the tumult, and turn it into speech, into song. But fate is something quite different. . . . I was never happy, Britomart. Desire is not song. It destroys and burns, like a snake, like the wind.

In Sappho's words there is also Pavese's destiny: he knew how to sing but did not know how to smile; he knew his "job of poet" but not the other "job of living." The image of the snake, then, brings us back to "that mysterious short circuit sex-death" of which Solmi speaks,[13] and which is the focus of the dialogue "The Mother." Hermes says to Meleager, referring to his mother's eyes:

The fact that those eyes grow old and die means that in the interval you become a man, and knowing that you offend them, you go somewhere else in search of them—live eyes, true eyes. And if you find them—and one always finds them, Meleager—the person they belong to is again your mother. . . . And no one can escape the fate that has marked him from birth with the sign of the fire. . . . The same death awaits them all. They all die of another's passion. In every man's flesh and blood, his mother rages.

Even the young woman whom Meleager loved had eyes like his mother's, in fact "she *was* those eyes"—those eyes that have within them life and above all death, as in Pavese's last poems.

The awareness of death grows more and more insidious in the dialogue "The Friends," and becomes Oedipus' destiny in "The Road."[14] To him, it is a destiny embodied in Mt. Cithaeron, the mountain of childhood, and it must be silently, painfully accepted: "This fatigue, this peace, after all the uproar of our destiny—they're perhaps the only things that are truly our own." This peace after destiny is also the theme of "The Werewolf," whereas in "The Inconsolable" destiny appears ineluctable; death destroys love, Orpheus turns deliberately in order to lose Eurydice, who could never be the same again:

The Eurydice I mourned was a season of life. I was looking down there for something very different from my love. I was looking for a past which Eurydice knows nothing of. I understood this among the dead while I was singing my song. . . . When I wept, I was no longer looking for her, but for myself. For a fate, if you like.

Actually, as the Bacchante says, by now Orpheus' thought is "only death." He confirms it when, desperately, he confesses what the knowledge of nothingness (juxtaposed with the joyous and drunken ignorance of the Dionysian rites) means to him: "Every time you invoke a god, you meet death. And you go down to Hades to bring something back, to violate a destiny. You don't defeat the darkness, and you lose the light. You're torn apart, like a man possessed."

In Pavese's interpretation, then, the knowledge of self coincides with everyone's destiny (one's own private hell) and with death. In some dialogues, however, Pavese's attention is focused on the awareness of others, and social life is described at its dawn. In this sense Prometheus in "The Mountain" is really a model:

What is a victory but pity turned gesture, saving others at your own expense? Everyone works for others, under the law of destiny. . . . Our fates are fused. By the world's law, no one goes free unless another's blood is shed for him. The same will happen with you [Heracles], on Mt. Oeta. . . . It will be the blood of the monsters which you now live to destroy. And the pyre you mount will burn with the fire I stole.

Prometheus' fire is thus an essential element of the human world (and of Pavese's mythology), in dramatic juxtaposition to the Vichian cycle of nature:

Titan is a name, nothing more. Understand me, Heracles. The world has its seasons, like the fields, like the earth. Winter returns, summer returns. How can we say that the forest dies, or remains the same? Before long, men will be the Titans.

In "The Guest," the seasons are juxtaposed with the rites of the peasants, who pretended to fertilize the earth with human sacrifices; Lityerses says to Heracles:

Before cutting up the body, we have to sweat him in the sun till he comes to a lather. And that's why we're going to put you to work, reaping and bringing in the sheaves until you're running with sweat. And then, at the last minute, when your blood is boiling pure and foaming like a living thing, that's the moment when we'll slit your throat. Yessir. You're a strong young man.

The reference to certain pages of *The Harvesters* is obvious, with their primordial and vaguely sacrificial violence. It will be remembered in this connection that in Chapter 3 we explained the references to pages of Vico that were more directly linked with the primitive world of the peasant (already mythological and ethnological), and especially those concerning "the fire that the heroes must have kindled with flints and set to the thorny underbrush on the mountain tops, dried out by the hot suns of summer . . ." and the "eternal property expressed in the saying that servants are the paid enemies of their masters." We can, in fact, see the social significance attributed to the bonfires—another of Pavese's myths—in the propitiatory rites of "The Bonfires."

Look, the gods are our masters. They're like the landowners. . . . Let's suppose a bonfire can make it rain, and burning some useless loafer can save the harvest. Well, how many owners' houses would you have to burn, how many owners would you have to kill in the streets to bring some justice back to the world and make us our own masters again?

The answer of the son, who feels a strong repugnance for such human sacrifices, is noteworthy: "I don't want to think about it. I won't. If that's the way we treated each other, then the landowners have every right to eat us alive. The gods are right to watch us suffer. We're evil, we're all evil."

The element of violence in the peasants' life concludes the first two groups of mythological dialogues. In them Pavese poetically relives the birth of the human world in all of its contradictory complexity. The complexity cannot be resolved in dichotomies such as Titanism-Olympicism or city-country, but is rendered with a richness of nuance that reflects the human reality born of chaos, which still tends toward order in a fatiguing daily conquest.

In the dialogues of the third group the central focus is the theme of love, and more precisely of love seen as a pretext for or cause of the contrast between immortality and happiness on one hand, life and suffering on the other. In "The Island," for example, when Odysseus complains of not being immortal, Calypso, who is in love with him, answers: "You will be, if you listen to me. What is eternal life if it's not accepting the moment that comes and the moment that goes? Drunkenness, pleasure, and death have no other aim. What else has your restless wandering been until now?" In "The Lake" Virbius-Hippolytus, who walks through Hesperia "as if he were a cloud," asks Diana "for life, not happiness."[15]

In "The Witches," Circe discovers the uselessness of the divine smile and would like to become mortal in order to have Odysseus. (Her attitude is already a prelude to the last group of dialogues.) "And as I sang, I went to the loom, and I put his home and his childhood into that harsh voice of mine, I gentled it, I was his Penelope."[16] Circe sees clearly the contradictions, but also the greatness of men:

You can't imagine the way death fascinates them. They're destined to die, of course, it's a repetition, something they know in advance. And yet they deceive themselves into thinking that it changes something. . . . That's the one immortal thing about a mortal, Leucò. The memory he carries with him, the memory he leaves behind him. That is what names and words are. When they remember, even men smile. A smile of resignation.

Or men act in order to be similar to the gods: this is the theme of "The Argonauts," perhaps the most Mediterranean of the dialogues, filled with light:[17]

Little Melita, you're one of the temple girls. Surely you all know that when a man climbs up there it's because he wants to become a god, at least for a day, for an hour. Because he wants to sleep with you as though you were the goddess. He always pretends he's sleeping with her; then he realizes it was only mortal flesh he was dealing with, poor human creatures like you and your friends up there, like all women. Then he flies into a rage and tries to be a god somewhere else,[18]

for example by going in search of the golden fleece, to discover a "virginity in things, more frightening than danger."

In "The Vineyard," too, there is a longing for immortality. The nymph Leucothea announces to Ariadne—the same Ariadne "made of earth and sun" abandoned by Theseus in "The Bull"—that a god will be sent to console her:

The youngest of all the gods. He has seen you, and he likes you. His name is Dionysus. . . . He was born at Thebes, and he courses the world. He is a god of joy. . . . He kills with laughter. Bulls and tigers walk beside him. His life is a festival, and he likes you.

Leucothea also explains to Ariadne that her abandonment by Theseus has taught her a great deal: "You've been afraid, you've suffered. You've thought of dying. You've learned what waking is. Now you're alone, and you're expecting a god." Leucothea concludes by announcing not so much the coming of a god, as immortality:

It will be like loving a place, a stream of water, an hour of the day. No man can give you this. The gods last as long as the things that make them gods. So long as the goats frisk through the pines and the vineyards, he will please you and you will please him. . . . The stars shine over the vineyards at night. The god who waits for you is a god of night. Don't be afraid.

The memory of the "young god" and of the "goat-god" of *Work Is Wearying* is fused here with the motif of the "festival night" in a repetition and a deepening of Endymion's symbolic sleep and awakening: love as death and immortality, reflected in nature.

In the dialogues of the last group there is indeed a "return to man"; they enhance the value of man in all of his poignant, imperfect, and fleeting *durée*, with all the feeling and the mystery of death, with the immortality given him, even more than by rare instants of love, by the word that becomes memory—story and poetry. In "Mankind" Kratos and Bia say:

But do you realize what men are? Wretched little creatures who are bound to die. More wretched than worms or last year's leaves: they're dead and they don't even know they die. But men do know and they talk about it; they never stop invoking us, trying to snatch a favor or a glance from us. They light fires to us—the fires they stole away in the fennel stalk. . . . Men are poor worms, but with them everything is unforeseen, everything is a discovery. You can understand an animal and even a god, but no one, not even we immortals, knows what is going on in the hearts of men. Some of them even dare to make a stand against destiny. Only if you live with them and for them can you enjoy the savor of the world.

This affirmation of man's value is emphasized by two motifs that mark crucial points in Pavese's search: the impossibility of knowing the human heart ties up with the essay "The Wood" (with the related mythological substratum), and the propitiatory fires echo practically the greater part of Pavese's work, culminating in the final scene of *The Moon and the Bonfires*. But in the dialogue "The Flood," the contrast between the human condition and the divine is seen above all in relation to death. Men live in time, and "the seasons of their life are festivals," but death is the main factor concluding these human seasons:

But dying is precisely this—no longer knowing that you're dead. And this is what this flood means: dying in such numbers that there won't be anyone left to know it. That's why they'll come to look for us. And they'll ask us to save them, and they'll want to become like us, like plants and stones—insensible things that are nothing but destiny. In them they will save themselves. When the waters retreat, they'll come forth as stones and trees, just as they did before. And this is all that mortals want, just as before.

We are reminded of a passage from Pavese's essays in which he outlines the "poetics of destiny":

Men do not have nature's immutability, its breadth of interpretation, its silence. . . . My poetry has tried in various ways to *petrify* them—by isolating them in their most natural moments, immersing them in things, by reducing them to destiny.[19]

But death cannot be escaped, and men are left with only "hope or destiny"; thus Pavese reasserts the fleeting value of life more than in any other of his works: a hamadryad, speaking of men, says:

Well, I hope this flood at least serves to teach them the meaning of festival and play. After all, there's a make-believe which destiny imposes upon us mortals and which we are aware of—why can't they learn to live their make-believe as though each moment of their wretched little lives was eternal? Why won't they realize that it's precisely the shortness of their lives that gives them their value? . . . They too will learn something tomorrow. . . . In the new world even the shortest lives will be in some way blessed.

Death is also the starting point of the dialogue "The Mystery." Everything men touch "becomes time. Becomes action. Waiting and hope. Even their dying is something," in fact it is something extremely important, as Dionysus, who almost seems an involuntary spokesman of much phenomenology, says: "But they wouldn't be men if they weren't miserable. Death is what they're born for. [Their only richness is death.] It's death that drives them to their efforts, to memory and foresight."

But man's true wealth, even more so than death, is the

word. As Dionysus says: "They have a way of giving names to themselves and things and us which enriches life. Like these vineyards that they've taught themselves to grow on these hillsides."[20] Demeter recalls the blood rites with which men found a transcendence[21] and expresses a wish to "give a meaning to their dying . . . by teaching them the life of the blessed," by making the word overcome death:

Teach them that they can become like us, beyond grief and death. But we'll tell them ourselves. Teach them that just as the wheat and the vine go down beneath the earth in order to be born again, so death is a new life for them too. Give them this holy story. Lead them upward by means of this story. Teach them a fate which is woven with our own.

From the Eleusinian-Christian mysteries to the poetical dialogue "The Muses," the theme remains the story, the word: Mnemosyne, whose "voice and glance are immortal," teaches Hesiod, whose existence is a Leopardian "weariness and unhappiness," how to transfix with a word the immortal moments, the divine models of daily life, the mythical archetypes of Pavese's search:

Have you ever asked yourself why an instant can suddenly make you happy, happy as a god? You are looking, say, at the olive tree, the olive tree on the path you have taken every day for years, and suddenly there comes a day when the sense of staleness leaves you and you caress the gnarled trunk with a look, as though you had recognized an old friend, and it spoke to you precisely the one word your heart was hoping for. . . . For an instant time stops, and you experience the trivial event as though before and after had no existence.

So, Mnemosyne concludes, "You know what immortal life is like"; and she suggests to Hesiod that he tell about work and the days, catching the ecstatic moments of life: "In everything you do, you renew a divine model. Day and night, there is not an instant, not even the most futile, that has not sprung from the silence of your origins." With the mention of the swamp of Boibei's, from which "at the beginning of time, in a seething bubbling silence" monsters and gods were born, Mnemosyne closes a circle: the circle of human destiny composed of chaos and light, death and immortality. And Pavese too closes poetically the circle that he began in the first dialogues.

In the pages of *Dialogues with Leucò* we find again the images and poetic motifs that enrich so much of Pavese's work: the taste for wandering and solitude, the attraction of an unknown and exotic world, the fires or bonfires, the hills or mountain of his childhood and imagination, the seasons and festivals, blood and earth, the fierce sun and the fateful moon, the clouds and the rocks, the vineyard and the stars, divine and pitiless smiles, eyes which bring happiness and death. His style, which is always clear and lively, is both classic and realistic in its symbolism. Pavese himself had wanted the *Dialogues with Leucò* to be his own *Short Moral Works*[22] ("with due proportions"), perhaps because, like Leopardi, he is examining and inquiring into the great questions of life and death, sorrow and unhappiness, and though he does not solve them he at least makes them universal and therefore more acceptable.

But Leopardi, even when he portrays himself in his characters (mythological or otherwise), faces reality and the absolute with a stubborn and stoic determination to achieve clarity, with a philosophical rationality not to be found in Pavese's dialogues. In the latter, the determination to achieve clarity often yields to the elegiac and imaginative, and for philosophical rationality is substituted mythological (and personal) irrationality. Both Leopardi and Pavese are pessimists when confronted with human destiny; but Pavese, writing

almost a century after Leopardi and familiar with the symbolists and with phenomenology, relies more explicitly on the
word to express the longing for eternity, the need to give a
meaning to death, whereas for Leopardi it was expressed in
his dramatic and "magnanimous" desperation. For both writers, however, the word is above all a consolation.

Another nineteenth-century author, Ugo Foscolo, should
be mentioned, for Pavese could have found in his poems,
instinctively more than rationally, a suggestion and an example.[23] Apart from the obvious mythical figures of the *Sonnets*
and *The Graces*, one should notice the conclusion of *The
Sepulchres*. For Foscolo, poetry overcomes time and death;
poets are the bards and priests of mankind. Something similar
can be found in Pavese: a religious feeling for the word,
which defines the poets as "oracles," as we shall soon see, and
makes the story a form of immortality, as we have already
seen. But Pavese has no Hector to celebrate as a vanquished
hero; the dead who are to be remembered are either unknown
or familiar—vanquished but not heroes: hence the crepuscular
or at least elegiac character of so much of his work, especially
the last novels.[24]

This absence of heroes is also important from a cultural and
historical point of view: it corresponds exactly to the failure
of D'Annunzio's *superuomo* and to the contemporary experience of Pascoli's meek and humble man. Pavese, who inherited
Leopardi's "traditional" and Foscolo's "decadent" classicism,
also inherits the last faded aspects of D'Annunzio's violence,
and as he echoes them in his own introverted and frustrated
way, develops them naturally in patterns and subdued tones
similar to Pascoli's. Thus, two conceptions of classicism and
two conceptions of decadentism find their focus—and their
transformation into a single *vision du monde*—in the complex
figure of Pavese. This *vision du monde* manages to give unity

to the poetry of Pavese, but nevertheless fails to reconcile the exigencies of poetry with those of life and again presents the problem and the tragedy of alienation. Pavese's poetics, which began with myth, become in *Dialogues with Leucò* a "poetics of destiny," which affirms both the value of man and of the word; the protagonists of the dialogues are, in fact, treated as "beautiful names charged . . . with destiny":[25]

The fountainhead of poetry is always a mystery, an inspiration, a perplexity in confrontation with the irrational—unknown territory. But the act of poetry, if we are permitted to distinguish, to separate the flame from the burning matter, is an absolute will to see clearly, to reduce to reason, to know. Mythos and logos.[26]

Pavese himself outlines the development of his search from myth to destiny, recalling the two dialogues "The Muses" and "The Gods." These dialogues and the essay "The Wood" ("We must accept symbols—everyone's mystery—with the calm conviction with which natural things are accepted. The city produces symbols like the country produces fruit") anticipate the most daring motif of such a poetics: the application to complex human relationships ("destinies," "the city") of this doctrine of a mythical scheme, of the atemporal contemplation of experience, which until now seemed only to be related to the childhood status of memory, to the making of certain universal, naturalistic symbols ("cloud," "wood," "country").[27]

Essentially, Pavese wants to transfix a temporal moment into an eternal meaning:

What is this destiny? The fact that acts, words, human life are seen as symbols, as myths, means that they seem to exist outside of time and yet discovered in each single instance as unique, as revealed for the first time. A life appears as destiny when, unexpectedly, it is shown to be exemplary, and fixed *ab aeterno*.[28]

This view of poetics was already foreseen in the words Pavese had dedicated to Edgar Lee Masters:

Each of us possesses an abundance of these things made into acts that are the symbols of our destiny: they are not in themselves valid, by their natural qualities, but they invite and call to us; they are symbols. For Lee Masters it might be said that death—the end of time—is the decisive moment that snatched one personal symbol from all the others and has welded and nailed it forever to the soul.[29]

Thus, the poet becomes "the oracle of his heroes' lives":

A whole work can be traced back to that one simple oracular sentence that contains its essence. This observation is important, because it links the completed poem to the mythical nucleus that shapes it. This nucleus, a destiny that is glimpsed in the midst of the indifferent reality, is by definition an oracular moment of supreme vision and bliss; it is not formed but gives form.[30]

We are brought back to "the beautiful names charged with destiny" of the dialogues, and particularly to the three poets of antiquity who appear as characters and stages in the poetic history of their author: Orpheus is seeking himself when he descends into Hades; Sappho looks unsuccessfully for happiness in song; Hesiod, who is incapable of happiness, finds immortality in words for himself and for others. Thus Pavese, in his simple and sublime dialogues with Leucò (i.e., Ino Leucothea, one of the "amorous Oceanine Nereids," the nymph who consoles), examines the most intimate aspects of himself; he recognizes the tragic unhappiness and fleeting, precious greatness of the human condition, and finally celebrates the works and days of mankind: love, work, festivals, and death.

It might be said that Pavese has solved his problem of human participation, in a completely abstract way and with a decadent taste directly proportional to the classical orderliness of his words and clarity of his style. At least for the moment, this is his finest contribution, more sincere than any political action, for which he was not suited. One is reminded of the words he wrote in his diary a few days before his death and their lapidary conciseness makes one shudder: "I have done my part by the world, as best I could. I have worked; I have given poetry to men; I have shared the sorrows of many."[31]

9

The Stranger in the Hills

"In gremium matris terrai. . . ."
LUCRETIUS

"I am too ripe for death; it seems too absurd and incredible to me, so dead am I spiritually, the fable of life so closed within me on all sides, to have to last longer. . . . I envy the dead, and I would only change my state with theirs."

GIACOMO LEOPARDI

In *Dialogues with Leucò* Pavese turned to classical myths in his search for universality; in *The Moon and the Bonfires* he turned to the hills of his childhood in his search for his own individuality, at a higher and more conscious level than in any of his previous works.

In the *Dialogues* Pavese "goes to the human kernel" of everyone of the classical myths; in *The Moon and the Bonfires* each of his personal myths is traced back to "memories of childhood and the world."[1] Together, the *Dialogues* and the last novel constitute the apex of Pavese's work, his fullness and maturity: they are the two endpoints of the same search, the two extreme moments of the same anxiety. After the universal and metaphysical experience of *Dialogues with Leucò*, Pavese could finally understand the sublunar world. He was now able to understand man's true nature, see himself in relationship with others, judge his own position in history, lucidly and tormentedly at first, in *The House on the Hill,* and then peacefully and poetically in *The Moon and the Bonfires.* In the latter novel there is total comprehension of himself in an historical context and, as a result, total acceptance of self and world. This acceptance and comprehension is expressed in Pavese's own poetic images. Thus, the poetic myths of *The Moon and the Bonfires* are meant to signify not mystify. They express precisely and definitively the dichotomy of contemplative man cut off from the world of action—a fundamental theme in poetry and narrative from Leopardi to Pirandello, and from Svevo to Montale. They are no longer an "escape into metaphor" but a whole life made into word, memory, poetry.

All the themes Pavese had put into his previous works and examined fragment by fragment with increasing depth are revived in *The Moon and the Bonfires* and totally encompassed in a supreme effort to understand the "monolith." In this novel all Pavese's great themes are fused into a poetic whole and only the exigencies of analysis (and therefore of clarity and critical comprehension) can induce us to separate them in order to reveal their components: solitude, poised between inability to communicate and participation; love and violence; work and holiday; childhood and death; nature and history; myth and destiny; maturity. This unity of themes contains within it and concludes, like a cycle, all Pavese's work and world vision. And since basically the cycle is a return, we shall begin our analysis of *The Moon and the Bonfires*[2] from the myth of return.

It will be remembered that the premise on which the myth of return is based, explicitly or otherwise, is the tendency to escapism, to daydream, the contemplative disposition of so many of Pavese's characters, such as the narrator of the emblematic story "Evocation" and perhaps more significantly the boy in the poem "Southern Seas" and the stories "Insomnia," "The Sea," and "Intimate History"—with the indispensible corollary of the admiration the boy feels for the person who has realized in life his own dreams, the boy mediated by the adult, a relationship frequently portrayed in the short stories ("The Leather Jacket," "The Hermit," "Mr. Pietro"). The myth of return derives from this premise and is exemplified first in the cousin in the poem we have quoted, in the protagonist of "The Langhe Hills," in Clelia in *Among Women Only*, in Corrado in *The House on the Hill*. Its profound significance as a search for self-awareness and a discovery of *durée*, of mythical timelessness, is poetically theorized in the pages of "Time," "The Field of Grain," and "The Vineyard."

As a preliminary we notice that the narrator of *The Moon and the Bonfires* is called "Anguilla," or "Eel," a nickname that in itself is emblematic, though perhaps unconsciously, in that eels swim back up the mountain streams and return to their birthplace, "to the paradise of fertilization" as Montale says. Anguilla has a tendency to escapism, a contemplative disposition:

. . . all these years . . . I had only to raise my eyes from the fields to see the vineyards high up on Salto and the way they sloped gradually down towards Canelli, towards the railway and the whistle of the train which ran along by the Belbo morning and evening, making me think of wonders, of stations and cities. . . . From the time when, as a boy, I leant on my spade at the farm gate at La Mora and listened to the chatter of people who had nothing better to do as they passed by on the main road— ever since that time, for me, the little hills round Canelli are doors opening on the world.[3]

This dreamy characteristic is fed and stimulated by the narrator's friend:

It was Nuto who told me that you can go anywhere by train and that where the railway line ends the ports begin and the ships have their own timetable and the whole world is a network of roads and ports, a continual coming and going of people, and some build and some undo what has been built, and everywhere there are people who can do things and others who can't. . . . And so some days when I was in the fields or in the vineyards above the road, hoeing away in the sun, and heard through the peach trees the train arriving and filling the valley with its noise as it came or went from Canelli, at these times I stopped and leant on my hoe and watched the smoke and the carriages and looked at Gaminella and the fine house they called Il Nido, looked towards Canelli and Calamandrana, towards Calosso too, and felt as if I had been drinking wine, and become someone else, as if I was like Nuto and every bit as good as him, and that one fine day I'd take that train, too, and set out on my travels.

Finally, by a particularly Pavesian switch, escapism is seen as destiny, in a moving, lyrical description:

In the sky there were long mare's-tails and white flossy clouds which seemed like the bright drift we see at night in the darkness behind the stars. I was thinking that tomorrow I'd be in the Viale Corsica when suddenly I realized that the sea, too, is veined with the lines of the currents and that when as a child, I watched the clouds and the path of the stars, I had already started on my travels without knowing it.[4]

There is a further indispensable element for the understanding of Anguilla's escapism: the desire for improvement, for confirmation that he could build his life, like Leopardi, who "would rather be unhappy than mediocre," and this we see when the adult Anguilla stands at the window of the *albergo dell'Angelo* and feels "like a mayor looking down from the balcony of the town hall":

I saw now that even when, as a boy, I chased the goat or broke the bundles of bushwood in a rage in the wintertime by putting my foot on top of them, or shut my eyes to see if the hill had vanished when I opened them again—even then I was preparing myself for what fate had in store for me, to live without a home of my own and always hope that there would be a village fairer and richer beyond the hills. As for this room at the Albergo dell'Angelo—I had never been there then—it seemed as if I had always known that when a signore, a man with his pockets full of gold coins, the owner of big farms, set out in his gig to see the world, he'd find himself one fine morning in a room like this and wash his hands in the white basin and write a letter on the old polished table, a letter which would go far away, to the city, and hunters would read it, and mayors and ladies with [parasols]. And here it was happening. In the morning I drank my coffee and wrote letters to Genoa, to America, I handled money, I employed people. Perhaps in a month I would be at sea again, following my letters.

It is interesting to note that all Anguilla's activity is completely external to the novel: it precedes it or is introduced by means of memories or allusions, but it is not an integral part of the narrative nor of the personality of the narrator.

In order to satisfy his longing for escape, Anguilla, the dreamy contemplative boy, had to leave; but the years have merely taught him the need to return, and this sets the tone of the novel from the very first paragraph:

There is a reason why I came back to this place, came back here instead of to Canelli, Barbaresco, or Alba. It is almost certain that I was not born here; where I was born I don't know. There is not a house or a bit of ground or a handful of dust hereabouts of which I can say: "This was me before I was born." I do not know whether I come from the hills or from the valleys, from the woods or from a great house with a balcony. Maybe the girl who laid me on the cathedral steps in Alba didn't come from the country either; maybe her people had a big house in town. . . . Who knows whose flesh and blood I am? I have knocked about the world enough to know that one lot of flesh and blood is as good as another. But that's why you get tired and try to put down roots. To find somewhere where you belong so that you are worth more than the usual round of the seasons and last a bit longer.[5]

It is very clear that the need to return causes suffering and is profoundly linked to the awareness of its limitation: Anguilla is a bastard and therefore his return is not a return to family or ancestors (after the manner of Herodotus),[6] but rather a search for his own individuality, in perfect harmony with his own contemplative nature. The death or absence of the father of the protagonist who is seeking self-affirmation is not a new theme either in Pavese or in Italian literature in general; through the rediscovery of the countryside, particularly, it reminds us of the childhood memories of Rousseau and of George Sand's *François le Champì*, and then of the rustic novel of Carcano, of Ippolito Nievo, right up to its various developments in Verga, Pirandello, Tozzi, Svevo, Morante, and Gadda. The return signifies the self taking root and becoming aware of human *durée* in contrast to the impassive cycle of the natural seasons. A similar antithesis is described in Pavese's diary in the following terms, only apparently paradoxical in this context:

In life, there is no return. As the seasons come around, the passing years color the same theme in ever-different ways. The beauty of our own discordant rhythm, moderation and invention, stability and discovery—is that age is an accumulation of equally important things, growing richer and deeper all the time.[7]

In life there is no return, because, even if one can return to the scene of one's childhood, there is no going back in time: on the one hand impassive nature repeats its vital cycles, and in this sense one can say "among the hills time stands still" and the narrator can delude himself into thinking he can find himself in the natural cycle, return to the womb of mother earth, in brief, ecstatic, mythical moments:

The sun is fierce up in these hills; I had forgotten how its light is flung back off the bare patches of volcanic rock. Here the heat doesn't so much come down from the sky as rise up underfoot, from the earth, from the trench between the vines which seems to have devoured each speck of green and turned it to stem. I like this heat; it has a smell, and I'm part of the smell—there are so many grape harvests in it, so many hay harvests, so many piles of stripped leaves, so many tastes, and so many desires that I didn't know I had any longer.[8]

But time really does pass, and in this sense the unchanging seasons stand in opposition to the years, which bring awareness, profoundity, maturity:

To make a long story short, I was a man too. I was someone else—if I had indeed found La Mora as I had known it the first winter, and the summer after, and then summer following winter again, day and night through all these years, I certainly wouldn't have known what to do with myself. Maybe I came from too far away: I didn't belong to this house any more, I wasn't like Cinto now, the world had changed me.

There come to mind the words that Verga puts in the mouth of 'Ntoni in *The House by the Medlar Tree:* "When someone leaves his home it's better never to go back, because everything changes while one is away, and even the faces with which they look at one are changed, and one seems to have become a stranger oneself." In fact, time silently influences the aspect of people and things, their very existence; Anguilla, no less a stranger than 'Ntoni, or Clelia in *Among Women Only* when she returns to her own district of Turin, recalls the old peasants who had brought him up and refers to them as being "like all the people who are gone now" as if there were no other people from his village:

I had come back. I had come out on to the road, I had made my fortune—I slept at the Albergo dell'Angelo and talked with the Cavaliere—but the faces, the voices, and the hands which should have touched me and recognized me were gone. They had been gone for a while. What was left behind was like a piazza the day after the fair, or a vineyard after the grape harvest or going back to eat alone after someone has let you down.

Even places have changed, and this is the first of Anguilla's disillusions on return, the first presentiment of the impossibility of refinding one's childhood: "The clump of hazels had disappeared and our closely cut patch of millet grass grown smaller. . . . But I had not expected not to find the hazels any more. That was the end of everything." Immediately, from the discordant rhythm of nature and time Pavese gathers the fundamental unity:

It was strange how everything was changed and yet the same. Not even a vine shoot remained from the old stocks, not even a beast; now the meadows were stubble and the stubble fields were vineyards and the people had moved on and grown up and died; the roots had come away and the trees had rolled down into the Belbo—and yet when I looked round at the great shoulder of Gaminella, the distant paths on the hill at Salto, the threshing floors, the wells, the voices, and the hoes, everything was just the same, everything had the taste, the smell, the color of long ago.

Equality and change, immutability and innovation are inter-twined and inseparable in things and persons:

One thing I always think about is how many people there must be living in this valley, and in the world for that matter, and the very same things are happening to them now as happened to us then, and they don't know it and never give it a thought. . . . That's how things are. They haven't changed a bit, boys or women or the world. They don't carry parasols any more, and on Sunday they go to the cinema instead of the festa, and they send their grain to the grain pool, and the girls smoke, and yet life is still the same and they don't know that one day they'll look round about them and for them, too, it will all be over.

So, rather than the myth of return, it is total comprehension of life and the world (in their mystery, ineffability, inseparability, and contradiction) that is the basis of *The Moon and the Bonfires*. Without a doubt it constitutes the deepest and truest maturity and poetry, in figures and rhythms that are unforgettable. A similar aspect of total comprehension is shown too in the sensory details that accompany descriptions, memories, and feelings; smells, colors, flavors, sounds reveal the real with a richness that goes beyond ordinary impression. In fact:

The more richly and diversely the life of the senses can be expressed, the more profound and comprehensive the resulting panorama will be, the spiritual wood that thrives and pushes within in order to reach the light. . . . Undesired things, multiplied by perceptive subtlety, provide an ever more abundant source of symbols.[9]

The environment of *The Moon and the Bonfires* is provided by the Langhe hills, with America in the background. The "bitter America" of Chapters 3, 9, and 21 (three key chapters in their symmetrical position in the novel, at the beginning, middle, and end), apart from echoing Pavese's literary debut as translator from the American, reveals to the narrator and clarifies for him his own solitude: from the "lights of San Francisco"—an echo of all the city lights in *Work Is Wearying*—and from the "din of the cicadas and frogs" in the hills of California, to the empty landscape of the desert—"As far as the eye could see there was an expanse of grey sand, full of thorns and little mounds that weren't hills, and the poles which marked the railway line," which seem to accentuate the hallucinating perspective—the American landscape always seems to arouse a feeling of tremendous solitude, which in itself immediately rouses fear, followed by thoughts of violence: "Then one fine day one of them wanted to touch something, to make his name, and so he strangled a woman, shot her in her sleep, bashed in her head with a spanner." Or again, with the musical background of animal howls "in the heart of America in a desert," after the train has crashed noisily past without interrupting his solitude, but even emphasizing it:

Later in the night a loud barking woke me with a start. The whole plain was like a battlefield or a farmyard. There was a reddish light and I jumped down, cramped and stiff with cold; a sliver of moon was piercing the low clouds and it looked like a gash from a knife and bathed the plain in a blood-red light. I stayed looking at it for a while. It terrified me.

Less dramatic but more desolate is the situation of Rosanne, Anguilla's American girl-friend, who wanted to become known but who "never appeared in the colored weeklies." Her solitude amid an environment indifferent to her dreams and projects seems to draw even tighter the thread of incommunicability first woven in *Among Women Only*. All the chapters on America, however, are very definitely detached from the body of the novel and emphasize, by contrast, a fundamental difference between America and Piedmont, between valleys and hills, between artificiality and nature, between chaos and custom; and yet, in their similarity they emphasize the fundamental analogies between Anguilla and Santa, between terror and death—as Peter Norton has shown.[10]

The hills, which have been the *leit motif* of Pavese's poetry since *Work Is Wearying*, are inseparable, even in the novel, from the human substance of the narrative; everything is dominated by Gaminella, "a hill like a planet, . . . all vineyards and overgrown watercourses."[11] It was in the hills that Anguilla first discovered the world: work and the toil of the fields, the joy of festivals with the bonfires, the first vague feelings of love for Irene and Silvia, violence and death, the lunar fixity of destiny. As always Pavese is at his best when he is describing a "festival night" or an "August holiday" in the hills, with the bonfires that are lit at night for the feast of John the Baptist.[12] However, the dichotomy of work-holiday has been overcome even in the description of the landscape, where vineyard and waste land coexist harmoniously and even evoke a feminine image that preludes the figures of Irene and Silvia:

And when I looked around me again, I thought of these clumps of trees and reeds and these spinneys and watercourses—all names of villages and houses round about—which are quite useless and don't yield any harvest, yet nevertheless have their own beauty —each vineyard has its own patch of scrub—and give you pleasure when your eye lights on them and you know there are nests there. Women, I thought, have something of the same charm.

Even the moon, the symbol of destiny and timelessness, is linked to the vineyard on the hill: "the vineyards lying white under the moon" often appear in the novel, giving it a shudder of tragedy. There is in fact a great deal of tragedy in the form of violence and death in the novel. It is primarily concentrated in the figure of Valino, "dark and thin, with eyes like a mole," who thought women should remain submissively at home and would beat them at the appropriate times like Vinverra in *The Harvesters*, and like one of Vico's peasants:

Nuto told me you could hear the women shrieking from the valley of the Belbo when Valino took off his belt and beat them like beasts and he thrashed Cinto too—it wasn't the wine—they didn't have as much as that—it was the utter misery and his rage at his life which never gave him a break.

There is little change in his attitude even when he is pointing out the dead in the fields:

Valino looked at me, his face dark, his eyes clouded and hard. "There are some there," he said, "there are some. All you need is the time to look for them." There was no disgust in his voice or pity. It was as if he were speaking about going to look for mushrooms or firewood. His face lit up for a moment, then he said, "No good came of them when they were alive, and none now they're dead."

In Valino is concentrated, physically even more than emblematically, the failure of the Resistance to shatter the *mezzadria*, sharecropping, the typical Italian agricultural and bourgeois institution, which has only recently been modified by the impetus of industrialization. Even after the Second World War it was often synonymous with exploitation and misery, especially in the not very fertile regions of the Langhe hills, and presented a continual source of stifled bitterness among the social classes. "To divide out the harvests with the scales" is not only unjust, but harmful on a psychological plane. In the figure of Valino, Pavese was able to describe this situation with brief touches of resentment and emotion, connecting it in an unexpectedly poetic and intense movement to Anguilla's destiny and the failure of his return to childhood:

[I] thought about the sort of life that Valino would have led all these years—sixty, was it? perhaps not even that—that he'd been working and paying half his rent in kind. How many houses had he left, how many bits of land, after he'd slept there and eaten there, and hoed the earth in the heat and the cold, carrying his belongings on a cart which was not even his over roads he would never tread again. I knew he was a widower, for his wife had died in the farm before this one, and his eldest sons had been killed in the war—he had nothing left except a young boy and his womenfolk. What else was he here for? He had never got out of the valley of the Belbo. Without meaning to, I came to a stop on the path and thought that if I hadn't run away twenty years before, this would have been my fate too. And yet I have gone on wandering about the world and he has wandered over these hills without ever being able to say, "This land belongs to me. On this bench I shall grow old. In this room I shall die."

Valino will disappear from the scene by hanging himself after having killed his women and burned his house out of desperation and misery—a tragic bonfire, not festive like those for John the Baptist.

Part of the violence of the hills is contributed by the animal howls, which are not only mythological echoes, as in "The Goat-God," but also recall the bestial howls beneath the moon of Doro in *The Beach* and Pieretto in *Devil in the Hills:* "I slept in the room at the back with the girls, and at nights we used to hear the wolf moaning because it was cold in the gully"; or:

There was the story of the dog whom they kept tied up without food and at night it smelt the hedgehogs and the bats and the weasels and leapt like a mad thing to catch them, and bayed and bayed at the moon that looked like polenta. Then Valino got out of bed and half-killed him, too, with blows and kicks.

The same anguished motif appears again in a very effective description of the dogs in the American desert.

But above all, when talking of violence we must notice how heavily the dead weigh on the narrative: the dead from the civil war, the Germans, the Fascists, and the partisans, all viewed with the same pity, starting with the final pages of *The House on the Hill*. They seem a repetition of ancient sacrifices, emblems of the idea of destiny, and yet a negative contrast, since so many of the bodies found remain unidentified; the man who dies unidentified dies without achieving individuality and awareness at least of the act that seals his life. (The episode of the gypsies is a good example of this.)[13] Moreover, especially in Chapters 12 and 13, it is from the discovery of the unknown dead and the political speculation that the local priest weaves around them that Pavese gets the impetus for one of the liveliest portrayals of our recent history, the transition from Resistance to peace, with all its compromises and the political-social involutions involved in it, of which Valino is the most tragic witness. Finally, it is the thought of the unknown dead that provides the emotional and psychological impetus, halfway through the novel, for the re-evocation of all the narrator's other unknown and beloved dead: especially Irene, Silvia, and Santa. Thus, an almost perfect fusion is achieved between individual and social datum, between the personal and the historical, between documentation and elegy.

At this point it would be best to concentrate on the three characters Anguilla, Nuto, and Cinto, in whom are embodied other Pavesian themes. As usual, these characters are not immediately disclosed in their totality; they gradually acquire substance and their physiognomy is outlined bit by bit as we see them act and talk, in relation to things and people. With Anguilla, the contemplative narrator, the bastard who "must be the son of a mountebank and a nanny-goat," the situation is immediately more complex: the boy and the man coexist in

him, almost like two characters, one of which explains the
other. There is the boy: "at La Mora I learnt a trade. . . . I
was Anguilla and I was earning my keep"; his working life
was calm, broken up by pleasant breaks, like the hours spent
naked with his companions on the banks of the Belbo. (It will
be remembered that in all the other references to nudism in
Pavese, it was considered an effort at identification of self with
nature and one's origins, whereas here there is no longer an
effort or even a trace of decadentism: "we *were* the whirlpool" of life, as boys, without knowing it):

The bank here is all sand and willows and short reeds like grass
and scattered clumps of trees that stretch as far as the cultivated
fields of La Mora. Sometimes in the hot weather when Cirino sent
me to prune or gather willow branches, I used to tell my chums
and we would meet on the riverbank; one came with a broken
basket and another with a sack, and we took off our clothes and
fished and played. We ran about in the sun on the hot sand.

On other occasions, however, there was no *festa* for him, and
there is an echo of Leopardi in the child's desperation: "On
nights like these, if I saw a light of a bonfire on the distant
hills, it would make me cry out and roll over on the cold
ground, because I was poor, because I was a child, because I
was nothing at all." The boy matures with the passage of
time:

I was a man now and the [overseer] no longer took his belt to me
and nobody called me bastard. . . . I was beginning to understand
all kinds of things: the scent of the lime blossom and the acacias
had a meaning for me, too, now that I knew what a woman was,
knew why the music at the dances made me want to roam about
the countryside like a randy dog.

As he grows older Anguilla gets to know the world, watching closely what happens around him; Nuto, his great friend,

helps him to learn. It is Nuto, for example, who suggests that he take up music, but Anguilla doesn't succeed and thinks only about travelling; it is Nuto who pushes him to study, with the same attitude as Pablo's in *The Comrade:* " 'They're books,' he said, 'read what you can of them. You'll never be anything if you don't read books.' " By reading this way, Anguilla learns a lot too about other people:

I liked these novels, but could Irene and Silvia, who were ladies and had never known Virgilia or cleaned out the stable, really like them too? I realized that Nuto was quite right when he said that to live in a hovel or in a place was one and the same thing, that blood is the same color everywhere, and that everybody wants to be rich and in love and make their fortune.

Or else, just his conversations with Nuto and his father would sow a seed:

"Do you remember those talks we had with your father in the shop? Even in those days he said people who don't know any better will always be in the dark, because the power lies in the hands of men who take good care that ordinary folk don't understand, in the hands, that is, of the government, of the clerical party, of the capitalists. Here at La Mora, it was nothing, but when I had done my military service and wandered through the vennels and the docks at Genoa, I realized what owners and capitalists and the army were. At that time we had the Fascists and you couldn't say that sort of thing. But there were the others as well."

As a boy Anguilla was always mediated by Nuto, and it was only as an adult that he was able to replace this relationship by a peaceful and reciprocal affection: "We walked like this along the main road beyond the village and discussed our lot in life. . . ." This motif is familiar: "walk the road and discover wonders," chatting, arguing, until dawn, in the city

streets or, as here, among the hills and vineyards, listening to
the moon.

But fundamental to our understanding of Anguilla's character is his attitude to Irene and Silvia, with whom his relationship is primarily and quite literally an Hegelian one of slave
and master, an inferior's relationship to a superior, composed
of timidity, embarrassment, and fear. This relationship gradually evolves into one of mediation, composed of admiration,
longing, and unconscious love, a relationship that nothing
henceforward can change, not Anguilla's *éducation sentimentale* acquired from his experiences in the world, nor his critical
awareness. The first time he finds himself near his young
mistress on the terrace, he reacts thus: "Irene said something
and they all laughed. All the time I held the ladder, I kept
looking at the wall and the cement, and to relieve my feelings,
I thought of what we boys talked about when we went to hide
among the reeds."

His attitude is expressed more explicitly and even more
poetically in a sentence that seems a fragment of Sappho's:
"When they walked past with their parasols, I eyed them
from the vineyard the way you look at a couple of peaches
too high on the branch." Or in a moment of anger because he
had been left at home on a festival to which everyone was
going (and the images in the dream strike one as ingenuously
psychoanalytic):

If I dared, I would have laid waste every flower in the garden.
And I thought of the faces of Irene and Silvia and told myself
that even they made water too. . . . The big carriage came back
very late at night after I had been asleep for a while and was
dreaming about climbing up Silvia's smooth back as if it was the
greasy pole. . . .

With the passing of time Anguilla understands the two girls
more and more, their motives, their desires, their frustrations

and caprices, which he always compares with his own experience:

And then they spent the whole day frittering away their time on the terrace or in the garden—they hadn't any work to do, any job to occupy themselves—they didn't even like looking after Santina. And so it was natural that their longing to leave La Mora and get into that park under the plane trees and be with the countess's daughters-in-law and grandchildren drove them [mad]—just as I felt when I saw the bonfires on the hill at Cassinasco or heard the train whistling through the night.

Or later: "I think Lugli was for her what she and her sister could have been for me, what Genoa and America were for me later."

On the other hand, Anguilla's feeling is clear, both for Irene and her sister:

But then, I said, it's easily seen she's in love, that she likes Cesarino, that he's the man she's longing to marry. And I'd have liked to be able to speak to her, to tell her to be careful not to throw herself away on that half-baked creature. . . . Silvia, at least, didn't waste her time like that but went about with someone worth while. If it hadn't been that I was only the farm boy and not eighteen yet, Silvia would perhaps have gone with me.

Nevertheless the two sisters seem to have influenced Anguilla's sentimental life in a decisive way, since the women he knew in the world after he left home always reminded him in some way or other of the two girls of his adolescence: "A few years later at Genoa where I was doing my military service, I had found a girl who was like Silvia; she was dark like her, but plumper and less straightforward, the same age as Irene and Silvia were when I started at La Mora." And the doubt occurs spontaneously that even Rosanne, the uninhibited and pathetic American girl, might only be a surrogate for a love he had lost forever.

A whole world, now dead, seems to live still in Anguilla's mind, despite his newly acquired awareness, his experience. For example, when the priest uses the dead as an excuse to preach a sermon:

And to think that when I was a boy and Virgilia took us to mass, I thought that the voice of the priest was a thing like thunder or the sky or the seasons, which helped the fields and the harvests, for the salvation of the living and the dead. Now I noticed that the dead helped *him*. We really shouldn't grow old or get to know the world.

The small world that provided a faith and a security, however illusory, a model of judgment even more than behavior, is deeply rooted in the child's mind, as is seen in several passages where the term of comparison is automatically the church: flowers, "real flowers like those in church"; old books "in Latin, like the missal"; or again, bunches of flowers "more beautiful than the stained-glass windows in the church or the priest's vestments"; or even the room at Il Nido "more beautiful than a church." With these comparisons Pavese underscores, consciously and with feeling, a whole spiritual condition and a received education, precisely at the moment when he recognizes rationally that they have been superseded and therefore lost.

Anguilla's importance would seem to be in the embodiment of the contemplative, solitary side of Pavese's personality; Anguilla does not get stirred up, does not get involved, does not marry, just like the narrator of "The Langhe Hills"; and at the end of the novel, he is ready to set out again, like 'Ntoni Malavoglia: " 'But I'm maybe going on a ship. . . . I'll come back for the festa another year.' " He is left without roots, alone, distant; it is the price he must pay for the knowledge he has acquired of the world, for being the witness and the narrator—and Pavese has to pay a similar price for his own poetic vocation; at the end of 1938, he writes in his diary:

Maturity is this, too; no longer seeking outside ourselves, but letting our inner life speak with its own rhythm—the only thing that matters. Then the outside world seems petty and materialistic, compared with the unforeseen, profound maturity of our memories. . . . Maturity is isolation that is sufficient unto itself.[14]

Nuto, instead, is just the opposite of Anguilla: sociable, active, involved, he is probably the calmest, most positive figure to appear in Pavese's work, one of the few characters who succeeds in "maturing and taking part in the human fray, assuming his responsibilities in it."[15] From the contrast between him and Anguilla originates a single vision of life and destiny that had never before been realized in a single figure. Nuto incarnates the difficult acceptance of humble, everyday reality, difficult because it consists of compromises, denials and limitations, intercourse with others, political faith, success in love and family life—all the things that were so difficult, problematic, and full of torment for Pavese.

Nuto, as opposed to Anguilla, remains in the hills; in him work and holiday are united, tools and clarinet: "winter was Nuto's season," just as summer was Anguilla's. His house still gives the same feeling of strength, of serenity and security (and the geraniums that decorate it seem to echo those at Sandiana's window, in "Intimate History"—the longing for a paternal home):

Now Nuto is married and a grown man; he works himself and has men working for him but his house is still the same, and in the sunshine it smells of oleanders and geraniums, for he has pots of them in the windows and in front of the house. The clarinet is hung on the end of the cupboard; underfoot are the shavings. . . .

Even as a boy Nuto had a strong, attractive personality; he was Anguilla's guide and model (like Gallo for the narrator of the story "The City," and like Candido for the narrator of "The Sea"):

[He] knew already how to whistle and play the guitar; his opinion was sought after and listened to; he argued with grown men and with us boys and he winked at the women. Even then I was always at his heels and sometimes played truant to go along the watercourse with him or even in the Belbo to look for nests. He told me what to do if I wanted to be thought well of at La Mora. . . .

A distinctive and characteristic trait in his personality is his ability to play the clarinet; the truck driver who recalls to Anguilla in exile the popular traditions of the Langhe hills ends by saying: "Nuto was in the middle and led them on the clarinet." (We are reminded of the friend in the poem "Smoking Cheap Cigarettes" and, again, Candido in "The Sea.")[16]

Basically, Nuto remains the same after twenty years: "He was only a bit more solid, a bit less of a dreamer. That cat's face of his was quieter and more surly." Of course, he is less of a daredevil and has learned to assume responsibilities: "After ten years of festas he laid aside the clarinet on the death of his father," and not "even for the Feast of the Assumption in August" did he want to take up playing again; instead he dedicated himself to his father's job of carpentering, to soothing the wounds of civil war, to rebuilding in a conscious fraternity (all of which cannot be realized by playing in a band.) Only he still had the habit of putting his lips the way he would when he played every time he was concentrating on expressing an opinion.[17] Nuto has a lot of ideas and he expresses them in a few rough words: above all he does not believe in violence; he doesn't like it and tries every way he

can to stifle and overcome it, and it is true he did not fight
during the Resistance but "had kept a wounded partisan hidden in a hole in the gully on Salto and carried food to him at
night. . . . Only yesterday when he met two boys on the road
who were tormenting a lizard, he took it from them." And as
a boy:

By this time he was going about all over the countryside and
could argue with anyone. . . . He knew [quite a] few people at
Canelli and when he heard they wanted to take it out of someone,
he called them all sorts of fools and told them to leave the job to
people who were paid for it. He made them think shame of
themselves. He told them it was only dogs that bark and go for
strange dogs, and men set on a dog because it suits them to show
that they are still masters, but if the dogs weren't dumb animals
they would come to an agreement with each other and start
barking at them. . . . [He said] you only needed to read the
papers that came out then to understand that the world is full of
people who set on their dogs . . . and have only to walk along the
streets to see people with papers in their hands and the headlines
as black as thunderclouds.[18]

Above all, Nuto's ideas on destiny are important, his faith in
the possibility of improvement in the world (like Leopardi's
Timandro, when he says, "The human condition can improve
considerably over what it is just as it has improved more than
can be described over what it was"). For example: "Nuto
would never have asked what use the war had been. We had
to fight it, that was our fate. Nuto has got this idea on the
brain, that something which has got to happen is everybody's
business, and the world is a botched job and needs remaking."
In his conception of human destiny Nuto is the exact (and
complementary) opposite of Anguilla, as is seen in the discussions about the bonfires, which in his opinion "are awakening
the earth":

"This is something new," I said. "So you believe in the moon too?"

"The moon—we must believe in the moon," said Nuto. "Try to cut down a pine tree when the moon is full and it will be eaten up by worms. You should wash a grape vat when the moon is new. As for grafting, unless you do it when the moon is only a few days old, it doesn't take."[19]

Then I said I'd heard a few stories in my travels but these were the most farfetched of the lot. There was no use having so much to say about the government and the priest's sermons, if he was going to believe in these superstitions like his great-great-grandmother. It was then that Nuto said very quietly that a superstition is a superstition only when it does harm to someone and if anyone were to use the moon and the bonfires to rob the peasants and keep them in the dark, then he would be the backward one and should be shot in the square.

For Nuto, in short, "we are in this world to transform destiny into freedom (and nature into causality),"[20] whereas Anguilla's position is considerably more negative, on the practical level, in that it is not a question of action but of comprehension and evidence:

Nuto, who had never really gone away, still wanted to understand the world and change it, and upset the cycle of the seasons. Or perhaps he didn't, and still believed only in the moon. But I, who didn't believe in the moon, knew that when all was said and done only the seasons matter and they are in your bones and they nurtured you when you were a boy. Canelli is the whole world —Canelli and the valley of the Belbo—and among the hills time stands still.

Despite their different ideas, Nuto and Anguilla are able to find a common ground and collaborate in bringing up Cinto, when, after running away from Valino's massacre of his family and destruction of his home by fire, "he seemed to wake up suddenly" almost to a new life, the young Asclepius with two Chirons at his side: "Nuto took Cinto into his house to make him learn carpentry and teach him to play the clarinet. We agreed that, if the boy turned out well, I would get him a job in Genoa in due course."

Cinto constitutes the dialectic synthesis between Nuto and Anguilla, between their contrasting world visions and ideas of destiny: he is a slender hope for the future, the new order which still limps but is full of possibility. The boy is seen for the first time "wearing a shirt and ragged trousers held up by broken braces," "barefoot," with a "scab under one eye and bony shoulders," and

one of his legs stretched out, kept apart from the other in a way that wasn't natural. He was lame and he had rickets, and I saw that his knee wasn't any thicker than his arm and he dragged his foot behind him like a weight. He would be about ten years old and to see him on that threshing floor was like seeing myself.

Even more than Dino in *The House on the Hill,* Cinto is the alter ego of the narrator, whose very mediation by Nuto is repeated in reverse with Cinto: "I was speaking to him as Nuto had spoken to me"; or:

What would I have said in my day if a big fellow like myself had appeared before me and I had gone round the farm with him? For a moment I had the illusion that the girls and the goat would be waiting for me at the house and that I would have boasted to them about it.

Moreover, in Cinto Anguilla finds both the return and the impossibility of return, memory and hope:

What would I have given to see the world still through Cinto's eyes, to start again in Gaminella like him, with the same father, with the same leg even, now that I knew so much and was able to look after myself. It wasn't that I felt sorry for him; sometimes I envied him.

At a subsequent level of interpretation, Cinto is, in Jesi's words, "the young boy bearing the sign like an initiate (he is lame), in whom Pavese sees . . . the charming boy-god who is the guide in the kingdom of the dead; and in fact the return to one's village is always a *katàbasis* in Pavese."[21] Certainly *The Moon and the Bonfires* is *katàbasis*; Anguilla does not refind his past; the old order is dead, dragging into ruin with it those who best represented it, Irene and Silvia, and she who marked the necessity of its passing, Santa, as John Freccero has shown.[22] To understand the fascination of the three girls in the second half of the novel, one must remember that all three are dead, like so many other people whom Anguilla no longer finds in his impossible return: therefore their re-evocation is born of the narrator's desperate awareness that time and violence have carried away his own youth. And so the re-evocation is carried out on two levels: the present with its cruel, critical awareness, its rational and practical logic; the past with its tender, irrational myths, its melancholy elegy. An example of the former:

I've realized that Sor Matteo's daughters weren't the prettiest after all—Santina, perhaps, but then I didn't see her when she grew up—they had the same beauty as dahlias, or roses, or the flowers that grow in gardens under the fruit trees. I've come to realize that they weren't very clever either, and that in spite of their piano-playing and their novels and their tea-drinking and their parasols, they couldn't manage their own lives—they weren't cut out to be real ladies and to lord it over a man and a house. . . . Irene and Silvia weren't peasants any more and they weren't real ladies yet, either. They didn't manage very well, poor things —that's how they died.

Such a judgment, though just and necessary, does not prevail. In the re-evocation of the girls, even before they are seen, they are heralded by the poetic motif of flowers and parasols seen by Anguilla for the first time at La Mora (a motif also found in the story "First Love"):

Under the lime trees, beside the gate, was the garden, full of zinnias and lilies and dahlias—I realized that you can grow flowers like fruit—they produced flowers instead of fruit and when they were gathered they were for the use of the signora and her daughters, who went out for them with their parasols and arranged them in vases when they were in the house.[23]

Flowers and parasols are the emblems of the girls who didn't bear fruit and who are immediately charming with their lightly sketched little figures, which are nevertheless very distinct and vivid. The narrator above all evokes the most beautiful age of Irene and Silvia, attentive to their loves and their caprices, secretly desiring both of them; but as he says, "These two daughters of Sor Matteo were not for me and not even for Nuto. They were rich and tall and beautiful."

Of the two, Irene is blonde and sweet, dressed in white; Anguilla particularly remembers two moments of hers. In the first it is difficult to say whether one is reminded more of Leopardi's "the quiet rooms were ringing" or of an image of Verga's (that of the Queen's hand, in the story "What is the King": "a hand so tiny that it seemed made to have nothing to do"):

As we crossed the landing we heard Irene playing the piano; on some fine sunny mornings the window was open and the sound of the piano came out on to the terrace among the lime trees. It always seemed strange to me that a piece of furniture that was so big and black with a sound that shook the windows should be played by Irene herself with her long white lady's hands.

In the second moment, he remembers a similar episode, described perhaps less successfully in a poem written twenty years earlier, "The Young Teachers":[24]

I stayed hidden behind an elder tree. Santina cried out and pointed to something on the opposite bank. And then Irene had laid aside the book and bent down, taking off her stockings and shoes, and kilting her dress above her knees, showing her white legs—she was so fair-skinned—she went into the water. She crossed the river slowly, feeling each step first with her feet. Then calling to Santina not to move, she picked some yellow flowers. I remember it as if it were yesterday.

About Silvia, "black-haired and dressed in red", "not so tall as Irene," with "dark burning eyes," who often "behaved as if she had gone off her head" for a man, Anguilla remembers particularly that she showed absolutely no signs of her loves (like other women in his poems, like the goddesses in *Dialogues with Leucò*, who always remain the same, unreachable):

I looked in Silvia's face for signs of what she and Matteo were doing together. When we started to harvest the grapes that September either she or Irene came into the vineyard with the green grapes, just as they had done in other years, and I crouched down under the vines and watched her, watched her hands feeling for the clusters, watched the curve of her flanks, her waist, her hair in her eyes, and, when she went down the path, how she walked, the spring in her step, the quick turn of her head—I knew all of her from top to toe, yet I could never say, "Look, she's changed. Matteo's been here!" She was the same, she was Silvia.

Both Irene and Silvia die tragically, Irene beaten to death by a violent husband, Silvia as the result of an unsuccessful abortion, at the end of their brief, happy, and useless life.[25]

Santa, the third sister, seems to combine the physical characteristics of both of them:

Her hair was turning out golden like Irene's, and she had Silvia's black eyes ["like the black heart of a poppy" Nuto would say] but if she bit her finger when she was eating an apple, or tore the heads off the flowers in a temper, or wanted us to lift her up on horseback whatever might happen and kept kicking us, we said she took it from her mother.

Her temperament is clearly defined from the moment we meet her—"They were killing the pig and the women had all run away except Santina, who was just learning to walk then" —and she is constantly shown as decisive and independent, a character like a destiny:

Santina had little red shoes and soft hair, so fair that it was nearly white; she wouldn't eat her bread and milk, and Emilia was trying to catch her and carry her into the house.

And Santina knew already that she made an impression when she stood behind the gate to let herself be seen, or came amongst us in the farmyard, or along the paths, and chattered away to the women.

At the wedding [of Irene] Santina was the beauty, all dressed in silk—she was only six, but she looked as if she were the bride.

And her proud and forboding words should be remembered: "They'd burn me if they could. They don't want a girl to make anything of her life. They'd like to see me finishing up like Irene and kissing the hand that strikes me. But I'd bite the hand the strikes me. . . ."

The last two chapters, among the most beautiful and most moving of the book, with Nuto's memories intertwined with and superimposed on Anguilla's, are dedicated to Santa: "I was thinking how everything happens again as it has happened before—I saw Nuto in the gig driving Santa up the slopes to the fair, as I had driven her sisters." Nuto then, as he climbs the slopes of Gaminella with Anguilla, tells him about Santa's end, about her playing a double game with the Fascists and the partisans without making up her mind for one or the other, as was necessary:

One morning Santa came back, under escort. She no longer wore the windbreaker and the slacks she had worn all these months. To come out of Canelli she had put on women's clothes, a light summer dress, again and when the partisans had stopped her up by Gaminella, she'd got a shock. . . . Then Baracca read out the sentence and told two of them to take her outside. They were more bewildered than she was. They'd always seen her wearing her jacket and belt and they couldn't get used to the idea that now they had a hold of her, she was dressed in white. They took her outside. She turned round at the door and looked at me and made a face just like a child. But, once outside, she tried to run away. We heard a cry and someone running and a burst of tommy-gun fire which seemed endless. We ran out, too, and saw her lying on the grass in front of the acacias.

What strikes us most in Nuto's account is the luminosity of the images: "one morning"; "a light summer dress"; "dressed in white"; "on the grass in front of the acacias." This luminosity gives a special emotive and lyrical power to the narration (or perhaps it would be more accurate to say re-evocation) particularly in that it fixes the temporal limits (a summer morning, the typically Pavesian time and season) and the spatial limits (the grass and the acacias in a field on the hill, near a vineyard, as we know from the context—the place too is a typical, mythical setting of Pavese's); and secondly, because it is contrasted with the "black, ruined walls" of the farm, still existing and visible reminder of the tragic events of the past, of violence, war, and death. But there is something else to notice, something that will not escape the attentive reader because it is repeated, emphasized, and specified: Santa first appears in "a light summer dress" and then is described as "dressed in white." The lightness of the dress seen vaguely in the distance is seen to be white when it is thought about later more intently. Unequivocally the whiteness of the dress is the center of the scene and therefore has an exceptional importance in the death of Santa. But why this white?

For an exhaustive answer we must begin by remembering other passages of Pavese's where the color white seems to have an emblematic value. Generally the lunar light that suffuses so many of Pavese's landscapes gives an almost distorted vision of reality, so that it provokes a shiver of fear rather than a feeling of serenity, or it creates a tense, dramatic atmosphere. It is sufficient to remember the "lunar horror" of the poem "August Moon" or the story "The Field of the Dead" to see the truth of this. More specifically we think of the cynical Moro in "Summer Storm," with skin "as pale as the belly of a fish," and "a flash of ill-temper in his eyes"; of Nora in "The Leather Jacket," who was "as pale as the belly of a fish" (and when she is killed by Ceresa, the narrator was "still thinking of Nora's white skin"); but most of all we think of Gisella in *The Harvesters*, when she is dying ("I could see the Grangia and the moon. . . . Between the candles and the moonlight, there lay Gisella on the bed, all swathed in bandages, with a white dressing on her forehead, but her nostrils and her mouth were black"): in each of these passages white is used to emphasize scenes composed of violence, evil, and death. Or we think of Clara in "First Love," who had "the dazzling white skin" and who was seen by the boy narrator when she was in the act of making love, "a white form lying" in the darkness of a shack in the vineyard; or of Artemis in "The Lady of Beasts," who looks, to Endymion, in the moonlight like a wild girl dressed in a (white) tunic that "barely reached her knees," or of Irene with her white hand, and dressed in white. In these examples white emphasizes feminine beauty and the mystery, evil, and tragedy that derive from it. Or again, we remember the dialogue "The Mares" in which the light of the Bright One, "cruel, blinding," exposes everywhere "sadness, wounds, the vileness of thing."

If then we turn to the beginning of Pavese's career, we remember the cousin in the poem "Southern Seas," "a giant dressed in white" who introduces the myth of return for the first time in Pavese's work, a theme that is constantly restated and culminates in *The Moon and the Bonfires*. There are obvious echoes in this poem of a work that Pavese had been translating, Melville's *Moby Dick*, and there are many passages of *Moby Dick* that concern our present examination; the whole of Chapter 42 is dedicated to "The Whiteness of the Whale," to the white color "mystical and well nigh ineffable," inspiring a "vague, nameless horror." It is one of Melville's very learned dissertations between encyclopedia and bible, in which Ishmael asserts among other things that:

Though in many natural objects, whiteness refiningly enhances beauty, . . . and though in other mortal sympathies and symbolizings, this same hue is made the emblem of many touching, noble things—the innocence of brides, the benignity of age . . . yet for all these accumulated associations, with whatever is sweet, and honorable, and sublime, there yet lurks an elusive something in the innermost idea of this hue, which strikes more of panic to the soul than that redness which affrights in blood.

In fact Ishmael asserts, with many examples which are not specifically interesting for our present purpose, that Nature numbers among her powers white, "this crowning attribute of the terrible" and that humanity cannot help but recognize in some cases "the supernaturalism of this hue," as in the pallor of the dead. Ishmael concludes that "though in many of its aspects this visible world seems formed in love, the invisible spheres were formed in fright," as whiteness shows us, because when we "consider that the mystical cosmetic which produces every one of her [Nature's] hues, the great principle of light, for ever remains white or colorless in itself, and if operating without medium upon matter, would touch all objects, even tulips and roses, with its own blank tinge—pondering all this, the palsied universe lies before us a leper."

So for Melville the color white is symbolic of grace and beauty, and of a vague feeling of mystical, puritanical, awesome religious feeling, and most of all of evil, grief, of the tragedy of the universe, in the life of man and things. Melville's affirmations appear to be echoed (and transformed by a sensibility that is different from his) in the passages of Pavese we mentioned. But to return to *The Moon and the Bonfires* and Santa's death scene, how much of Melville did Pavese find in himself, in his own "reflected culture," to be in agreement with his own poetic and human sensibility, and with his own myths?

Above all, the color white is certainly a symbol of noble and moving sentiments: it is an image of innocence, underscored by the face that Santa makes "like a child" and confirmed by the memory of the time when Santina, at Irene's wedding, "looked as if she were the bride," a child of six dressed in silk—very much Melville's "the innocence of brides." As for religiosity, in Pavese it is not so much mystic, puritanical, and awesome, as it is in Melville, but rather mythical and secular: if we think about the name of the girl, *Santa*, then the white of her dress becomes the color of the sacrificial victim who will be burned on the final, ritual, and propitiatory bonfire, like those of the primitive peoples in *Dialogues with Leucò.* Finally, the tragic quality of white: on the literal level, Santa puts on women's clothes, a white dress, almost as if she foresees her death; but Pavese shows her dressed in white almost as if he sees in her a much greater tragedy than that of the character. On the one hand, in fact, he has become "aware of history" (the war, the Resistance, the post-war period, the passing of people, the changing of the social classes and of ideologies); on the other hand he has realized the impossibility of his own return, the impossibility of regaining childhood, and therefore the impossibility of attaining the absolute in the sublunar world ("The palsied universe lies before us a leper," empty and meaningless as it is for Rosetta in *Among Women Only*): the "burst of tommy-gun fire which seemed endless" would seem to suggest and fix cruelly, as one bullet after the other penetrates the tender and proud body of Santa, in her white dress, the inevitability of history and death, the double awareness of Pavese. Thus, even though in Pavese there is not the same powerful inspiration, eloquence, and grandiosity as in Melville, he has created an image that is hard to forget, an image all his own, inserted in the texture of his themes and myths, an image that concentrates elegy, judgment, and symbol.[26]

In fact, the white figure of Santa seems to stretch even into the last scene of the novel, constituting the premise for it in the richness of its meaning. It is precisely in relation to Santa that Anguilla (like Corrado at the end of *The House on the Hill*) in a pause in Nuto's account, can express his elegy and also his judgment, his feelings of grief, his pity for all those who are no more: "[Rather than Nuto,] I saw Baracca—he had been hanged, too, until he was dead." And it is thanks to the white dress of Santa's that the end of the story can achieve its mythical meaning, which is completely immersed in Pavese's poetic world: this dress, because it makes Santa more

beautiful, makes her desirable, even though dead, and to avoid
any possible necrophilism—with all the morbidity and obscu-
rity there are in such a thought—Nuto and Baracca decide to
burn the body of the woman they loved and, without knowing it, consecrate her:

Nuto had sat down on the wall and looked at me with his
obstinate eyes. "No, not Santa," he said. "You won't find her. You
can't cover a woman like her with earth and leave her like that.
There were still too many men who wanted her. Baracca saw to
that. He made us cut a lot of twigs in the vineyard and we piled
them on top of her until we had enough. Then we poured petrol
on the pile and set fire to it. By midday, everything was burnt to
ashes. Last year the mark was still there, like the bed of a
bonfire.

So, Santa really becomes "earth and death," like Gisella in
The Harvesters, but with a difference. By making a mistake,
she finally transformed her destiny into freedom: she betrayed
both Fascists and partisans, but only in an effort to understand, to be herself, disregarding and transcending historical
contingency. Like Coronis, in the dialogue "The Mares,"
Santa "walked through the vineyards and she played with the
Bright One till he killed her and burnt her body," but at least
"she found herself as she died." Moreover, like an echo of the
ancestral human sacrifices in the dialogue "The Guest," her
ashes in the bed of the fire contribute to the earth's fertility, to
the fertility of the hill Gaminella, green with vineyards and
thickets, "like a planet" that shelters all of humanity. Again, as
in that other mythological dialogue "The Bonfires," we can
think of her sacrifice as serving "to bring some justice back to
the world," the aim that the Resistance had achieved only partially. We think in fact of the desperate fire lit by Valino,
the last whisper of violence, the last protest against injustice;

and we see Cinto, who escaped from that fire, appearing like a young Asclepius born on the funeral pyre of his mother: thus Santa, on her bonfire-funeral pyre, culminates, within the novel's time, all the violence of the war, and can be considered the mother-symbol for Cinto—the uncertain yet hopeful future. But for Anguilla, the narrator who is not interested in that future, as is seen by his ending the story there, Santa is the final term, the seal of his *katàbasis.*

Pavese's last novel ends with Santa's death and the image of the bonfire, and it can truly be said that in it "myth is linked directly to poetry without passing through theory or action," and Pavese has achieved a style that can be so identified with things that "it destroys every barrier between the ordinary reader and the most dizzying symbolical and mythical reality."[27] *The Moon and the Bonfires,* in fact, contains, even in the title, various symbolical references embedded in the two images that compose it: the moon as cycle of nature and the seasons, the bonfires as moments of human time, as an echo of escapism, joy, and festival for the young narrator, and as a sacred part of human activity and work, for they serve to awaken the earth, and they are also the ancient propitiatory rites; the moon as an impassive force of destiny, the bonfires as man's acts—of destructive violence (Valino burns his own house in rebellion against an unfair destiny), and of compassionate love (Baracca and Nuto burn Santa, consecrating individuality in the face of destiny); the moon as immanence, the bonfire as transcendence. In the words of Freccero, who is emphasizing primarily the mythical roots of Pavese's world, especially in reference to *Dialogues with Leucò:*

To propitiate the gods is in a sense to manipulate them, to answer their crushing force. If the victory of such a revolution seems pale, and the fire a little thing against the moon, it is nevertheless all that man has, the only weapon against fate that he has been able to fashion from the gift given him by Prometheus.[28]

Finally, there remains the need to underscore the novel's epigraph, taken through F. O. Matthiessen from Shakespeare's *King Lear:* "Man must endure / his going hence e'en as his coming hither. / Ripeness is all."[29] This epigraph contains the hidden meaning not only of *The Moon and the Bonfires* but of all Pavese's work: total comprehension of human life, from birth to death; virile acceptance of the mystery behind life; the maturity that derives from understanding and acceptance. On the artistic plane, ripeness is realized both in the lyrical expression of *durée* and in the epic surpassing of it: individual destiny in time, self-recognition, pure elegy; destiny as seen in history, recognition of others, sublime compassion. All the elements that remain separate and opposed up to the end of *The House on the Hill* are blended into one in the last novel.

Unfortunately the epigraph becomes tragic on the human plane: Pavese kills himself right at the time of his greatest maturity as a writer, perhaps because that maturity was not sufficient in an absolute sense for the man.

The idea of maturity had always interested Pavese greatly. Beginning with some of the poetic images of *Work Is Wearying* (such as those in "Grappa in September"), again in the essay on Matthiessen entitled "American Maturity," and even in his last critical essay "The Art of Maturing," his preoccupation becomes clearer, increases in intensity, becomes more profound and wider. He writes in one of his last pages:

Our century has forgotten that genesis is merely the point of departure, that one is born to live and grow old, and that between birth and death there is a period of just maturation, of perfect and virile equilibrium. . . . There are cultures that grow on an inferior level of history—for them the problem of maturing, of rising to that virile tragic moment that is individual and collective equilibrium, is the same as is the problem of growing up to be a tragic hero, aware of history, for the rebellious anarchist in short socks.[30]

What Pavese wrote of culture is *a fortiori* valid for the poet and writer, and above all is valid for Pavese himself, who by nature was always attracted to "angelism" and tended to look on childhood as the real world, but at the same time was always able to resist the temptation and integrate it consciously into his literary and civic duty. That he himself grew into a "tragic hero, aware of history" is fully proved by his narrative works; so much so that Natalino Sapegno, defining him as "a character in a tragedy," wrote:

No one more than he, in a closed culture such as ours with its tendency to easy and soothing solutions, has expressed that basic reluctance for life, that internal laceration and anticipated ruin of all the feelings and ideals that go towards its composition, that primordial vocation for death which is at the root of so much of our civilization.[31]

Since our civilization basically goes back to romanticism (of which decadentism is only one aspect), it is to romanticism that we must refer if we are to understand it, especially "that passive availability for experiencing life,"[32] which is fundamental to the contemplativity and introspectivity of so many greater writers, the latest of whom is Pavese. One of his lucid earlier pages should be reread in this connection; it is ingenuous but extremely valid for the categorical quality of its affirmations:

I am one of the many decayed sons of the nineteenth century. That century was too great in thought, feeling, and action; and by the laws of history, equally great must be the dejection of those who can no longer believe in its ideals and cannot resolutely find new ones. I should say: *are afraid* to find new ones. That's the way I am. . . . My spirit is, in other words, a faithful copy of what the world would be if all the ideals of the nineteenth century were more or less realized, without the opposition of the twentieth century.[33]

The figure of Carlo Michelstaedter comes to mind, a man who had much the same experience as Pavese, at the beginning of the century; in a note written in 1905, five years before he committed suicide, Michelstaedter described himself as a person who "sees too much," in whose "embittered mind the source of feeling has dried up" nor is it possible "to reacquire the lost spontaneity, passed enthusiasms": "With the habitual cruel sincerity towards himself he examines his own interior, analyzes it, then with calm and reasoned resolution kills himself, thereby restoring to mother earth the energies that struggled within him uselessly."[34] In Pavese, as in Michelstaedter, the inability to adhere to romantic ideals, the sterility, the frustration, the falling back on himself led to an examination of existence and the absolute which could not be satisfied.

There is no doubt, therefore, that Pavese, in his "reluctance for life," in his "passive availability for experiencing life," reached his own artistic maturity in the sense he himself indicated: in his works, especially *The Moon and the Bonfires*, man and history, nature and destiny are seen with a "monolithic" total comprehension, as "symbolic reality."[35] Pavese reached this comprehension gradually and combined in his last novel all that he had accumulated in his years of research (poetics, style, psychology, and mythology.)

In his work Pavese succeeded in interpreting contemporary exigencies, exigencies that are also universal and permanent.[36] In his feeling for what is beautiful, he was a part of the tradition which started with Foscolo and Leopardi, developed through Verga to D'Annunzio and Pascoli (not to mention

Baudelaire and the symbolists), and with the aid of American writers (largely thanks to Pavese, as well as Cecchi, Vittorini, and Montale) widened into an extremely rich, subtle, nuanced prose that is both lyrical and essential, concrete and symbolic, classical and familiar. Certainly the same cannot be said of many other styles: it is in fact a prose in which are fused the best aspects of classicism, Italian *verismo*, American realism, and European decadentism to form a very individual whole.

With his examination of existence, Pavese made a completely original contribution to the literary currents of the twentieth century that range from psychoanalysis to German expressionism, from Pirandello's irrationalism to ethnology, currents that can be traced back to the childhood of Rousseau and the myth of Vico. Pavese drew these currents together and continued them with a constant, determined, integral effort at depth and clarity. He absorbed and went beyond his experience and convictions in his constant anxiety to acquire more knowledge. Thus, the decadent and sensual images inspired by D'Annunzio's *superuomo* are to be found in Pavese, but in a more tormented, psychoanalytical form, as if depleted by his anticipated awareness of failure; we find too the myth of childhood, but dramatically, of a problematic rather than consoling childhood; we find that nature does not offer shelter and peace as in Pirandello and Michelstaedter, but is rather divided between order and chaos, between civilization and the wild, containing the mystery of human origins.

Furthermore, Pavese knew how to express man as a social creature. His characters are the spokesmen of his own irresolute but spontaneous political engagement, his own incapacity for action, of which he was ashamed, his own populist feelings resolved in a watchful and lucid historicism. But primarily he dealt with the asocial side of man, the crisis of the inidividual torn from society and contemporary reality: solitude, the inability to communicate, which is suffered and yet at the same time self-determined, the contemplativity of the writer isolated in his ivory tower yet tormented by awareness and remorse that this tower of his (as Virginia Woolf wrote) would henceforward overlook burning fields on all sides.

Pavese was able to lift himself out of the lucid and painful individual portrait to the universal framework of the contemporary epoch, expressing it in his myths and images even more than in his critical reflections. Although his teaching perhaps remains limited by the lack of a precise ideology to meet the contemporary contradictions that he interpreted so well, precisely because of this, since even we have not resolved and overcome these contradictions, Pavese is so close to our affections that in the years to come he will be the voice of our generation and of our conciousness. And he will be so above all because of his recognition of our limitations, as when he wrote:

When one is gloomy, cynical, sceptical, and disenchanted, to recover one need only look around and, in the case of a culture, look at other cultures or past ones. We in Italy today are provincial; all the ideas that control our political, scientific, and philosophical life, etc., are of foreign origin (democracy, idealism, historicism, etc.): one has only to study these fields thoroughly and understand them critically, instead of accepting them all broken up for us as they are by the journalists, and deceiving oneself into thinking we are the ancient Romans. Italian culture *today* does not exist: there is a European, and maybe even a world culture; and one can only say something valid if one has digested the whole of contemporary life.[37]

Pavese's characters and writing reflect tragically the condition of a culture that is "provincial" (or peasant or archaic), which is tending to become "European" or "world" (or civic and modern) and which nevertheless does not succeed in surpassing its own origins but maintains them in constant tension with present developments.

There can be no doubt, however, that the tragedy of Pavese's maturity is to be found in his own life and not on the cultural plane. His yielding to the "primordial vocation of death," to the *vizio assurdo* that had always haunted him, can be traced during the period between the conclusion of *Among Women Only* and the beginning of *The Moon and the Bonfires* "when his myth has become *figura*, and he, unoccupied, can no longer believe in it but cannot yet resign himself to the loss of that good, of that authentic faith that kept him alive, and he makes another attempt at it, turns it inside out and becomes disgusted by it."[38] We read in fact in the diary: "Probably this is your most intensive period, and it is getting past its best."[39] Perhaps (if we agree with these conjectures) Pavese felt that his most intense and mature season could not have lasted.[40] After *The Moon and the Bonfires*, in fact, he only wrote some essays and the poems of *Death Will Come and Its Eyes Will Be Yours*, and these too, like the novel, are dedicated to "C.," the woman who reminds him of the years of his youth and renews for him the torment of a love that has failed ("All is the same / time has gone by").[41] Moreover, he felt perhaps he was to blame for not being capable of political engagement. Remember that Pavese, in an obvious allusion to Peter's betrayal, gave the title *Before the Cock Crows* to the volume containing *The Political Prisoner* and *The House on the Hill*, the premise and the conclusion of his disengagement:

My happiness of '48–'49 is paid for in full. Behind that Olympian contentment lay my impotence and my refusal to become involved. Now, in my own way, I have gone down into the abyss: I contemplate my impotence, I feel it in my bones, and I am caught in a political responsibility that is crushing me. There is only one answer: suicide.[42]

However, it was not failures, or apparent failures, such as these that drove Pavese to suicide; if anything they were the fortuitous cause of it: they perhaps confirmed the relativity and imperfection of the sublunar world (remember, again, the anguish and disgust of Rosetta in *Among Women Only*, re-echoed in the penultimate sentence in Pavese's diary: "All this is sickening"); death, deliberately chosen and determined, signified for him the act that opens the way to the absolute, so long sought after in childhood and in love, pursued in myth, longed for in the smile of the gods. Fernandez writes:

Suicide is not a break but the ultimate point of maturity, the moment when subjectivity—after having fought long with moral and social laws, and having fought also with its own desire to know and love the world, its adversary—abandons the world to itself and retires within itself to realize itself to the full.[43]

Since even the word is part of the world, Pavese finally commits the act that will negate the word and destroy the relationship between literature and life, which till then had been held in a difficult balance: the ultimate maturity, for him, will not be a book but silence. The relativity of books and days is succeeded by the absolute of silence outside of time, a silence that keeps the enigma of Pavese's work, its authenticity, its myth.[44]

The few, moving testimonials of his friends tend to confirm, in their evocation of the figure of Pavese, the reasons for his suicide. Natalia Ginzburg, especially, confirms them in her description of Pavese's solitude, and his authenticity as tragic hero, his passing among things and men "like a stranger,"[45] his mistake (if mistake it was) in "not wanting to bend himself to love the daily course of existence: thus he was left with everyday reality to overcome; but this was forbidden him, impossible for him who had both a thirst for it and a horror of it; and so he could only look at it as if from an unlimited distance."[46]

On the basis of Natalia Ginzburg's words, there come to mind with a new and higher resonance, like a seal, those other words spoken by the narrator of *The Moon and the Bonfires*, spoken with the calm certainty of knowing that it was impossible to stay in his own village, on the hills: "I came from too far away."

Notes

Introduction

1. The notion of the separation of self and world in general is analyzed in György Lukàcs, *Die Theorie des Romans* (Neuwied am Rhein: Luchterhand, 1963). The derivations and application of a similar notion in Italian culture and society during the period with which we are concerned is explored in Gian Franco Venè, *Letteratura e capitalismo in Italia dal '700 ad oggi* (Milan: Sugar, 1963), especially in Part III. Venè bases his study on the premise that bourgeois society is inadequate to meet the individual's demands and that literature for its part fails to understand that inadequacy. Carlo Salinari's *Miti e coscienza del decadentismo italiano* (Milan: Feltrinelli, 1960) is on the same topic, especially page 10: "The awareness of crisis, the solitude of the artist dislodged from his natural historical *humus*, the desperation of modern man, these are the great themes through which the artists of every nation become aware of the alienation of society from their contemporaries."

2. Cesare Pavese, *La letteratura americana e altri saggi* (Turin: Einaudi, 1959), p. 231. Piero Gobetti died in Paris in 1926 after being beaten up by the Fascists; Mussolini had given orders "to make life difficult" for him. Antonio Gramsci died in Rome in 1937, after eleven years in Fascist prisons had undermined his health irremediably. Of Gramsci, Pavese says: "I know only *Lettere dal carcere* and *Materialismo storico*, which are published. The other notebooks containing some more essays are in the hands of the editor and nobody knows anything as yet. But I don't think democratic America will allow the translation of these pages: they were written in a

Fascist jail by a fighter who, were he alive today, would, for instance, be forbidden entrance to the USA" (*Lettere 1945–1950,* edited by Italo Calvino (Turin: Einaudi, 1966), p. 6, letter to Sanford J. Greenburger, April 3, 1948).

3. *Lettere 1924–1950,* edited by Lorenzo Mondo with the collaboration of Davide Lajolo and Italo Calvino (Turin: Einaudi, 1966), January 12th, 1930, p. 164 (in English in the original). The best and most direct evidence of Pavese's contribution to American studies is his volume of essays on American literature cited above.

4. *La letteratura americana,* p. 189.

5. *Ibid.,* pp. 194–195: "American culture during those years offered us the spectacle of our own drama played on a gigantic screen. It showed us a frenzied, conscious, endless struggle to give meaning, name, and order to the new realities and new instincts of individual and collective existence, to adapt man's former meanings and words to a world which has been transformed at a dizzying pace. . . . We could not openly participate in the drama, in the legend, in the problem, and so we studied American culture somewhat as one studies past centuries, Elizabethan drama or poetry of the *'stil nuovo'!*"

6. Calvino, "Preface" to *La letteratura americana,* p. xiv.

7. *Ibid.*

8. *Ibid.,* p. 28. Also on p. 34 Pavese explains: "There is a very clear and real parallel. One is reminded of what the discovery of regionalism meant to Italian literature, as it developed side by side with the efforts to obtain national unity during the last part of the eighteenth and the whole of the nineteenth century. All the Italian writers, beginning with Alfieri, who are trying, often unconsciously, to achieve a more profound national unity, constantly probe their regional character, their *true* nature; thus they are creating a human conscience and a style which was rich with the blood of the regions and with all the dignity of a renewed life."

9. An exhaustive and sensitive biography of Pavese is Davide Lajolo's *Il "vizio assurdo": Storia di Cesare Pavese* (4th ed.; Milan: Il Saggiatore, 1961). A brief biography in English is Stuart Hood's "A Protestant Without God," *Encounter,* XXVI (May 1966), pp. 41–48; a general critical evaluation is Leslie A. Fiedler's "Introducing Cesare Pavese," *Kenyon Review,* XVI (Autumn 1954).

10. Fulvio Longobardi, "Ancora Pavese," *Belfagor*, XX (November 1965), pp. 693–716. The quotation is on page 693.

11. The best essay is Sergio Solmi's "Il diario di Pavese," in his *Scrittori negli anni* (Milan: Il Saggiatore, 1963), pp. 243–255. Psychoanalytical interpretations are given by Michel David, *La psicoanalisi nella cultura italiana* (Turin: Boringhieri, 1966), pp. 511ff., and by Dominique Fernandez, *L'échec de Pavese* (Paris: Grasset, 1967).

12. Roland Barthes, *Critique et vérité* (Paris: Aux éditions du seuil, 1966), pp. 59–60.

13. Susan Sontag, "The Artist As Exemplary Sufferer," in her *Against Interpretation* (New York: Farrar, Straus and Giroux, 1966), pp. 39–48.

14. A more direct and exhaustive approach to Pavese's cultural and historical background is taken in the special issue of the review *Sigma: Pavese*, I (December 1964) and in Armanda Guiducci, *Il mito Pavese* (Florence: Vallecchi, 1967).

Chapter 1. *Where Myths Are Forged*

1. *Lavorare stanca* (*Work Is Wearying*) was published for the first time by Solaria in Florence in 1935–1936, and in a new edition by Einaudi in 1943. It has now appeared together with various unpublished poems and *La terra e la morte* (*Earth and Death*) (1947) and *Verrà la morte e avrà i tuoi occhi* (*Death Will Come and Its Eyes Will Be Yours*) (1950) in a new volume: *Poesie edite e inedite*, edited by Italo Calvino (Turin: Einaudi, 1963). It should be noted that no distinction is made in my text between published and unpublished poems. Between the two appendices to *Work Is Wearying* (also included in the above-mentioned volume) one should place the pages of the "Secretum professionale," which form the opening to Cesare Pavese's diary *Il mestiere di vivere* (*Diario 1935–1950*) (4th ed.; Turin: Einaudi, 1960; latest ed., 1965). Quotations are taken from the English translation by A. E. Murch, *The Burning Brand* (New York: Walker and Co., 1961). There are numerous passages in the diary that refer to *Work Is Wearying*: among these, it is enough to mention the two contrasting examples of critical reflection on November 20, 1937, pp. 68–71, and May 16, 1938, p. 103. In addition,

some of Pavese's letters make special reference to *Work Is Weary-ing*: January 24, 1936, to Carocci (I, p. 496), with its jubilation and also its "feeling of emptiness" over the future publication of his poetry; June 8, 1941, to Einaudi (I, p. 592), with the offer of a new edition; and above all the letter to Giuseppe Cassano (who had criticized the immorality of *Work Is Wearying*), in June 1936 (I, pp. 520–523): "This will probably astound you, but I must confess that of all the critics of my book I am the one who is most convinced of a moral blemish in it, a weakness, a human insufficiency that now make even its smell odious to me"; after offering some explanations to justify and clarify his poetic and human intent, Pavese continues: "After making these objections I'll get back to your criticism: the moral timbre of my book smacks more of *perversion* than *health*. I will be very sincere with you and confess that I've always feared this; I've always been concerned about the frequency and compla-cency with which I touched on erotic topics . . . and now it has been judged and my suspicions confirmed: *perversion*. What should I say to you? In your disinterestedness you were precisely the oracle for which I was waiting. Ethically and therefore aesthetically, the book was not a success; it is ambiguous, confused, and needs to be completely rewritten." But he expresses a completely opposite opin-ion in his letter to Fernanda Pivano, February 13, 1943 (I, p. 674): "I was so much more a scoundrel and so much more intelligent at 25. I wrote a book then that nobody thought was worth a penny, and yet I'll never write anything better than that book." This opinion is confirmed in his letters to Giovanni Nicosia, August 6, 1945 (II, p. 23): "*Lavorare stanca* is worth more than you seem to consider"; and to Mario Motta, January 23, 1950 (II, p. 470): "a book which is enough (I'm not kidding) to save a generation."

2. *La letteratura americana*, pp. 246–247; on p. 293, Pavese confirms that his work was "begun coyly right at the time of the hermetic poets and *prosa d'arte*, when the castle of the closed Italian literary culture remained impervious to the bold winds of the world."

3. *Ibid.*, p. 218. The historical reason for an attitude such as Pavese's is explained later: "The best of us, touchy and despairing as they were, often found themselves, as the years went by, imagining that only one thing could save them: a plunge into the crowd, a sudden feverish quest for experiences and proletarian or agrarian

interests, for which the special, refined illness injected into us by fascism finally ends in the humble and practical health of everyone" (p. 226). Again, Pavese was obsessed with this same preoccupation when he wrote: "For a writer, for a 'workman of fantasy,' who ten times a day runs the risk of believing the whole of life is books, his books, it is necessary to have a constant cure of violent shocks, of people, and of concrete reality" (p. 238). Pavese's "workman of fantasy" is very like Antonio Fogazzaro's expression *nous ouvriers de la prose* in "Le grand poète de l'avenir," now in *Discorsi* (Milan: Mondadori, 1941), p. 140. As for Cowley's definition, it is in his introduction to Walt Whitman's *Leaves of Grass: The First (1855) Edition* (London: Secker and Warburg, 1960), p. viii: "the proletarian bard"; as all definitions, this one too is inevitably partial but nevertheless useful.

4. *Ibid.*, p. 143. In Pavese's diary, February 19, 1940, *The Burning Brand*, p. 169, there is the following observation: "The characters in your poems tend a little too much to have odd, i.e., picturesque, ways of earning a living"; and November 10, 1935, p. 34: "If there is any human figure in my poetry, it is that of a truant running back, full of joy, to his own village, [after many different experiences, all of them strange;] a man who likes to work as little as he can; finding great pleasure in the simplest things; always expansive, good-natured, set in his views; incapable of deep suffering; happy to follow nature and enjoy a woman, but also glad to be free and on his own; ready every morning to start life afresh. As in *Mari del Sud*." Italo Calvino adds the following to this last observation (*Poesie edite e inedite*, p. 218, n. 1), to explain the Piedmontese dimension of Pavese's wanderings: "Monti contrasted . . . the virtue of the Piedmontese *sansôssì* (which consisted of thoughtlessness and youthful irresponsibility) with the virtue of the solid Piedmontese workman, long-suffering, hard-working, and taciturn. Pavese, in his early work (and maybe always) moved between these two extremes; don't forget that one of the first authors he read was Walt Whitman, who praised both hard work and a vagabond's life. The title *Lavorare stanca* would be, precisely, Pavese's version of Augusto Monti's (and Walt Whitman's) antitheses, but without the gaiety, which he could never really share: a young boy in an adult world, jobless in a working world, womanless in a world of love and family life, weaponless in a world of fierce

political struggles and civil duties." When he was a student, Pavese wrote a eulogy of Whitman, now in *Lettere*, I, p. 17; *passim* there are various references to the American poet and his influence on the cultural (and human) formation of the Piedmontese. See especially his letter to Piero Jahier, December 3, 1948 (II, p. 318), evidence of his old loyalty: "The news that you are translating Whitman fills me with my former nostalgia."

5. *Poesie edite e inedite*, pp. 195–197. These experiences can be summed up as follows: "Studies and translations from the North American," "some short, almost dialectal stories," and "an amateur collection of pornography"; but, once this is said, it should be clearly kept in mind what Pavese writes in his diary, October 11, 1935, p. 28: ["My writing is not in dialect".]

6. In *Poesie edite e inedite*, p. 206.

7. February 16, 1936, p. 41. Pavese had already emphasized the city-country opposition in Sherwood Anderson: "For Anderson, the whole of the modern world consists of a contrast between city and country, genuineness and empty deception, nature and small men" (in *La letteratura americana*, p. 36). He refers to it frequently in his diary in his efforts to evolve a conceptual and imaginative unity in *Work Is Wearying:* "the idea of a mysterious connection," and "a wealth of associations that skillfully arrive at an assessment of value" (October 28, 1935, p. 32); "I am always wondering how to arrange my little poems in such a way as to be able to add to their number and make their significance complete" (November 9, 1935, p. 33); or "The mind, in all its manifestations, strives toward *unity*"; "It is good to go back to Homer" (February 17, 1936, p. 43).

Basically it is the same search in "The Poet's Job," where Pavese refers not only to Whitman but also to D'Annunzio (*Alcyone*) and Baudelaire (*Les Fleurs du Mal*). Pavese even copied Baudelaire's "*La rançon*" into his diary as an "epigraph to everything" in 1937 (December 31, p. 86). On the preceding page he had written: "Two things interest you: the technique of love and the technique of art." Also in the *Lettere*, I, there are references to the unity (or at least non-fragmentation) of *Work Is Wearying;* for example, p. 110. Interesting too are the observations on poetry as totality (pp. 4, 38) and as a means of "correcting" reality (p. 32), as well as Pavese's intention of *being a poet* (pp. 11, 15, 20, 28).

8. The mention of ancestors brings to mind Walt Whitman: "My

tongue, every atom of my blood, form'd from this soil, this air, / Born here of parents born here from parents the same, and their parents the same."

9. For example: "The Sad Wine (2)," "Simplicity," "Fatherhood," "The Star," "Revelation," "The House."

10. *8 poesie inedite e quattro lettere a un'amica* (1928–1929), with a piece by Enrico Emanuelli (Milan: Scheiwiller, 1964), pp. 18–23. Other examples of the same images are: "In the halo of lights / of the city by night / the poet in his frenzy is like / cosmic hurricanes in strength" (December 17, 1928); and "Silent lights stud the night like jewels / necklaces of lamps along the avenues" (February 10, 1929). The letters to Ponina Tallone have now been published in *Lettere*, I, pp. 149, 153, 162, 163. Cf. also p. 102 ("and the faces of the lamps in the asphalt") and p. 271 ("The bordering fields, with houses in the distance, an occasional street lamp, and on the horizon the denser lights of the city . . ."). There are other examples in *Work Is Wearying* that contain variations of the "lights" theme: "Smoking Cheap Cigarettes," "Two Cigarettes," "Sand-blasters' Dusk," "City in the Country," "People Who Don't Understand" (the latter has a Leopardian graft "with her bundle of grass" onto Pavese's poetic stem), "Night Pleasures," "Ancient Discipline," and "Poetics."

11. "This is the day when the mists rise from the river / in the beautiful city, in the middle of the fields / and hills, / and evaporate like a memory. . . ." The theme of fog in the city reappears in several stories and in the novel *The Comrade*.

12. "A Generation" and "Revolt" have at least one theme in common: "They have covered the bloodstains in the street" and "Yet the stars have seen blood in the street." The events alluded to in this poem are described by Lajolo, *Il "vizio assurdo"*, pp. 36–39. Pavese mentions "Green Wood" in a letter to his sister Maria, July 8, 1935, sent from the prison Regina Coeli, *Lettere*, I, p. 401: "I, who had never been in prison and never thought I would come to prison, once wrote a poem in which I described in detail the thoughts of a man in prison. What do you think of that for intuition?"

13. ". . . As each new morning came / I would go out in the streets looking for colors." The same theme is found in "Summer (1)": ". . . The anguish of the gentle handshake has rekindled colors / and summer and warmth under the brilliant sky."

14. René Girard bases his theory of mediation on the Hegelian

concept of master and slave. See his *Mensonge romantique et verité romanesque* (Paris: Grasset, 1961); English translation by Yvonne Freccero, entitled *Desire, Deceit and the Novel: Self and Other in Literary Structure* (Baltimore: Johns Hopkins University Press, 1965). In Pavese the two relationships are often merged or superimposed: for example, in *The Moon and the Bonfires* there is literally a master-slave relationship between Sor Matteo's daughters and Anguilla, and there is also mediation. Notice how important the exotic element is in this relationship. In this connection it would be wise to draw attention to the end of the poem, where there is an explicit reflection on the work which Pavese had just been translating and which we shall be talking about later, *Moby Dick* by Melville:

> "Only one dream
> is left in his blood: he once crossed,
> as fireman on a dutch fishing boat, the *Cetaceo*,
> and saw the heavy harpoons fly in the sun,
> saw whales fleeting in a foam of blood,
> and saw them followed and their tails raised and struggling
> with the harpoon."

A possible reference to the "huge greenish stamp" is in Pavese's letter to Antonio Chiuminatto, April 5, 1930, *Lettere*, I, p. 186: ". . . to receive letters with such strange stamps that cause janitors to stare a bit of a time. . . . I noticed what a waste of 'Golden Gates' and 'Liberty's Statues' you are practicing in your mailings of books. . . ." See too pp. 246 and 304 on the "myth" of the Southern Seas which was realized in the poem of the same name.

15. It is not possible to quote all the places in which hills appear; we will simply mention the following poems: "Southern Seas," "The Young Teachers" (with its image of the little parasols which appears frequently in Pavese's narrative; also the image "a house on top of a hill," which seems to anticipate the title of one of his novels), "Encounter," "Landscape I," "Uprooted People," "Landscape II," "Atlantic Oil" (with the image of the vineyard on the hill), "House under Construction," "Green Wood," "Later" ("The hill is stretched out and the rain impregnates it in silence," a prelude to the play on the images hill-woman-rain), "Landscape V," "Landscape," "The Widow's Son," and finally "Earth and Death," as for example, "You

don't know the hills"; furthermore, in the diary entry for July 30, 1949, p. 342, are quoted several lines crossed out of "Smoking Cheap Cigarettes," the last of which is "all around great hills were rising. . . ."

16. Note that nudism is one of the themes of Whitman's poetry (connected with Timber Creek), and all its premises are also to be found in the sensual summer of D'Annunzio's poetry, as for example "*Stabat nuda aestas,*" "*Furit aestus,*" and especially one of the *Madrigali d'estate,* "*Nella belletta*": in fact, Pavese uses its setting for the nudism of some of his short stories and for *The Devil in the Hills.*

17. Of the many references in Pavese's diary to this poem the following seem worth quoting: November 19, 1939, p. 158: "Reading Landolfi makes it clear that your motif of the goat was the motif of the *bond between man and the animal kingdom.* Hence your taste for prehistory, the period that gives a glimpse of a community of interests between man and wild beasts. Hence your own research into the origin of imagery at that epoch." It is evident that the roots of *Dialogues with Leucò* go very deep. Other references are in *Lettere,* I, pp. 471 and 439: "I have taken note of the advice of the Ministero Stampa and am removing, as you see, 'The Goat-God' (regretfully)."

18. It is interesting to bear in mind that the motif of drunkenness and wine, linked with inns, vagrancy, picturesque types, is also found in the two authors Pavese refers to in "The Poet's Job": in Baudelaire ("*Le Vin*"), and in D'Annunzio ("*L'otre,*" "*L'offerta alla terra*").

19. See also "Unconvinced People":

> "But, above the scent
> of the earth, a sterile musty smell of flowers
> sucking up water, and among the flowers the villas
> dripping with rain. Only from the other side,
> a smell of vines is carried on the wind."

"Green Wood": "The hills taste to him of rain: it is the faint smell / wafted into prison by the wind sometimes."
"The Country Whore":

> "In the gradual awakening there often comes back
> that old, faded smell of distant flowers,

of stable and sun. No man knows
the subtle caress of that bitter memory."

20. Cf. the letter written by Pavese "to a girl, Turin," September 17, 1927, at night (*Lettere*, I, p. 86): "And, child, you have come and stirred it up for a moment [my heart] and intoxicated it again, with those exalted words, and made it come alive with their music 'alone.' Like one of those clouds which used to pass in the sky, child, I love you now, my slender dream with eyes lost in blond hair."

21. For example Franco Mollia, *Cesare Pavese* (Florence: La Nuova Italia, 1963), p. 176, speaks of "the gradual depletion of an objective vein, even though it is transformed into images, and its replacement by a lyrical contemplation that is felt as an escape from the 'subject' and from the commitment, but is aesthetically valid: as can be seen in the poems of 1945 and 1950 and in a very few of them written in the years '31–'38." On *Earth and Death*, there is an entry in Pavese's diary, December 17, 1949, p. 350: "an explosion of creative energies which had been pent up for years."

22. The passage from Pavese dealing with "not naturalistic but symbolic" reality is as follows: "In these poems the facts will take place—if they take place—not because reality wants it but because intelligence decides it. Single poems and *canzoniere* will not form an autobiography but a judgment. As in fact is the case in the *Divine Comedy* (we always get back to that) but remembering that your symbol would correspond not to Dante's allegory but to his imagery."

23. Pavese's meter is analyzed in Massimo Mila's preface to Cesare Pavese, *Poesie* (Turin: Universale Einaudi, 1961): particularly interesting is the "ternary rhythm" of the thirteen-syllable lines.

24. The same motifs of morning, light, sky, and eyes are in "Creation" and in "Summer (1)" (both from *Work Is Wearying*) and in "The Mornings Go by Clear" (which repeats in a different key the line "Mornings go by clear and deserted" of "Grappa in September") and in "Death Will Come and Its Eyes Will be Yours" (the title poem of the volume which contains both these poems): respectively: "It makes one shiver to feel the morning quiver / still virgin, scarcely anyone of us awake"; "a motionless sky is gathered / coldly, in those eyes"; "It is dark, the morning which

passes / without the light from your eyes"; "your eyes / will be a
meaningless word, / a stifled cry, a silence. / Thus you see them
every morning / when you bend them on yourself alone / in the
mirror." In "The Carter," too: "There will be those eyes that stir the
blood."

25. Perhaps it is worth noting that the theme of woman and earth
goes far back in Pavese's culture and thought and is directly linked
with the theme of ancestors that we find from the time of his
"discovery" of America; in *La letteratura americana*, p. 37, Sherwood Anderson's grandmother is described as "the resolute Italian
woman, *earth and blood,* a drinker and a centenarian" (italics
added).

26. Cesare Pavese's diary, March 25, 1950, p. 361. On March 23,
Pavese had written: "Love is truly the great manifesto; the urge to
be, to *count* for something, and, if death must come, to die valiantly,
with acclamation—in short, to *remain a memory.* Yet [the] desire to
die, to disappear, is [always] bound up with [love]: perhaps because
[love] is so magnificently alive that, if my being could blend with
[it], my life would have more meaning than before." The last note in
the diary corresponds with the last line of poetry quoted above
(August 18, 1950, p. 366): "Not words. An act. I won't write any
more." See also November 28, 1949, p. 347: "Night comes, when I
begin to feel drowsy. Every noise . . . stirs up a kind of whirlpool in
my brain, a sudden, swirling whirlpool, in which my mind and the
whole world are swept to ruin. . . . It is not unpleasant—a light
buoyant feeling, as though I had been drinking, and when I recover,
my teeth are clenched. But what if, one day, I do not recover?" We
are reminded of Pascoli in *"Era nuova": "*But I remember some vague
and fleeting moment in the shadows of the night: the giddy descent
into an endless whirlpool, weightless, breathless, beingless. . . ."

27. Concerning "You, Wind of March," there is an entry in the
diary written much earlier than the composition of the poem, which
can nevertheless explain the origin of one line: "But to you she is life
itself, and death" writes Pavese, January 3, 1938, p. 86, about one of
his women, whose name it is not important to know. On May 16,
1950, p. 363, Pavese wrote: "Now even the morning is filled with
pain." Pavese's state of mind in January, 1938, is described in his
terrible letter to Enzo Monferini, *Lettere,* I, pp. 533–534.

28. *Ibid.*, p. 49. It is important to note that the italics are Pavese's. The words quoted are in the following context: "Have I ever in my life done anything that was not the action of a crack-brained fool? A fool in the banal, incurable sense of the word. A man who has *no idea* how to live, who has not developed morally, a futile dolt, propping himself up with thoughts of suicide, but not committing it." Again in the diary, July 14, 1950, p. 364, we find some lines from "Last Blues, to Be Read One Day" after this note: "Stoicism is suicide. People are dying in battle again. . . ." Cf. also Pavese's letter to Augusto Monti, August 23, 1928, *Lettere*, I, p. 104: "I can't fling myself into living, I can't. To live one needs strength and understanding, an ability to choose. I've never been able to do this. Just as I don't understand politics, I don't understand all the other activities of life."

29. The words are Pavese's in "The Poet's Job," and he is referring to Whitman's free verse. Cf. the excellent second chapter of Lorenzo Mondo, *Cesare Pavese* (Milan: Mursia, 1961) on the poetic value of *Work is Wearying;* the conclusion, p. 23: "The last image to be obtained from *Lavorare stanca* is that of an ardent workshop, where names and myths are fashioned for a prevailing narrative vocation."

30. Lucien Goldmann, "Introduction" to Lukàcs, *op. cit.*, Italian trans., *Teoria del romanzo* (Milan: Sugar, 1962), p. 26.

31. *La letteratura americana*, p. 248. The fundamental unity of Pavese's poetical inspiration is stressed by Anco Marzio Mutterle, "Appunti sulla lingua di Pavese lirico," in *Ricerche sulla lingua poetica contemporanea* (Quaderni del circolo filologico-linguistico padovano, n. 1; Padua: Liviana, 1967), pp. 261–313.

Chapter 2. *Solitude*

1. The *Racconti* of Cesare Pavese (Turin: Einaudi, 1960) includes, in chronological order, *Notte di festa, Feria d'agosto*, the unedited short stories, and some fragments. Giorgio Zampa has rightly expressed reservations about this volume in the *Corriere della sera*, March 3, 1960, p. 5. Some of these short stories have appeared in English translation by A. E. Murch: *Festival Night:* "Land of Exile,"

"Wedding Trip," "The Intruder," "The Three Girls," "Festival Night," "Friends," "Gaolbirds," "Suicides," "The Villa on the Hill," and "The Cornfield" (London: Peter Owen Ltd., 1964); and *Summer Storm*: "The Evil Eye," "Misogyny," "Summer Storm," "The Idol," "First Love," "Loyalty," "The Beggars," "Evocation," "The Family," "The Name," "Freewill," and "The Leather Jacket" (London: Peter Owen Ltd., 1966). The quotations in this chapter are taken from the translations by A. E. Murch whenever they exist.

Opening words are very important for Pavese, as he says in his diary, July 22, 1938, p. 114: "Once the first line of a story is written, the whole is already decided—style, atmosphere, and the sequence of events." One should remember, too, that "Pavese gives little attention to 'creating characters.' Characters are a means for him, not an end. He merely uses characters to construct intellectual fables whose theme is the rhythm of what happens: the astonishment as of a fly trapped under a glass, in *The Political Prisoner*. . . ." These are Pavese's words about himself in a "Radio Interview" now published in *La letteratura americana*, p. 294.

2. *The Burning Brand*, p. 78, December 5, 1937, and *Lettere*, I, p. 441, September 17, 1935, respectively. Other examples are in the diary, p. 79 ("the innate, ravening loneliness in every man," December 15, 1937), p. 96 ("True loneliness, when one has to endure it, brings with it a desire to kill," February 9, 1938), and p. 120 ("The art of being alone," October 9, 1938); and in *Lettere*, I, p. 489 (to his sister Maria, December 27, 1935): "As for me I am now used to fate and I let the days go by like someone who is already soaked lets the rain fall on him. I am used to asthma, to solitude, and to uncertainty." Pavese's tremendous existential solitude is made very clear in a self-portrait he sent to Fernanda Pivano on November 5, 1940, which ends with these words: "Life takes revenge in real solitude. Let life be as it will": in Lajolo, *op. cit.*, pp. 256–259, and *Lettere*, I, p. 572ff; also see *Lettere*, II, p. 69, letters to Bianca Garufi, March 27, 1946 ("Here I live alone and tragically. With your ability to make friends even with a broom, you have no idea what it's like to be alone *every* evening. But I'm used to it. . . .") and April 17, 1946, p. 75 ("I'm alone, as I said, and what's more it's the beginning of my bad season—spring—when I've never been able to write anything.")

3. On December 22, 1937, p. 180 of the diary, Pavese refers to

"Land of Exile" in almost the same words: "Each of your stories is a combination of figures moved by the same passion expressed in different ways in their individual titles. '*Notte di festa*,' celebrating the festival of the Saint; '*Terra d'esilio*,' all men imprisoned. . . ."

4. The theme of feminine infidelity is developed fully in the work of Pavese from "Gaolbirds" (whose portagonist is the wild and evasive Concia) and "Loyalty" (typically bitter even in its title) right up to *The Comrade*.

5. *The Burning Brand*, January 13, 1937, p. 63.

6. Notice that the thought of suicide, corollary to solitude, constituted a tragic constant in the spiritual evolution of Pavese, marking the crucial points in the swing of the pendulum, in his diary: April 10 and 24, 1936; November 6 and 30, December 4 and 23, 1937; January 8 and 16, February 5, March 23, 26 and 27, May 31 and November 10, 1938; January 1, 1946—without counting the last months before the end in 1950. Besides the diary, see *Lettere*, I, especially the following letters: to Mario Sturani, February 4, 1926 (p. 19), January 9, 1927 (p. 48), April 8, 1927 (pp. 53–54), already published in Lajolo, *op. cit.*, pp. 66, 74–76, 82–83 respectively; to Giorgio Curti, October 27, 1926 (p. 44: "Finally you should know that I am thinking about suicide"); to Tullio Pinelli, July 12, 1927 (p. 58: "At the back of every exaltation of mine is the supreme exaltation of the thought of suicide. Oh, one day I'll have the courage for it! I long for it, trembling, from hour to hour. It is my last consolation. Let me hear from you, I need to hear from you, I am so alone, I'm confused"); to a girl, Turin, September 9, 1927 (p. 83: "For a year now I have been thinking about suicide too much. . . . But if sometime—not now, I swear to you on the present memory of your little blonde figure—I have the courage to kill myself it will be a long time from now—and a long way from you—so that you need not have the slightest remorse, because all that is wrong is inside me and what will kill me will be the disillusionment of life, not you"); to Ponina Tallone, October 3, 1929 and January 2, 1930 (pp. 149–150 and 163), both published in Cesare Pavese, *8 poesie inedite e quattro lettere a un'amica*, *cit.*, pp. 34 and 39; to Augusto Monti, September 11, 1935 (p. 436: ". . . at least if my hand doesn't slip, some morning when I'm tieing my tie"), already cited by Lajolo, *op. cit.*, pp. 181–182; to his sister Maria, November 5, 1935 (p. 460: "Here I lead a

life somewhat like that of the author of the book I described to you [*Autobiography of a Suicide*]. If only it won't end the same way"); to Enzo Monferini, January 1938 (pp. 533–534: ". . . I made a half-attempt at suicide, with gas. . . . In other words I live with the idea of suicide, which is much worse than a suicide which has taken place, which is only a sanitary operation"). In *Lettere*, II, the letters of the last period reflect the same "collapse" as the diary (see especially the letter to Aldo Camerino, June 16, 1950, p. 540), and in their entirety provide "a series of advance notices of death."

7. In reference to this story Dominique Fernandez, *Le roman italien et la crise de la conscience moderne* (Paris: Grasset, 1958) pp. 142–144, mentions the name of Gide: "The youthful novel *Viaggio di nozze* . . . relates the failure of a marriage and the remorse and grief of the man who has sacrificed his gentle, meek companion to his own need to be alone: a theme which brings to mind *L'immoraliste*."

8. Pavese notes in his diary, December 31, 1937, p. 85, in reference to this story: "Hitherto you have made the protagonist speak in the first person, without bothering to characterize him and give him his own mode of expression. Now you must also concern yourself with his individuality, create him as a person, not leave him a neutral version of yourself (and that will be *Volgarità* or *Suicidi*)"; an entry on September 21, 1938, p. 118, concerns the narrative technique of "Friends."

9. Cf. Pavese's diary, April 10, 1936, p. 47: "And even where my work is concerned, have I ever been anything but a hedonist? I enjoyed working feverishly by fits and starts, under the spur of ambition, but I was afraid, too; afraid of getting tied up"; and January 15, 1938, p. 88: "Your salvation . . . lies solely in [cowardice], creeping back into your shell, never running any risk. But if the risk seeks you out? And how long will your shell last?"

10. The quotations from *Il carcere* are taken from the English translation, *The Political Prisoner*, by W. J. Strachan (London: Mayflower-Dell Paperback, 1966). It will be remembered that *The Political Prisoner* was written during the years 1938–39 but not published until ten years later together with *La casa in collina* (*The House on the Hill*) in a volume entitled *Prima che il gallo canti* (*Before the Cock Crows*, Turin: Einaudi, 1949). See in this connec-

tion *Lettere,* II, the letters to Emilio Cecchi, January 17, 1949, p. 340 ("*Il Carcere* . . . hasn't been retouched since 1938 except for the proper names—for reasons of discretion. . . . The curious thing is that until now I had always been ashamed of it, and only when I realized that *Casa in collina* complemented it was I convinced that I should publish it"); to Gianni De Francesco, March 3, 1949, p. 362 ("The similarity [of *Il carcere*] with *Conversazione* [*in Sicilia* by Elio Vittorini] makes me proud, when I think that that book is the best to be thought up in the last twenty years"); and to Lalla Romano, April 6, 1949, p. 373 ("But the most extraordinary thing is the pre-dawn quality you attribute to my book. . . . Actually when I gave the book its title I was thinking of remorse and judgment and in fact gnashing of teeth, but all the time, without realizing it, I was dreaming about the joyous hope of the morning"). For the events of Pavese's personal life, in the years preceding and during the writing of *The Political Prisoner,* see two chapters of Lajolo's biography: 10, "Lettere dal confino" (pp. 174ff.) and 12, "Da *Il carcere* a *Paesi tuoi*" (pp. 218ff.) All his correspondence from prison and from political exile has been collected in the first volume of *Lettere* from p. 377 (to his sister Maria, [Torino, Carceri Nuove,] May 16, 1935) to p. 519 (telegram to his sister Maria, [Brancaleone,] March 17, 1936).

11. See the diary, December 28, 1936, p. 62: "The point is that reality is a prison, where, in just the same way, one vegetates and always will. All the rest—thought, action—is just a pastime, mental or physical. What counts then, is to come to grips with reality. The rest can go."

12. Cf. *The Burning Brand,* November 29, 1938, p. 138: "Who can feel at home with a cell?"; and the previous November 26, p. 138: "Still in a stupor and just out of prison in an unfamiliar town, you see someone else—already dear to you—go to jail, and the obsessive idea of this second prison is colored by the strangeness of the town that shows its hidden face in your new loneliness." Perhaps it is interesting to remember too, that Pavese, when speaking of the central mythical image of various writers, remarks "in Stendhal the isolation of prison life" (September 15, 1943, p. 241).

13. In this connection Alberto Asor Rosa, *Scrittori e popolo* (Rome: Samonà e Savelli, 1965), pp. 234–235, notes that in Levi

"even the large part given to the magical and irrational aspects of the primitive world represented appear as a form of understanding and comparison, as a necessary experience, as an indispensable key to reach the heart of it. Doubtless there is a profound difference between Pavese's way of using ethnological instruments and Levi's: the former has a tendency to reduce interior reality to a series of ancestral symbols, which therefore acquire a significance and a validity in themselves, as pregnant as if they were of an autobiographical or intellectualistic content, all the more capable of explaining the secret ways of the artist's intimacy; the latter constantly tries to utilize myth as an interpretive instrument, granted it is of an imaginative and analogical nature, in the comparison of environmental situations which, *by definition,* cannot fall under logical and historical criteria. In the case of Levi, therefore, the fact that the author's culture is characterized by irrational implications does not constitute a restraint on his consciousness but if anything gives it dynamic impetus."

14. Cf. the letter to E., September 15, 1932, *Lettere,* I, pp. 346–347: "I don't know how to weep for love, E.—I weep to hear of an injustice, a cruelty, a child's grief—and I cannot even devote you tears in return for the immense gift you have given me during these days. Maybe I shall cry when I think back—later—of the wonder of the love thus squandered, on someone who wasn't worth the trouble: it's true he's letting it die without even being moved, without lifting a finger to save it or deserve it. It's no use lieing: in love what counts is the body, the blood, the struggle, *life,* and we must stand apart, we must be sensible, we must be reasonable. . . . But where will we end up, Elena? Is there anything more absurd than love? If we enjoy it to its last drop, then suddenly we're tired, disgusted; if we look up to it so that we can remember it without remorse, there will come a day when we shall regret our stupidity and our cowardice in not having dared. Love only asks to become a habit, a life together, one flesh in two bodies, and, as soon as this happens, it dies."

15. Carlo Salinari, *op. cit.,* p. 70. The sentence actually refers to D'Annunzio, from whom Salinari quotes the following passage, an excerpt from *Il piacere:* "He embraced her again, laid her down, covered her with wild kisses, blindly, desperately, with a devouring ardor, without speaking, smothering the moan on her lips, stifling on

her mouth the almost uncontrollable impulse that came to him to shout the name of Elena. And on the body of the unconscious woman he committed the horrible sacrilege." Note, apart from the obvious differences, it is the contemplation which distinguishes Pavese's Stefano from D'Annunzio's Andrea Sperelli; in fact, though he is thinking of Elena Muti while he is with other women, particularly Maria Ferres, Sperelli is above all a man of action. In his diary, April 26, 1936, p. 54, Pavese speaks of his own "habit of self-contemplation"; and his letter to Carlo Pinelli, July 14, 1928, *Lettere*, I, p. 95, contains the programmatic excerpt: "One should always be ready to examine, analyze and synthesize oneself, to explain to oneself every movement of one's spirit, sentiments, ideas, and all the rest. In other words to make a self-examination."

16. After finishing his novel Pavese wrote in his diary, April 26, 1939, p. 148 (Garofolo is the original name of Stefano, and Oreste that of Giannino): "As long as Garofolo wants to break down his isolation or strengthen it (the first nine chapters), he damages only his hands; when he thinks of something else, relaxes, welcomes the spring, thinks of his fantastic past, grows humble and considers himself one of many (an identification with Oreste in prison and the banished anarchist), then he grows serene and lighthearted (the last two chapters)." But whether his solitude is tortured or serene, the terms of the problem don't change: human relationship remains inside, in the conscience. Besides, Pavese wrote on December 26 of the preceding year, p. 143: "Imprisonment is bound to seem like the end of every kindly impulse, the point when human sympathy congeals. In fact, during the ascending phase, one's mind soars beyond those walls (do not take the strangeness of that new world as final. Use it as a means of stimulating wonder and curiosity), and in the descending phase one thinks with sympathetic horror of the next prisoner to be confined there, for whom that strangeness will increase the burden of loneliness."

17. Cf. the diary, November 29, 1938, p. 138: "Knowing about the invisible cell makes us feel that everything is provisional, even in the human circle to which we belong."

18. October 9, 1935, p. 26.

19. *Ibid.*, p. 26.

20. Cf. Giovanni Pascoli, *"L'aquilone,"* from "The bushes were bare, thorny" to "among the rough leaves of the ditch."

Chapter 3. *Violent Types*

1. The translations in this chapter from Pavese's *Racconti* are by A. E. Murch, for those stories contained in *Summer Storm* and *Festival Night*. See Chapter 2, note 1.

2. Concerning Rocco's act, we are reminded of a similar one made by Faulkner's character Lucas (Mondo, *op. cit.*, p. 44). References to American authors have already been thoroughly traced by Pavese's critics, from Mondo to Guiducci. Gianfranco Contini writes in his "Saggio introduttivo" to Carlo Emilio Gadda, *La cognizione del dolore* (Turin: Einaudi, 1963), p. 26: "Emilio Cecchi has rightly noticed that the combination of interior monologue and local color achieves a slangy and regional effect, *almost as if Pavese were a Faulkner of the Langhe* . . . and almost like another *Malavoglia* enriched with French naturalism" (italics added). Concerning the story "Gaolbirds" it is interesting to note that on June 18, 1937, Pavese jots down in his diary (p. 65) the following plan: "1. A rabble—a priest—speeches (Afternoon). 2. Flight—the street—the sound of a whistle (Dusk). 3. Investigation—the priest at prayer. 4. The woman and the priest (In the dead of night). 5. (Morning) Investiture—Return."

3. Unlike the picturesque idlers in *Work Is Wearying*, the Professor in this story is described as a contemplative idler.

4. Giacomo Leopardi, *"La sera del dì di festa"*: "a song heard in the lanes, / dying away in the distance gradually . . ."; and too, from *"Le ricordanze"*: "the song / of the frog far off in the country."

5. Pavese's diary, December 22, 1937, p. 80: "*Primo amore*, all men moved by the discovery of sex"; also September 22, 1938, p. 118: "The true [story] (*Primo amore* and *Campo di grano*) treats time as a material, not as a limitation, shortening or lengthening it as it chooses, in no way concerned with stage directions, which are time and vision of real life."

6. *The Burning Brand*, June 3, 1943, p. 238.

7. *Ibid*, December 25, 1937, p. 81.

8. *Ibid.*, January 16, 1945, p. 276. Also, in a letter to Tullio Pinelli, December 4, 1939, *Lettere*, I, p. 548, Pavese states: "Personally, I consider that the evocation of the peasant world is not the definitive

aim of my little work. The motif of *Paesi tuoi* is 'an encounter with stupidity-incarnate, which neither subtlety, nor humanity, nor self-defence can make a dent in.' This encounter should be explained, on the first and crudest plane, as a comparison of city and country and it doesn't matter if the city background remains in the pen; it is enough that there is a subtle city man (convinced of his subtlety) who is constantly made a fool of by a stupid peasant (and known to everyone as stupid)."

9. The quotations from *Paesi tuoi* are taken from the English translation, *The Harvesters*, by A. E. Murch (London: Peter Owen, 1961). Pavese's letter to Mario Alicata, July 1941, *Lettere*, I, pp. 598–599, discusses Alicata's critical review of the novel.

10. In fact, Pavese, reading Vico, has noted in his diary all the passages concerning the world of the peasant: November 5, 1943, pp. 251–252. Note especially, in reference to Vinverra's blows (and Valino's in *The Moon and the Bonfires*): ". . . [they]would beat their sons within an inch of their lives, so that they often fell dead in agonies of pain beneath their fathers' blows." Or in reference to certain pages of *Dialogues with Leucò:* "The fire that the heroes must have kindled with flints and set to the thorny underbrush on the mountaintops, dried out by the hot suns of summer"; ". . . eternal property expressed in the saying that servants are the paid enemies of their masters. . . ."

11. Mondo, *op. cit.*, p. 129 (note 45 *bis*), recalls "some typical places" in *The Harvesters* that are reminiscent of Anderson's *An Ohio Pagan*, as "the stupefaction caused by the country"; "The smell of the cows particularly aroused in him a sort of drunkenness. It was as if he had drunk strong wine."

12. "The place could have been a cowshed with a calf inside. He looked like the calf . . ."; "When he was not laughing, Talino looked like a goat himself."

13. In a letter written from prison, Pavese quotes a fragment of Ibico's poetry in which love is expressed in a similar way: "And in spring the quince / watered by the currents / of the rivers where lies intact / the garden of the nymphs, and the buds of the vines, / grown under the shady trellis / of the branches, flower; for me instead / in that time of calm, in the same way as the Thracian wind / springs up between the lightning flashes, love / rushing on Venus' behalf with

arid frenzy / sombre with passion / violently shakes my reason to its foundations. . . ." (in Lajolo, *op. cit.*, p. 192, now too in *Lettere*, I, p. 489).

14. Cf. Pavese's fragment entitled "Il sangue" ("The Blood"): "They had backed up; the pool of blood was enormous and filled the whole space between the tramlines, and the grooves were overflowing with it" (*Racconti*, p. 432).

15. *Ibid.*, p. 471.

16. A sentence of the diary comes to mind: January 3, 1938, p. 86: "Your eyes drank in her beauty while she ate her *brioche*. She wished you all the good in the world, as far as her nature allowed. But to you she is life itself, and death. Yet, of the two of us, she will always be the one to be penalized." Later in the novel the *polenta* motif is again resumed with the same effectiveness: "Down in the kitchen, Vinverra still had not moved from where he sat. With his hat on his head and his eyes fixed on the table, he looked like an old man in a tavern, overcome by wine. Keeping my eyes away from that basin, I cut myself a slice of pudding and ate it. It tasted of earth and cold soup, and as I gulped it down my thoughts were still with Gisella."

17. György Lukàcs, *A lélék es a formák*, Italian translation *L'anima e le forme* (Milan: Sugar, 1963), p. 59.

18. *La letteratura americana*, p. 68.

19. Pavese's diary, December 14, 1939, p. 162.

20. *Ibid.*, December 10, 1939, p. 160. On the same subject there are the passages for November 5, 1938, pp. 130–132, and February 6, 1944, p. 256: "A cypress and a house on the crest of the hill, dark against the crimson sky—the place that evokes your passion for this land of yours. Ethnology sprinkles such familiar places with blood, shed irrationally, mythically." The latter passage is particularly important in revealing the connections between classicism and decadentism, ethnology and mythology, violence and sex, blood and nature, D'Annunzio and the Americans in Pavese's formation and sensibility; see too Giorgio Bàrberi Squarotti, "Pavese o la fuga nella metafora", in *Sigma, cit.*, pp. 165–188.

21. Diary, October 14, 1939, p. 155.

22. *Ibid.*, December 4, 1939, p. 160. On the same date Pavese wrote a letter to Tullio Pinelli in which the affirmations here quoted recur

on a broader context (*Lettere*, I, p. 549). In one of the "dialogues with a friend," on *The Harvesters*, Pavese explains simply the meaning of his novel (in *La letteratura americana*, pp. 259ff.)

Chapter 4. *Attempts at Love*

1. May 15, 1939, p. 151. Even more than the diary, the *Lettere* bear evidence of the constant attempts made by Pavese in his life to establish a real and lasting relationship with a woman: especially his love letters to Milly, to a friend, to E., to "Signorina*", to Fernanda Pivano in Vol. I; to a friend, to Bianca Garufi, to Constance Dowling, and to Pierina in Vol. II. In a letter to the latter written in August 1950, II, pp. 559–60, he wrote: "Love is like grace from God —cunning is of no use."

2. The translations from the *Racconti* are by A. E. Murch, for those stories contained in *Festival Night* and *Summer Storm* (see Chapter 2, note 1).

3. October 15, 1940, p. 195. In this connection the beginning of the fragment "Wanda" (in *Racconti*) resumes the theme of women as masters or slaves, typical of Pavese's "amorous dialectic": "Here I am ringing the doorbell, and if, instead of a hesitant, surprised Wanda the door is opened by a disdainful Wanda who asks what I want and whether I think all I have to do is put in an appearance to put my hands on her and spend the night breathing beside her, I should bend my head down."

4. John Freccero, "Zeno's Last Cigarette," in *Modern Language Notes*, LXXVII (January, 1962), p. 20.

5. September 17, 1938, p. 116, and December 25, 1937, p. 82, respectively. Further evidence is given in the notes for December 31, 1937, p. 84 ("Their little secret seems improper, insufferable."), and January 26, 1938, pp. 93–94 ("You felt like this as a child when you saw two grown-ups gazing at each other, [shameless] but blissfully content. In those days you didn't quiet understand what they were thinking of doing, and you were not thirty years old. You're just the same now, except that you know the dreadful truth behind their embraces, and you are thirty. You will never *grow* up."): thoughts that confirm the situation of the story we are examining and reflect

with more anguish and immediacy the unhappy autobiography of Pavese.

6. The entry of Pavese's diary for November 17, 1943, p. 253, states: "There is a risk that your idea of ambivalence (avarice-prodigality, laziness-activity, love-hate) may become a rule in all your life; the *same* energy that produces an effect is corrected by the opposite effect."

7. May 15, 1939, p. 151. This reflection can be considered an indirect answer to a note on August 30, 1938, p. 116: "My stories are always about love or loneliness. For me, there seems no way of escaping from loneliness except by 'picking up' a girl. Possibly nothing else interests me? Or is it that the erotic relationship is more easily link[ed] in my mind with mythology instead of with any particular person?"

8. Reference to this beautiful short story is in the diary, June 3, 1943, p. 238: "Your classical knowledge stems from the *Georgics,* D'Annunzio, and the hill of Pino. To that background you added America, because its language is rustic-universal (Anderson, *An Ohio Pagan*) and because it is the place ("The Cornfield") where town and country meet."

9. The city is the subject of two of Pavese's letters to Tullio Pinelli, *Lettere,* I, September 1, 1926, p. 35: "Now as for me, I don't know whether it is the influence of Walt Whitman, but I would give twenty-seven countrysides for one city like Turin. The countryside is good for a temporary spiritual rest, good for a landscape to look at and run away again quickly in an electric train, but life, real modern life, as I imagine and fear it is a big city full of uproar, of factories, enormous apartment buildings, of crowds and beautiful women (although I don't know how to approach them)"; the second letter, November 6, 1939, I, p. 546: "I live long and tender days, misty and tingling, suffused with gold and rose and the scent of vines, days which make of Turin the city that is ours alone and we were born for her." Another important reference to Turin is in the diary, November 17, 1935, p. 36: "City of fantasy, through her aristocratic culture composed of elements new and old; city of decorum, through the complete absence of any jarring note, material or spiritual; city of passion, in her kindly indulgence towards idleness; city of irony, through her own good taste for life; [an exemplary] city, with her

calm rich in underlying tumult. A city virgin in art, like a girl who has already seen others making love but, for her own part, has tolerated only caresses so far, yet is now ready, if she finds the right man, to take the step. The city, in fine, where I [was] spiritually born when I reach[ed her] from outside: my lover, not my mother nor my sister. And many others feel this same relationship with her. How can she fail to exert a cultural influence? And I form a part of a group. The conditions are all present."

10. Quotations from Pavese's *La bella estate* are taken from the English translation *The Beautiful Summer* by W. J. Strachan, in *The Political Prisoner* (London: Peter Owen, 1966). The significance of the festival at the beginning of *The Beautiful Summer* (as well as of *The Devil in the Hills* and *Among Women Only*) is analyzed by Furio Jesi, "Cesare Pavese dal mito della festa al mito del sacrificio," introduction to the latest edition of Pavese's *La bella estate* (Turin: Einaudi, 1966), pp. vii–xx. Two entries in the diary concern the novel: February 1, 1940, p. 168: "Just like Proust: when you had to do without coffee, you no longer found the serenity of nerves that you needed before you could use your imagination. Then you got accustomed to it (*Paradiso sui tetti, Paesaggio*, and the plot of *La tenda*). Now there is coffee, and it seems to you to counteract imaginative serenity." More interesting, the "recovery" of August 22, 1949, p. 342: "From rejections (failures '41–'47) this beginning (of 15th November, '39): 2) Cinina was not thinking about the fog, and still she walked as if she were alone in the road. The feeling that nobody was near or around her was sweet and Sunday-like. 1) Cinina was walking in unforeseen directions, vaguely following the patches of fog which the morning was clearing away. She stopped when she came to a square . . . (preparation for the *Curtain* or *The Beautiful Summer*)."

11. Pavese's diary, June 3, 1938, p. 107; and his letter to Leone Ginzburg, August 20, 1929, *Lettere*, I, p. 122: "a feminine gloved hand, resting on the steering wheel, is something more beautiful and modern than any skyscraper."

12. The importance of the nude is analyzed by Fernandez, *Le roman italien, cit.*, p. 187: "A naked body, symbol of what is radically 'other,' as a stone is or broad sunlight. . . ."

13. *The Burning Brand*, December 22, 1937, p. 80.

14. Cesare Pavese and Bianca Garufi, *Fuoco grande* (Turin: Einaudi, 1959), English translation by W. J. Strachan, *A Great Fire*, in *The Beach* (London, Peter Owen, 1963). In a letter to Bianca Garufi at end of February 1946, *Lettere*, II, p. 61, Pavese speaks of "Giovanni's cannibalism."

15. *Ibid.*

16. In the second volume of *Lettere* the letters to Bianca Garufi emphasize in an agonizing way the ambivalence, the ambiguity, the interchange of art and life typical of Pavese. For example, in the letter quoted, p. 61: "Now I am unduly obsessed with the personal 'revelation' in your chapter—the ferocious things Silvia's stupid ferocity make me do. I was well aware when I started on this book that the undertaking would bring to the surface all the pus we have inside us, and I am not afraid of the words—but I also know that these words express a subconscious that has had for us and still has a significance that is not only literary. Add to it your letter and this larva of Roman life we have lived. All of this is atrocious"; but in another letter, on the following page: "Remember that the succession of our chapters is based on an illusion. For example *you* related the conversation on the cliff; I pick it up again and allude to the conversation *as if I had related it*. What I mean to say is that each of the two protagonists is not writing continuously as if he didn't know about the other; by this device the novel avoids the possible unpleasantness of a double autobiography: ours is a work of art not of unburdening"; then again, March 27, 1946, p. 69: "From now on I shall live with visor down with everyone, you included. To some I'll even show my moustaches, to others only my eyes, but the fact is this: I trust no one. One day I won't even trust myself, then peace." At this point it is a question of misogynism rather than inability to communicate.

Chapter 5. *The Honey of a Problematic Mind*

1. Salinari, *op. cit.*, p. 172. On the following page the author explains that in the context of the poetic under consideration, Pascoli's myth of childhood "cannot be confused with Leopardi's desperate contrast of illusion with reality, nor with Carducci's momentary

pause in the eternal brawls that burn in his heart, and which he doesn't want to and cannot placate, nor again with Pavese's much later one, richer in intellectual ferment and more troubled by sexual inhibitions and fed by historical footholds." Observations on Pirandello and nature are on pp. 28off.; cf. also his conclusions on Pavese and European decadentism in Salinari's other book *La questione del realismo* (Florence: Parenti, 1960), pp. 54–57 and 89–99.

2. *Feria d'agosto* (Turin: Einaudi, 1946) is the only collection of short stories published in Pavese's lifetime; it has the following introduction: "It is not always novels that are written. One can construct a reality by bringing together and exposing efforts and experiences which have pleased us each individually, and yet, since they tend to free us from the same obsession, become adventure and counter-adventure. Here, as in all adventures, it is a question of blending two fields of experience. And the answer could be this: only when one is a man does one know how to be a boy." The quotations from the short stories in this chapter are based on the Italian text in *Racconti*, except for the translations by A. E. Murch for those stories contained in *Festival Night* and *Summer Storm* (see Chapter 2, note 1). On *August Holiday* there are two interesting letters by Pavese to Silvio Micheli: January 22, 1946, *Lettere*, II, p. 55: "Don't you get the feeling of the hick who has come to town? Except for 'First Love,' which was written in '37"; and August 14, 1945, II, pp. 24–25: "I too am purely a countryman in origin and tastes, but an impenitent city-dweller in life. I find that each of these surroundings brings regret for the other and therefore helps one enjoy the other."

3. Other examples are in "Freewill": "Alexis is obsessed by the idea that, subconsciously, every child is constantly testing and probing within himself the instincts, the desires, the voices he will follow when he is grown up"; and in "The Langhe Hills": "I don't know who said that we must go carefully in making plans when we're boys, since they will be realized when we are mature. If this is true, I want to repeat that the whole of our destiny has been formed already in our bones, even before we reached the age of reason." But even more than Pavese's short stories, *The Burning Brand* is full of observations on childhood, destiny, and adulthood. For example: "Whatever happens to a man is conditioned by his whole past" (April 10, 1936, p.

47); "Almost all men, it seems, can retrace, in their childhood, the signs foreshadowing their adult agony. To investigate this hotbed of retrospective discoveries, alarming as they prove to be, is to see the sufferings of the grown man predicted by the irreparable acts and words of his infancy. *I Fioretti* of the Devil. Contemplate this horror always: what has been, will be" (November 26, 1937, p. 73); "One cannot change one's nature" (January 5, 1938, p. 87); "I wish I could always be sure, as I am this morning, that since the will power of an adult is conditioned by the hundred thousand decisions he took as *an irresponsible child*, it is ridiculous to talk of free will. One gradually acquires characteristics *without even knowing how*, and beyond question, one acts in this way or that according to one's personality" (January 16, 1938, p. 89); "What one does, one will do again, indeed has probably *already done in the distant past*. The agonizing thing in life is that it is our own decisions that throw us into this rut, under the wheels that crush us. (The truth is that, even before making those decisions, we were going in that direction)" (April 4, 1941, p. 210); or April 25, 1938, p. 102 and May 24, 1938, p. 104. Finally, in a letter to Carlo Musso, March 15, 1948, *Lettere*, II, pp. 224–6, Pavese describes the screenplay of a film: after portraying plot, characters, and themes, he concludes: "As you can see, it is the story of *destiny that cannot be escaped:* the same thing happens to each one of us, we meet the same people, and are faced with the same situations."

A different aspect of childhood is seen in the following entries in Pavese's diary: "The keen interest K. P. Moritz takes in *childhood recollections* is a method of discovering evidence of a state that existed prior to life. During infancy it is still fresh in the memory and leaves traces. . . . Hence their anxiety to identify themselves with The [Whole], which appears to be the same as pre-natal reality" (May 22, 1941, pp. 212–213, on Béguin); "Modern art—for what it is worth—is a return to infancy. Its perennial theme is the discovery of things, a discovery that can come about, in its purest form, only in the memory of infancy" (February 12, 1942, p. 220); "As a child one learns to know the world not—as it would seem—by immediate initial contact with things, but through signs of things: words, pictures, stories" (August 31, 1942, p. 229. It will be remembered that a similar attitude inspired J.-P. Sartre's *Les mots*.)

4. In this connection there is an interesting observation in Pavese's

entry in his diary for September 17, 1939, p. 154: "We give alms to a beggar to rid ourselves of the sight of the poor wretch; and if such a one upsets us by his display of utter misery, appealing to our sense of some obvious, undeniable kinship with him, then we loathe him with all our might." One will remember Stefano's similar attitude in *The Political Prisoner* to the picturesque beggar.

5. We are reminded of Pavese's words referred to by Lajolo, pp. 11 and 13: "I'm a vine that has been overfertilized. Perhaps this is why I feel the parts I thought were healthier rotting inside me. You, who come from the hills like me, you know that too much manure makes the worms multiply and destroys the harvest." And then later: "Now the worms have devoured all the roots, and the vine, yellow with Phylloxera, is dead. It's time to end. I want to do it like a stoic, but am I a stoic?" Compare, too, the poem "Atavism" (in *Poesie edite e inedite*, p. 103):

> "The boy wanted to go out
> naked like that—the street is everyone's—and drown in the sun.
> It's not possible in the city. One could in the country,
> were it not for the depths of the sky over one's head,
> which terrify and depress one. There's the grass, which is cold
> and tickles one's feet, but the shrubs gaze
> unwaveringly, and the tree trunks and bushes are severe eyes
> for a weak and pallid body that's shivering.
> Even the grass is different and becomes repugnant to the touch."

Remember, too, the poem "Dina's Thoughts" (*ibid*, p. 46). With reference to the short story we are examining, Pavese writes in the diary, September 2, 1944, p. 271: "You have dealt up till now with two kinds of savage. In "Nudism" you have touched upon what is savage to the adult, the virgin countryside, that which has not yet been spoilt by the human hand (and here it is implicit that any work, any rite, can justify nature). In *Storia segreta* you have described the savage that is in a boy, something that is remote and evasive, even if, and in fact more so, others succeed or have succeeded in seizing it. (In both cases this is what we are missing, 'that which we do not know.')"

6. There is a very important passage in the diary, December 17, 1949, p. 350: "Generally speaking you must remember that in the

years between 1943 and 1945 you were reborn in isolation and meditation (in fact during 'that' period you theorized and lived your infancy)." Another note synthesizes the development in Pavese's thought: "Your conviction that what one was as a child he will be as an adult, and never will the 'span of his bridge' become shorter or longer, has now lost all its dreariness and has moved into the realm of the search for the fantastic roots of the 'instant-eternity' " (May 22, 1944, p. 262).

7. Among the critics who have emphasized the importance of childhood in Pavese, R.-M. Albérès, *L'aventure intellectuelle du XXe siècle. Panorame des littératures européenes 1900–1959* (Paris: Editions Albin Michel, 1959), p. 336, notes that Pavese, Vittorini, and Elsa Morante "always present the same problem: how is the transition effected from that absolute that is the world of childhood to the illusionism and *imbroglio* of lies that constitutes the world of adults? One Italian writer at least died because of this problem: Cesare Pavese." Also, Giorgio Pullini, *Il romanzo italiano del dopoguerra* (Milan: Schwarz, 1961, then Padua: Marsilio, 1965), p. 12, elaborating on Salinari: "The theme of childhood as an ideal, lost age, which is the pivotal point of Proust's narrative and of Joyce's, at least in *Dedalus*, i.e., of the two most representative authors of the twentieth century avant garde in Europe, not to mention the *illusione* of Leopardi and the *fanciullino* of Pascoli, is at the source of almost all of Pavese's work, and has been fully theorized by him in his critical writings." Leopardi, in *Zibaldone* (I, 1259), had written: "Often a boy knows quite a bit more than the philosopher, sees truths and motives clearly which the philosopher only sees confusedly or doesn't see at all."

8. *Lettere*, II, pp. 637–639. Also, in a letter to Alberto Carocci, December 27, 1935, *Lettere*, I, p. 488, Pavese, referring to his friend's book *Paradiso perduto*, said it pleased him also "because of a certain vein of similarity (the paradise of *childhood* and of adolescence, seen not so much for its milk and honey, nor examined intently, but viewed in its human interest and wonder)."

9. Furio Jesi, "Cesare Pavese, il mito e scienza del mito," in *Sigma*, pp. 95–120. Jesi's article is not only essential in finding and defining the sources of Pavese and of a whole historical-cultural climate, but it is also a sensitive interpretation of Pavese's soul, his attitude

towards art and death, which was partly determined by that climate: "The only mystification to which he didn't want or know how to resort was the one that would enable him to recognize explicitly his own actual ability to attain those myths. To give it the name of its greatest author, it was the mystification of Thomas Mann. Contrary to Mann, Pavese did not acknowledge that the Faustian compromise was an acceptable way to art, and he remained orthodox in his religion of death, and in his more nihilistic aspects" (p. 120). Jesi is even more successful in his comparison of mythical figures such as Concia in *The Political Prisoner* and Cinto in *The Moon and the Bonfires.*

10. *Ibid.*, p. 106.

11. The quotations in this section are taken from Pavese's *La letteratura americana,* which contains four pieces originally included in *August Holiday:* "Of myth, symbol and other things," "State of Grace," "Adolescence," and "Job-Sickness." They were considered essays and not included in the volume of *Racconti.*

12. The beginning of the passage "Of myth, symbol, and other things," was sketched in Pavese's diary, September 17, 1943, pp. 241–242; among the parts omitted in the definitive version there is the following passage: "Here again we see that the return to childhood is like satiating the thirst for myth. . . . Could these feelings be our religious emotions?"

13. *The Burning Brand,* February 12, 1944, p. 257. Also December 28, 1944, p. 276: "The very suggestion that the subconscious may be God, that God lives and speaks in our subconscious mind, has exalted you. If, with this idea of God, you review all the thoughts of the *subconscious* scattered here and there in this work—don't you see? —you are changing all your past and discovering many things. Above all, your toilsome research for the symbol is illumined by its infinite significance." These notes mark the most explicitly religious moment of Pavese's life; but we also notice that his religiousness is felt mostly as the function of his own art: "It must not be forgotten that *God* means also a technical cataclysm—symbolism built up through years of following the gleam" (January 9, 1945, p. 276).

14. *Ibid.*, November 6, 1938, p. 132. The entries for November 19, 1939, p. 158, and January 1, 1940, pp. 164–5, concern the image-story. Lienhard Bergel, "L'estetica di Cesare Pavese," in *Lo Spettatore*

Italiano, VIII (October, 1955), pp. 407–421, especially p. 415, analyzes the passage in myth from *langue* to *parole;* Enzo Noè Girardi, *Il mito di Pavese e altri saggi* (Milan: Vita e Pensiero, 1960), especially pp. 16ff., writes on "Individual Myth," "Infancy and Memory," and "Myth and Presence."

15. This thought of Pavese's can be compared with a similar concept expressed by Alfieri in his *Vita scritta da esso:* "Now behold, reader, in me the little man that I am, the portrait of both you and of all those men who have been and will be; we are all always, if we think about it, perpetual children"; there is no need to point out Alfieri's debt to Rousseau.

Chapter 6. *The Hubbub of Actions*

1. Marcel Raymond, *De Baudelaire au Surréalisme,* p. 48, transcribed by Pavese into his diary, February 10, 1941, pp. 206–207.

2. The quotations in this section are from the *Racconti* (except for A. E. Murch's translation of "The Villa on the Hill," in *Festival Night*), and from *The Beach,* translated by W. J. Strachan (London: Peter Owen Ltd., 1963).

3. The seafaring background is found in another of Pavese's short stories, "The Adventure," in which are found such refined images as the following: "Nanni was standing in the strip of sun and smoking a cigarette. In its rays the smoke spirals looked like silk, or like the veins of some precious wood."

4. Pavese never considered *The Beach* important, as the essay "The Influence of Events," in *La Letteratura americana,* p. 248, shows: "*The Beach,* on the other hand, a short novel of mine that is neither brutal, proletarian, nor American—and which fortunately few have read—isn't a chip of the monolith. It was a diversion of mine, a human one, and, in other words, I would be ashamed of it if it were worth the effort. It is what is called an open experiment in style." Nevertheless, in the diary, January 18, 1941, (missing from the American edition) he notes: "*The Beach* is finished," and later he will take up again "the short novel" in relation to *The Devil in the Hills.* Then there are two interesting passages in *Lettere,* I: the first is a biographical note of Pavese's, p. 620: "Four men hover around

the woman and to each his own world is felt like a presence, an uneasiness outside of what is happening"; the second is in a letter to Fernanda Pivano, July 21, 1943, p. 717: "In 1940 I felt an aesthetic enthusiasm for you (whence the poetry) which, with effort, I transformed into a moral attachment (whence the little novel *The Beach*)."

5. Mario Praz, *La carne, la morte e il diavolo nella letteratura romantica*, translated by Angus Davidson, *The Romantic Agony* (London: Oxford University Press, 1933). In listing examples of romantic-decadent sadism in the work of Delacroix, Praz describes precisely "the bloody corpse of the beautiful youth Saint Sebastian, from which a woman's delicate fingers are plucking the arrows" (p. 141).

6. *The Burning Brand*, February 21, 1938, p. 98. Remember Eugenio Montale's poem *"Falsetto"* in *Cuttlefish Bones*, where the poet describes Esterina swimming in the sea while he remains ashore.

7. Leone Piccioni, *Lettura leopardiana e altri saggi* (Florence: Vallecchi, 1952). A confirmation of Fitzgerald's influence on Pavese and an idea of its extent can be gained from a letter Pavese sent to Lajolo together with a copy of *The Beautiful Summer:* "Do you remember my speaking to you about Fitzgerald? When I brought you *Tender Is the Night?* I think I spoke even more about Fitzgerald with Maria Livia Serini. I myself didn't want to translate this man's books for the publisher's because I was too fond of them and also because I was already intent on writing something on the same lines myself": in Lajolo, p. 340.

8. The quotations in this section are taken from *The Devil in the Hills*, translated by D. D. Paige (New York: Noonday Press, 1959). For the women see the following passages from the novel, which are all pervaded with a certain misogyny: "I didn't tell her, but I was glad that the women in the house were all elderly or only children"; " 'The great thing is the way they keep their women,' Pieretto said. 'We were outside drinking and telling stories and they and the brats were in the kitchen, but they weren't breaking their hearts' "; "Also, the fact that Poli had a wife disturbed me at the moment. All our past with him became prohibited ground, became an obstacle. What could we talk about any more?"; " 'The fact is, they [the women] lack any sort of interior life. They lack liberty. That's why they're

always running after someone they never find. . . . There are real *Femmes damnées.*'"

9. "We talked about Poli as a boy and of the need for solitude that sooner or later seizes everybody"; or "Lights were blazing all over and gave me a sense of solitude"; this last sentence vaguely echoes the streetlights in *Work Is Wearying*.

10. "Towards evening little old women, street pedlars, the uprooted, always sat on those benches . . . ; and they were bored, they waited, they grew old. What were they waiting for? Pieretto said that they were waiting for something enormous, the collapse of the city, the apocalypse. Sometimes a summer storm drives them away and washes everything clean"; "Going home to study was senseless; I was too accustomed to live and argue with Pieretto and wander about the streets; in the air, in the movement, even in the dark of the avenues there were more things than I could understand and enjoy"; "What! . . . And night and day you're thinking about how to get out of the squirrel cage. Why do you suppose we go beyond the Po? . . . Only you're mistaken: the most unforeseen things happen in a room in Turin, in a café, on a tram . . .'"; and the diary, November 11, 1948, p. 327: "Another discovery: the pleasure of going into a suburban café you have never seen before, watching the gamblers and the few customers, savoring the life of a world that you have always felt outside of, that yet seems to hold so much of your own past and the hopes you had then."

11. *The Burning Brand*, January 30, 1941, p. 204.

12. *Ibid.*, May 22, 1941, p. 212.

13. "Then Pieretto—I heard him take a deep breath—threw out that awful shout, lacerating it in his own manner and then laughing scornfully. A trampling of feet in the house followed, doors creaked, and from a distance Oreste's faint voice replied."

14. In the diary, March 17, 1940, p. 175: "If it were possible to have a life absolutely free from every feeling of sin, what a terrifying vacuum it would be! It can be said that this feeling ('the forbidden thing') is in life what the difficulty of the material is in art."

15. *Ibid.*, December 6, 1935, p. 38.

16. *Ibid.*, September 2, 1944, p. 272. This reflection is prepared by others: July 13, 1944, p. 266: "Nature becomes savagery when some forbidden thing happens; bloodshed or sex. . . . [Wherefore it is

plain that that which is savage is not what is natural but what is violently superstitious. What is natural is impassive.] . . . If a man falls from a fig tree in a vineyard and lies prone on the ground in his own blood, that does not seem to you 'savage,' as it would had he been stabbed or sacrificed." And again, August 23, 1944, p. 269: "To fall from a fig tree and lie stretched in a pool of blood is not an unnatural event, not 'savage,' but becomes so if it is regarded as a law of life. If, in one way or another, blood gushes forth in torrents on the ground and [if *by nature* beasts devour each other] and if the fallen man has no rights of appeal, that is savage because our feelings would prohibit such a thing; a mere event, not a law. Here one's natural feeling is to blame nature, which, by its very lack of feeling seems to be performing a rite and to be, itself, superstitious. Every inadequate theodicy is superstitious. When any vindication of the justice of God is superseded, it becomes superstition. Justice, as long as it is just, is natural."

17. Praz, *op. cit.*, p. 102. This may be the moment to note that Pavese, when he speaks of his own literary formation, emphasizes his own "discovery of Baudelaire" (diary, July 4, 1943, p. 240).

18. Pavese, "The Villa on the Hill" in *Festival Night*. Moreover, the following are examples from the novel, chosen from many possible ones: " 'These fields have a flavor of the sea,' I said, putting my head down to tie open half of the shutter. 'Look down there. It even looks like a sea' "; "The voices retreated under the moon. I sniffed the odor of the pines in the still warm air. It was nearly a seaside odor, pungent."

19. July 30, 1944, p. 268.

20. May 1, 1948, p. 322.

21. In *The Beach*: "We also ascended a stretch of the main road which crossed the valley. By then it was towards evening when the sun already low over the plain filled the air with fine sunbeams and the acacia flowers were beginning to shiver in the breeze."

22. July 25, 1944, p. 268.

23. The narrator had said: "All that remained of my infancy were those summers. The narrow streets which led into the fields on every side, during the day and in the evening, were gateways to life and the world. It was a great marvel when a motor car, coming from God knows where, honked its way through the main street of the town

and went on, God knows where, to new cities, towards the sea.
. . ."

24. Another example is the following curious and beautiful image: "We looked about for a moment in the cool and colored shade. At the far end the altar gleamed whitely, like a piece of nougat; and there were many flowers and a small lamp."

25. In this connection Pavese states in his diary, August 19, 1944, p. 269: "What is so charming about Vico is his constant wandering between what is savage and what is rustic, each trespassing in the other's field. The whole of history is reduced to this germ."

26. *Ibid.*, February 3, 1941, p. 206.

27. *Ibid.*, October 23, 1940, p. 197; and on October 22, p. 196: "A person counts for what he *is*, not for what he does. Actions are not moral life; the way we treat others is only well or ill. Moral life is the eternal, immutable existence of the ego. Actions are only the ripples on that sea, whose real depths are revealed only in tempests, or not even then." In the polemic with Professor Augusto Monti, who had reproached him for having presented "people to be hated rather than loved" (*Lettere*, II, p. 461), Pavese asserted, in reply, that he wanted to make a distinction between the "humanity of someone who works and is useful for something and the humanity of someone who, because he does not work and is not useful, goes to rot and stinks" (*Ibid.*, p. 460, already quoted by Lajolo, p. 344); it would seem that Monti was right in seeing beyond Pavese's expressed and conscious intentions, that he was fascinated despite himself by that very bourgeois and futile world he wanted to stigmatize and to which, ambiguously, he found he belonged himself. Cf. also Italo Calvino's letter, *Lettere*, II, p. 409, note: "In order to write well about the elegant world one must know it and suffer it to the marrow like Proust, Radiguet, and Fitzgerald; loving or hating it doesn't matter; what matters is to know exactly one's own position in respect to it. You aren't clear about that, and it can be seen from the way you return to the theme so persistently, it isn't true that you couldn't care less. . . ."

28. In the diary, September 17, 1942, p. 230: "We live in a world of things, facts, deeds, which is the temporal world. Our ceaseless, unconscious effort is to reach out beyond time towards the ecstatic moment when our liberty will be realized."

29. There are many entries in the diary concerning *The Devil in the Hills:* July 24, 1948, p. 325: "Lovely company—a cry in the night" (the motif of the first chapters); October 7, 1948, pp. 325–326: "On 4th October, *Diavolo in collina* was finished. It has the air of something big. It is a new language; dialect[al], written with an atmosphere of culture and introducing 'student discussions.' For the first time you have really set up symbols. You have revitalized *La Spiaggia*, putting into it young men who make discoveries, the liveliness of debates, mythical reality"; and December 18, 1948, p. 330: "R. says: 'Neither the proletarians nor the bourgeois will like it.' [Well]. . . ." Pavese's reactions to the first reviews by famous critics are interesting: January 19, 1949, p. 333: "Well? I shall not say: 'Is that all, and now what?' I knew what I wanted, and I know what it is worth now that I have it. I wanted to go on, take it further, absorb another generation, become everlasting, like a hill. Hence no delusion. Only a confirmation. . . . Yet, what sound insight I had, what a coincidence of will and destiny! What if the value lies in this and not in the works?"; and December 1949, p. 351: "R. has told you (talking of *Diavolo sulle colline*) that your work gives the impression of a young man, and is rather alarming because of that; you are handling a material that may fly to bits. I did not quite understand this. But was it entirely complimentary?" Finally in *La letteratura americana*, p. 294: "the examination of the paradox of what is country and what is the civilized life of the city, what is the elegant life and what is vice, in *The Devil in the Hills*."

30. Cf. Chapter 2, note 5. On suicide in the life and work of Pavese Solmi has sharp and sensitive observations, *op. cit.*, pp. 251ff.

31. Quotations in this section are taken from *Among Women Only*, translated by D. D. Paige (New York: Noonday Press, 1959). On the opening of the novel, there is an interesting passage in the diary, December 25, 1948, p. 331: " 'I came to Turin at carnival time, as students and mountebanks used to, in olden days.' " With reference to *Among Women Only*, in *Lettere*, II, pp. 408–9, there is the exchange of letters between Pavese and Calvino, who had defined his friend's novel as "one of Gulliver's journeys, a journey among women, or better still, among strange beings half woman half horse"; "a new way of seeing women, and of getting even with them lightheartedly or sadly." He goes on to observe that lesbianism in the novel "is only a magic word for indicating something obscure or

forbidden practised by the woman-horse. One is reminded of Pasiphae rather than Sappho: or of strange rites with a horse penis made of beechwood." Calvino concluded: "And the true message of the book is an intensification of your teaching of solitude with something new added on the sense of work, on the system work-solitude, on the fact that human relationships not based on work become monstrous, on the discovery of new relationships born of work." Pavese replied: "Horse qualities and penis of beech are pure and lovely invention. . . . You—squirrel with a pen—you, you calcify an organism when you dissect it into fable and *slices* of life. Shame on you."

32. On Gozzano's Turin the final observations are by Mondo, *op. cit.*, pp. 103ff.

33. Pavese wrote in his diary, October 15, 1940, p. 195: "We obtain things when we no longer want them"; and in more detail, February 8, 1949, at S. Stefano Belbo, p. 334: "For glory to bring us pleasure, the dead would have to rise, the old grow young again, absent friends return. We have dreamed of it in a tiny setting, among familiar faces that for us were all the world, and we want, now we are grown up, to see the reflection of our deeds and words upon those faces, in that little place. They have vanished, scattered, died. They will never come back. Then we despairingly look around, trying to re-create the little world that left us alone but wished us well, and now should be amazed at us. But it no longer exists." The motif of the impossible return often reappears in the novel: "If they weren't dead, they'd make you laugh now. What could you have in common with them any more?" Momina asks Clelia, in a cold and distant tone, then teasingly; and again: "You get these things when finally you can live without them." And finally in a letter to Doris Dowling, July 6, 1950, *Lettere*, II, p. 543: "The trouble about these things is that they always come when one is already through with them and running after strange different gods" (in English in the original).

34. Reference to the *haute* is in the diary, August 21, 1940, p. 191: "Whatever people say, the fastidious, formal manner of the upper classes is preferable to the slovenly easygoing behavior of the common middle class. In moments of crisis the first know how to act, the second becomes an uncouth brute."

35. Cf. the diary, November 2, 1940, p. 198: "If a man does not save

himself, no one can save him." A manuscript variant is identical with the sentence quoted in the text. And in a letter to Fernanda Pivano, January 17, 1943, *Lettere,* I p. 667: "You must save yourself by yourself: it is the only way one can save oneself"; again in a letter to Monti, January 21, 1950, in Lajolo, p. 343, now *Lettere,* II, p. 468: "If one doesn't save oneself, no one will."

36. There comes to mind an observation from the diary, November 6, 1938, p. 132: "I spent the whole evening sitting before a mirror to keep myself company. . . ."

37. In this connection there is a letter to Monti, January 18, 1950, in Lajolo, p. 344, now in *Lettere,* II, p. 460: "The girl who committed suicide [Rosetta] is basically an ingenuous victim; she is the most innocent of them all, and if she dies it is precisely because, of them all, she is the only one still able to feel what is missing (except of course Clelia)."

38. *The Burning Brand,* March 23, 1949, pp. 336–337: "Without seeming to, I have begun my new novel: *Tra donne sole.* A clear-cut, assured work that presupposes a sound construction, inspiration that has become habit. (It takes up again the theme of *La Spiaggia, La Tenda,* and several poems about women.) It should bring out something new"; April 17, 1949, p. 338: "Discovered today that *Tra donne sole* is a great novel; that the experience of being engulfed in the false, tragic world of high society is broad and congruous, and blends well with Clelia's wistful memories. Starting from her search for a childish, wistful world that no longer exists, she discovers the grotesque, sordid tragedy of those women, of Turin as it is, of her own realized dreams. Her discovery of herself, and the emptiness of her own world, which saves her ('I've got everything I wanted')"; May 26, 1949, p. 340: "Today, *Tra donne sole* is finished. Each of the concluding chapters written in a day. It came with extraordinary, questionable facility. Yet it clarified itself little by little, and the great discoveries (journey through a world dreamed of since she was a little girl, and now vile, hellish) came to me after about a month, in early April. I tackled it with a good heart. But I wonder whether I was playing with lay figures, miniatures, lacking the grace of a stylized creation. But the basic idea, was it not tragic?"

39. Letter to Ponina Tallone, January 2, 1930, in *Corriere della sera,* November 17, 1963, now in *8 poesie inedite e quattro lettere a*

un'amica, p. 39, and in *Lettere*, I, p. 163. In one of the first entries in the diary, October 2, 1936, p. 61, Pavese speaks of his "hatred of noisy crowds . . . disgust at spiteful actions."

40. April 10, 1949, pp. 337–8. Cf. the letter to Sturani, May 10, 1926: "The only support left me in the world is the hope that my pen is worth, or will be worth, something. But then if I think about it, even that seems empty. . . .": in Lajolo, p. 67, now in *Lettere*, I, p. 20. Also the self-portrait Pavese sent to Pivano, November 5, 1940, seems important in this connection: "For all P.'s belief that art and life should be kept completely separate, that writing is a profession like any other . . . he hasn't succeeded in accepting his existence as anything other than a gigantic spectacle that *he* is performing. But whoever compares life to a spectacle usually means that the spectacle isn't to be taken seriously, that life is a toss-up, and things like that. Instead it happened that P. performed with a terrible seriousness. . . . He has the appearance of a tragic poet who rises among his characters to kill or be killed. Now, P., who is a hermit without a doubt, because when he became an adult he realized that one could do nothing that was worth anything unless he went far from the business world, is the living martyr of these contrasting needs," in Lajolo, p. 257.

Chapter 7. *The Others*

1. Most of the quotations from the *Racconti* of Pavese in this chapter have been taken from the English translation by A. E. Murch, *Summer Storm*. The quotations from "Vespa," "The Castle," and "The Captain" are from the original text. The passages from *Il compagno* are taken from the English translation by W. J. Strachan, *The Comrade* (London: Peter Owen, 1959). The passage quoted above continues: "Garofolo opened the counter and took the little bottles of perfume out of the glass showcase. As they sniffed at them, her own subtle perfume pervaded the air, warmer and more delicate. After the cologne came violet, then the 'Notturno.' . . ." We are reminded of a poem Pavese wrote in high school, the one in which he describes how, standing in front of the window of the perfumery, he gazes fondly at the women, at their "proud image gathered into a

small space": "They make up my big garden of life" (in Lajolo, pp. 86–88).

2. Later: "So the days went by. There was often snow or fog, and it was nice and warm in the cinema." We remember the poem "Landscape VI": "This is the day when the mists rise from the river / in the beautiful city, in the middle of the fields and hills. . . ."

3. In the same short story there is yet another of Pavese's typical motifs: "Corradino . . . always kept a certain distance from Vespa, not from pride but for his peace. He didn't want Vespa to get too used to people like them and become too intrusive. Their relationship with each other was that of officer and sergeant."

4. The same theme as in "The Captain" is also explored in the fragment "The Group" but less successfully.

5. Pavese has notes on this novel in his diary, October 26, 1946, p. 298; November 7, 1947, p. 312; and especially October 8, 1948, p. 326: "I opened *Compagno* at random and reread some of it. It was like touching a live wire. Its tension is well above average, due to the smooth cadence of the phrases; a surging forward constantly frustrated, a breathless excitement."

6. Compare the following passage in *La letteratura americana*, p. 256: " 'Tomorrow [Pieretto] tells us what he has done and what he has said,' grumbled Masino, and we laughed. 'He likes the telling more than the doing.' 'Like those who write' I said. 'Masino, would you like to know how novels are written? This way. You go off your own and go for a walk. You pretend nothing happens. Then you come back and tell a story. Not what has happened, something a little less and something a little more. That's how you write novels.' "

7. For example: "I walked for half an hour without meeting anything but carts. I could hear them in the fog and then their lamps appeared just above road level. . . . I finished the night in the station café. All the streets were empty, and it was the only café open. Here the only fog was the steam from the espresso machine; a colder smell came from outside. . . . We dawdled round the lake in the car. Linda remarked—not to me—'How beautiful it is!' Even Lubrani turned to look at the reeds and the mist over the water"; and Linda's words too: " 'I recall one morning when there was a thick fog and it seemed as if the whole world was cut off from me. You couldn't even hear footsteps. . . .' " Finally, an entry in Pavese's diary, May 31, 1946, p.

294: "I noted the abstract shapes of the long, high city streets; smelt, this morning, [the constant dampness of the mist that coats everything with haze]. Here there is nothing of the dryness or the sharply defined colors of Rome." This observation reflects well the sharp distinction between the two parts of *The Comrade,* the Turin episode and the Rome episode.

8. Pavese wrote in his diary, August 5, 1940, p. 189: "It is a [sure] sign of love to want to know, *to relive,* the childhood of the other"; and again, August 30, 1942, p. 229: "Love is desire for knowledge." Moreover, we must remember the memories of Linda herself, among which we find another typical motif of Pavese's, nudism: "She told me about how when she was by the sea at San Remo she had gone to bathe alone from a boat and once she had got away from the shore had removed her swimsuit and sun-bathed in the nude. 'It was wonderful,' she said. 'We all ought to be naked. If people went about the streets naked, it would be much better.' "

9. Similar thoughts reappear later in reference to Gina, the blonde proletarian girl: "[Other] times while I chatted and joked with the others I would suddenly feel [a wave in my blood and knew] that she was expecting me. It became more [beautiful] to hang about with the others until late."

10. Pavese wrote in his diary, July 10, 1947, p. 309: "You sigh for the country, for 'the savage,' but you appreciate the good sense, the moderation, the clear understanding of people like Berto, Pablo, the man in the street."

11. Also the following passage: "That day I understood that the press can convince as well as threaten. It hadn't occurred to me before." The quoted passages show clearly that Pavese is anxious to link politics and culture, culture and life. One could paraphrase Pavese's own definition of Melville: "a *peasant* who has studied, who is well-read": and apply it to him (in *La letteratura americana,* p. 95).

12. Also, p. 81: "Some days I tried to imagine [old things], that this woman was not la Bionda at all and that we could stay together. I had the same kind of feeling you have when you are getting over a fever: the slightest thing touched me in my blood"; and p. 93: "I [thought that nothing] was new and that some one else [was] going round with me in Rome instead of Gina, and we would laugh and

drink wine together. . . . I was bound to see her again one day; something would happen. Then I remembered Amelio and I felt upset."

13. For example: "The evenings by this time had a smell of the country in them. I would have given my eyes to have gone along to the Paradiso as I had done before. Those had been the nights for love-making"; in Rome, "in the restaurants we saw road-menders and masons; there was a smell of lime and all day long we could hear the thud of the rams and pickaxes"; "I was near the piazza Venezia and I could smell [that stink] and hear [that] voice [i.e., Mussolini's]. You could smell and hear it all as you looked at the vast buildings and newspapers—the passers-by seemed to bear it along with them too. I turned the corner and got into narrow and noisome streets. Had not the Romans done their [pissing] there since time immemorial? I passed down the via Lungara to see the prisons. The same odor [broiling in the sun] was there too"; "I could hear children shouting on every side and there was the same smell of litter, food and warmth that you got on the crowded beach"; or finally, one of the last times that Pablo and Linda meet: "We ascended the Spanish Steps, and there was no one else there. We kissed under the trees for a while. 'How wonderful it is,' she said. Mingled with the scent of the trees was her own."

14. *The Burning Brand*, January 8 or 9, 1940, p. 166. For confirmation, cf. some of Pavese's letters, *Lettere*, I: to his sister Maria, June 24, 1935, p. 393 ("Everyone knows that I have never been concerned with politics, but now it seems that politics are concerned with me"); to Alberto Carocci, October 24, 1935, p. 454 ("The only thing that doesn't interest me—*ab aeterno* and I'm speaking with my hand on my heart—political literature"); to Fernanda Pivano, August 2, 1943, p. 719 ("I am not a politician and have nothing to gain from politics"); to Giaime Pintor, August 23, 1943, p. 728 ("Dear Pintor, on the whole I'm nauseated by the publishing house's involvement in politics, which has held up work for a month"); and in Vol. II, to a friend, November 25, 1945, pp. 39–40 ("And now I'll confess some other things I'm ashamed of. . . . I have to make an effort to listen to politics").

15. *La letteratura americana*, p. 237 (from "Communism and the Intellectuals"), italics added.

16. *Ibid.*, p. 243 (from "Concerning a New Literature").

17. *Ibid.*, p. 218 (from "Return to Man"); and in his letter to Fabrizio Onofri, September 9, 1947, *Lettere*, II, p. 162: "It would be enough if one could succeed in getting the intellectuals and the proletariat to live together without suspicion and repugnance, in giving the intellectual classes a taste for mixing with the working crowd."

18. *La letteratura americana*, p. 242: "We move in the midst of bloody realities, and a man of good will can let his conscience suggest the choice of alternatives. Collaboration with others, with one's neighbor, can be exhausting, desperate—never impossible. The presence of others and the position taken by them shows us the way" (from "Concerning a New Literature").

19. *Ibid.*, p. 221: "One must understand others, have compassion for others, since this is the only way of understanding and loving oneself: this is where culture begins" (from "Reading").

20. *Ibid.*, p. 232: "Even Italian history of the last few years demonstrates for whoever wants to see that the intellectuals can find in communism the most useful means of realizing a concrete intellectual freedom. The direct experience of the war of liberation has discredited many of the more banal calumnies which fascism circulated successfully concerning communism. Men of all parties . . . in collaborating with the Communists have noticed their directness and humanity, which had been unknown. But most of all they have come into actual contact with the political concreteness and consistency of these comrades" (from "Communism and the Intellectuals").

Elio Vittorini had similar affirmations (in *Il Politecnico*, a critical anthology ed. by Marco Forti and Sergio Pautasso (Milan: Lerici, 1960), pp. 165–167: "I did not register with the Italian Communist party for ideological reasons. When I registered I hadn't yet had the opportunity of reading a single one of Marx's or Lenin's or Stalin's works. . . . I was joining a struggle and men, . . . the best that I had ever known, and the best in everyday life too, the most honest, the most serious, the most sensitive, and at the same time the happiest and most alive. . . . "

Finally on the same subject there is an entry in Pavese's diary for March 5, 1948, p. 320: "Fundamentally, humanistic intelligence—the fine arts and letters—did not suffer under fascism; they managed to follow their own bent, cynically accepting the game as it was. Where fascism exercised vigilance was in preventing intercourse between the intelligentsia and the people, keeping the people uninformed. Now the problem is to [get out of] the privilege we enjoy[ed]—servitude—and not to *approach* the people but to *be* the people, to live by a culture that has its roots in the people and not in the cynicism of the free Romans."

21. *La letteratura americana*, p. 219: "To speak. Words are our job. . . . Words are tender things, intractable and alive, but they are made for man and not man for them. . . . Our task is difficult but it is a living one. It is also the only one that has meaning and hope. They are men who are waiting for our words, poor men like we all are when we forget that life is community. They will listen to us with firmness and trust, ready to incarnate the words we speak" (from "Return to Man").

22. *Ibid.*, p. 238, already partially quoted in Chapter 1, note 4. In this connection one should remember also the letter to Massimo Mila, November 10, 1945, *Lettere*, II, p. 34: "I have finally regularized my position and registered with the Communist party and am in that much a better position to sustain and maintain the vitality of the Turin branch [of the publishing house Einaudi] which I think of as my fief from birth"; the letter to Ernesto De Martino, November 18, 1949, p. 438, in reference to editorial policies: "If we have to be rigorous even in this matter, then we should first decide whether we are Marxists or idealists, and I would be the first not to know how to answer"; and the diary, February 15, 1950, p. 357: " 'Pavese is not a good Communist.' . . . Tales of intrigue everywhere. Shady counterplots, that could then be the talk of those who are nearest your heart."

23. *La letteratura americana*, p. 244 (from "Concerning a New Literature").

24. About "The Family" Pavese noted in his diary, April 4, 1941, pp. 209–210: "Nothing is more essential when beginning a work of art than to make sure of a *richly productive standpoint*. . . . A good example would be my discovery this morning that the story of Corradino could be told in the third person, but surrounding the events with an atmosphere of the first person plural, which not only gives a setting, a background to the over-free Corradino, but—an

immense advantage—enables one to treat him ironically." On the novel, there are two entries, the first of which seems to reflect the moment of solidarity and participation, the second the solipsistic withdrawal (emphasized by the title "Fear," which was never used but which reflects so much of Corrado's character): November 11, 1947, p. 313: "The *Casa in collina* may be the experience that has culminated in *Ritorno all'uomo*"; and October 8, 1948, p. 326: "Strange. The women tolerated and hated in *Paura* have names beginning with E; the desired and intangible ones have names beginning with C: Elena, Elvira; Concia, Cate." Still on the topic of the novel are the entries for January 12, 1948, p. 316, and December 15, 1949, pp. 349–350. Many critics, especially Asor Rosa (*op. cit.*, p. 214) and Bàrberi Squarotti (*op. cit.*, pp. 185–188) have emphasized the beauty and importance of *The House on the Hill* among Pavese's works.

25. The quotations from "The Family" are taken from A. E. Murch's translation in *Summer Storm* and those from *The House on the Hill* are taken from the translation by R. W. Flint, included in *The Selected Works of Cesare Pavese* (New York: Farrar, Straus & Giroux, 1968).

26. In his diary solitude is seen to be the basic and constant essence of Pavese's existence. It is sufficient to remember the sentence that became tragically familiar: "I spent the whole evening sitting before a mirror to keep myself company" (November 6, 1938, p. 132).

27. An autobiographical entry in the diary might be mentioned here; it was written January 26, 1938, p. 94: "Didn't you once act just as badly yourself? Remember how you got rid of E. . . ." Once again it is a clear example of the master-slave dialectic.

28. Cf. an entry in the diary, September 30, 1937, p. 65: "The only women worth the trouble of marrying are those a man cannot trust enough to marry."

29. Also from "The Family": "I've never had a child to support. . . . Never got involved with anyone. That's the way I'm made. I've known plenty of women and always left them in the end"; "I discovered—and this is the point—that I had always treated people, especially women, in the same way: known them and dropped them. With no one had I made common cause; I had shirked all my responsibilities"; "The few women he had known began passing

through his mind, creating a crescendo of remorse. . . . He had treated all those women in the same way, gently; he was incapable of talking to any one of them like a man; he was too wrapped up in his self-isolation. He might at least have treated them roughly, mastered them, raped them. That morning he felt he had violated them all by letting himself be violated; first, the prostitutes, with whom he always passed for a man of good position, a gentleman of distinction. . . . And all of them . . . ended by breaking away from him, angered and disappointed by his unconquerable indolence." In addition, in the diary, April 10, 1936, p. 47: "afraid of getting tied up," Pavese writes, referring to his own work; or again April 20, 1936, p. 49: "My need is to avoid responsibilities"; September 6, 1936, p. 58, taken up again on March 23, 1938, p. 100: "You will . . . never become obsessed by one of those ideas worth dying for, as you know from past experience."

30. An example, in *Racconti*, pp. 506–7: "It didn't seem possible to me that all that had happened. There would come a day when life would be safe and stable like it was that moment. I had forgotten about it for too long. The bloodshed and pillaging couldn't go on forever. . . . I didn't see a living soul in the little square and the little heaps of brown roofs that yesterday had seemed to me such a safe hiding place now looked like dens to me from which one would smoke out the prey. The problem was just to go on resisting the flame until one day it was burnt out. One had to go on resisting so in order to find hope intact one day."

31. Furthermore, in the same novel (*The House on the Hill*): " 'This kind of war is nothing new.' I said. 'A day comes when we all find ourselves alone.' " And later the description of the state of mind of the teacher Castelli and his colleagues: "Furthermore, to be honest about it, hadn't he already been living, stubborn and solitary, as if in a cell? But now we were all living like that, behind four walls in fear and expectation, and every step, voice, every unexpected move caught us by the throat."

32. For example: "Many women used to intimidate me, but not Cate. With her you could easily lose your temper without losing her. It was a little like asking for something to drink at a country inn: you don't expect a great wine but you know what you're getting. Cate sat still and let you make love. Then she would get panicky lest anyone see us. We didn't have much to say, and this encouraged me.

It wasn't necessary for me to talk or make promises. . . . [Some]times, to her great delight, I bought her a stick of rouge, and it was then I understood that one can support a woman, educate her, give her a good life, but as soon as one knows too much about what her elegance is composed of, then goodby magic. Cate's dress was threadbare and the leather of her handbag cracked; it was touching to listen to her, so great was the contrast between her life and her desires. But her joy in the rouge got on my nerves, made me realize that for me it was all mainly sex. . . . The idea of being tied to her or of owing her something for the time she had given weighed on me always."

33. Other examples: Cate "said that now we had to unite—shout, strike, make ourselves felt. For a while, she said, there shouldn't be any raids and we had to make the most of it, force a peace from the government. She already knew how little the government was worth. 'They're all the same,' she said. But this time they were afraid, had to save their skins. All they needed was a shove." Or when Cate's old woman says, "Go and tell that to someone who works. If you have your loaf of bread and can stay on the hill, the war is a pleasure. It's people like you [the narrator] who brought on the war." Or again the narrator: "This war is bigger than it may seem. The people have seen their former masters running away and now nobody is in charge. But you can take my word for it, they mean revenge not only on the Germans, not only on them; they have it in for the Fascists, too. It's not a war of soldiers that might end tomorrow; it's a war of the poor, the war of people desperate with hunger, poverty, prison, corruption."

34. An entry in Pavese's diary is extremely important in this connection: "My stories—in so far as they succeed—are tales by an onlooker who watches things greater than himself take place" (February 21, 1942, p. 221).

35. We are reminded of Pavese's reaction to the news that his friend Leone Ginzburg had died in prison: "I had the news on 1st March. Do others exist for us? [I wish it were not true in order not to suffer.] I am living in a sort of fog, thinking of him all the time, but vaguely. I shall end by making a habit of this state, always postponing real grief until tomorrow; so one forgets, and has *not* suffered" (*The Burning Brand*, March 3, 1944, p. 258).

36. In *Il sentiero dei nidi di ragno* (Turin: Einaudi, 1947), re-

viewed by Pavese, October 16, 1947, now in *La letteratura americana,* pp. 273ff.

37. This is what Pavese wrote about Edgar Lee Masters' feelings about his Spoon River dead: in *La letteratura americana,* p. 55. We should also consider the evidence of Lajolo, who had given Pavese his own diary to read on the war of the partisans, and got this answer: "Your pity for the dead enemy pleased me" (in *Il "vizio assurdo,"* pp. 287–88). Pavese himself emphasized the protagonist's significance in *The House on the Hill* in several letters addressed to friends or critics who were interested in the book: especially in the letters to Monti, January 21, 1950, *Lettere,* II, p. 467, already in Lajolo, p. 343, ("The story curves from the protagonist's proud solitude, through the example of others' simple sacrifice and the human enormity of the events, to the compunction and humble simplification of the ending, to his pity for the dead"); and to Rino Dal Sasso, March 20, 1950, p. 496, already in Lajolo, pp. 348–9 ("I wanted to portray a hesitant person, a solitary man who, through or despite his cowardice, discovers values or at least understands by intuition that there are new values [such as a meaning in death, humility, understanding of others etc.]").

38. In the essay "Concerning a New Literature," in *La letteratura americana,* p. 242, Pavese states that the work of the writer "seems destined to bring with it separation, isolation"; "to get on with this work we must isolate ourselves, and not just materially: the effort we exert on ourselves to listen in, tends to . . . put us in opposition to material things, to make us indifferent, unaware of them. We set out to understand and possess the very depths of reality and the result is that we are enclosed in a fictitious world that resists reality. And so of course we suffer. . . . We remain, or become again, adolescents." Finally, it seems to be significant that the only protagonist of Pavese's who was really able to sacrifice himself for others remains only faintly sketched in a script for a film in 1950 ("Due sorelle" [Two Sisters], in *Cinema Nuovo,* n. 141, September–October 1959): it is a sketch of a mature woman (like the woman in *Among Women Only*) who lets herself be humiliated and sacrificed in order to protect her younger sister, ending with the final emblematic embrace. Other documents on this subject are Pavese's diary, May 12, 1950, p. 363, and the correspondence between Pavese and Constance

and Doris Dowling, *Lettere*, II, pp. 494 and 513ff., March–May 1950: after many changes in title and content, the film script sketched out for the two sisters never came to anything.

39. The fragility of Pavese's position is very clearly shown in one of his letters to Fernanda Pivano, June 4, 1943, *Lettere*, I, p. 706: "One understands that, roughly speaking, others don't even exist; but one must make a gift of oneself precisely because it is the only way to make them exist, and so not be alone any longer. . . . *To give oneself* means *to respect oneself*, above all, that is to spend the day nurturing one's own virtues, one's own strength, one's own soul and culture in order to make them *of use* for something."

40. *Lettere*, II, pp. 490–1, already in Lajolo, pp. 347–8. Also in his letters to Emilio Cecchi, January 17, 1949, p. 340, and to Carlo Muscetta, May 11, 1950, p. 521, Pavese rightly refutes the strictly political connotation of his book (as well as of *Tiro al piccione* by Giose Rimanelli).

Chapter 8. *The Smile of the Gods*

1. *La letteratura americana*, pp. 321–323.

2. *Dialogues with Leucò* was a book Pavese was very fond of, and he described it in one of his essays as "perhaps the least unsuccessful thing I have put on paper" (*La letteratura americana*, p. 293). In his diary there are numerous passages that refer to or prepare the dialogues. There are meditations on the wild or the superstitious (pp. 256, 266, 269–272, 299, 308, 309), on ancient peoples and gods (pp. 276, 281, 289, 297, 298, 301, 302, 314, 315), personal echoes and landscape references (pp. 88, 284, 285, 293, 301, 311), observations on the form and significance of these dialogues (pp. 297, 304, 310, 346–7). On the last point in particular there is an interesting entry on July 10, 1947, p. 309: "You preach order by describing disorder."

Also in his *Lettere*, II, there are numerous letters that announce, accompany, or follow the publication of the dialogues: to Neri Pozza, undated, p. 49 ("These little pieces of dialogue that I am writing condense for me an experience and a deprivation that have existed for years"); to Bianca Garufi, February 26, 1946, p. 60 ("This

morning I sent you another little dialogue, 'In the Family,' which I
think you will like. It deals with the same old problem of the *femme
fatale* but with irony"); to Bianca Garufi, March ? 1946, p. 72 ("My
dialogues express fundamental sentiments through an extremely dangerous play of literary allusions. . . ."); to Franco Fortini, October
27, 1947, p. 189 ("*Leucò* the big scandal"); to Paolo Milano, November 25, 1947, p. 196 (". . . my *Dialogues,* that heretical book I'm so
fond of"); to Tullio and Maria Cristina Pinelli, December 3, 1947,
pp. 200–201 ("I must explain to you that not being involved in
politics is one form of involvement; . . . not to study language is one
way of studying it, etc. . . . Must I explain to you? This being said, I
don't give a damn about *The Comrade.* Are you happy? By now you
have received *Dialogues with Leucò,* which I knew you were very
anxious to get, but not to this extent. Seeing them in print gave me a
bad impression: they are small, stunted, and cute. . . ."); to Bona
Alterocca, December 11, 1947, p. 203 ("*Leucò* is a book with a curse
on it and nobody dares make a pronouncement on it. . . ."); to
Antonio Giolitti, November 26, 1948, p. 312 ("It doesn't seem possible that *Leucò* isn't understood, but that makes me happy. It means
it's just like the second *Faust*"); to Billi Frattini, July 20, 1950, p. 553
("Perhaps you are trying to tell me that you see *Leucò* as my visiting
card for my descendants? Few understand it"). See also Lajolo, p. 315
and ff.

3. The cultural climate in which Pavese's interest in mythology
matured can be traced back, as we have seen in Chapter 5, to German
poetry of the late nineteenth century, then to Thomas Mann and the
expressionists on one hand and to the ethnologists on the other.
Among the latter, the main ones are Lévy-Bruhl, Frobenius, Frazer,
and Walter Otto, from whom Paula Philippson and Karl Kerényi
(with his Jungian component) derived; Robert Graves should also
be mentioned. For Pavese, Vico is naturally the link between the
ethnologists and classic authors.

On Pavese's sources and their meaning there are two important
essays: Maria Luisa Premuda, "I *Dialoghi con Leucò* e il realismo
simbolico di Pavese," in *Annali della Scuola Normale Superiore di
Pisa,* Series II, Vol. 26, fasc. 2 (Pisa: 1957), pp. 221–249 (on the
derivations of many of the dialogues from Frazer's *The Golden
Bough*); and Eugenio Corsini, "Orfeo senza Euridice: I *Dialoghi con*

Leucò e il classicismo di Pavese," in *Sigma*, pp. 121–146 (on derivations from Nietzsche, Otto, Philippson, and Kerényi, especially in relation to the contrast between chaos and order, Olympicism and Titanism, and also, for Kerényi, the Olympic characteristic of the smile of the gods; remarkable, too, for the distinction between a "classicism of the traditional type" and a "restless and morbid classicism" of a decadent type to be found in all of Pavese's work, starting with "The Goat-God").

There are numerous references to classicism and ethnology in Pavese's diary; for example: "Your classical knowledge stems from the *Georgics*, D'Annunzio and the hill of Pino . . . and could easily become prehistoric ethnography," June 3, 1943, p. 238 (and further to p. 242); also pp. 60–61 (Lévy-Bruhl), 155 (Lavelle), 158–9 (Landolfi; Lévy-Bruhl), p. 265 (Herodotus, Homer, Vico), 272–3 (Herodotus), 275 (Vico), 278 (Mann and Vico), 293 ("ethnology"), 296 (Frazer), 309 (Nietzsche, Dionysus), 309–310 (Harrison, Nilsson), 314 (Harrison), 348 (*Specimens of Bushman Folklore*). In Pavese's *Lettere*, II, he writes in detail of all the motifs, names, and interests mentioned above; the amount of editorial correspondence for the ethnological series is impressive, particularly the letters to Mario Untersteiner and to Rosa Calzecchi Onesti, pp. 241ff. (on the translation of Homer, and also Philippson's influence on "The Mares"); the letters to Giuseppe Cocchiara (for example, p. 347 on Robert Graves, and p. 474 on *Specimen of Bushman Folklore*) and to Ernesto De Martino (for example p. 406, on Frazer, "the book which converted me to ethnology"). In Vol. I it is enough to mention the letter to Fernanda Pivano dated June 27, 1942, p. 640, in which Pavese, referring to the *Georgics*, asserts, "They are not beautiful because they describe the life of the fields with feeling . . . but because they imbue the whole countryside with a secret mythical reality; they go beyond appearances; they reveal even in the act of studying time or sharpening a scythe, the vanished presence of a god who has done it or shown how to do it."

4. *The Burning Brand*, p. 256, February 7, 1944.

5. Cf. Eugenio Corsini, *op. cit.*, p. 146: "He [Pavese] is rather like the Orpheus of his dialogues, who descends into his hell and contemplates all the horror of death and dissolution. But from this descent into Hades he returns alone, without Eurydice, i.e., without being

able to understand others and communicate with them, alone with himself and his myths, empty shells and dried-up forms incapable of blossoming and receiving the fertile graft of reality."

6. The quotations from the dialogues are taken from Cesare Pavese, *Dialogues with Leucò,* translated by William Arrowsmith and D. S. Carne-Ross (Ann Arbor: University of Michigan Press, 1965). With little formal variations, the preface to the dialogues is in Pavese's diary, February 20, 1946. The last Italian edition of the dialogues (Turin: Einaudi, 1965) includes some unedited notes on the preparation and chronology of the individual dialogues.

7. Gaspare Giudice, *Pirandello* (Turin: UTET, 1963), p. 278. Another important example of natural images for the problematic in question can be found in the short story *"Canta l'epistola":* "To have no more awareness of being, like a stone, like a plant; . . . to gaze at the blue sky and the dazzling white clouds, swollen with sun; to hear the wind, which makes a noise in the chestnuts in the wood like the sea, and in the voice of that wind and in that roar as from a distant infinity is the vanity of everything and the agonizing boredom of life." The same passage is repeated almost word for word in Book II, Chapter 9 of *Uno, nessuno e centomila;* even the end of the novel has the same tone, the same poetic images, the same significance: trees, clouds, wind, whilst "the city is distant"; the pantheism becomes explicit in the last lines: ". . . because I die every moment and I am born again, without memories: alive and whole, no longer in me but in every thing outside of me."

In this connection Salinari, *Miti e coscienza del decadentismo italiano,* p. 280, writes: "In Pirandello the motif of defeat, which only appears on the fringe of D'Annunzio's *superuomo,* is asserted with complete awareness at the heart of his work. And the other motif appears indirectly, that of nature as a place and condition to contrast with society: where the one is chaotic, the other is organic; where the one is tormented in its self-awareness, the other is simple, ignorant, and happy. It is worth while to say that in him are found the two extremes of the struggle of contemporary consciousness." Cf. too a note of Carlo Michelstaedter made in 1906 (in his *Opere* [Florence: Sansoni, 1958], p. 440, note 1): "I need to expand, to get relief from the filth, to shake off the weight of vanity, to be mirrored in someone like myself but better, greater, in nature itself. If only I could communicate with nature, obliterate myself, and identify with it, feel the spiral of an infinite superhuman expansion of all that stirs within me and makes me suffer. . . ."

8. It is worth noting that Hyacinth is completely mediated by Apollo. For example: "Didn't he perhaps think of the god as a model, an older friend, a brother he trusted and looked up to?"; Apollo "treated Hyacinth like an equal, like someone of his own age, and the names of Aglaia, Eurynome, and Auxo, distant smiling women, young women, who had lived with the god in strange intimacy—he spoke their names casually, calmly, with an idle relish that made Hyacinth shiver. This was how the boy lived, and felt. When he was with the god, everything seemed easy and clear. He felt he could do anything."

The same relationship of mediation can be seen in the words of Sappho, in the dialogue "Sea Foam": "How can you accept a force that seizes you and turns you into desire, into shuddering desire that struggles over a body, a man's or a girl's, like the foam between the rocks? And this body rejects you and crushes you, and you fall and long to embrace the rock, to accept it. Sometimes you are the rock yourself, and the foam and the tumult are twisting and turning at your feet. No one is ever at peace."

In his diary, February 15, 1938, p. 96, Pavese gives himself some advice about the way to behave towards a woman: "Be the rock and no longer the wave." In reference to Apollo, in the diary, July 28, 1947, p. 310, Pavese describes him as "the sender of all evils. Cf. *Fiore* [and] *Cavalle*, where he appears in such a guise and only in such a guise."

9. Cf. *Lettere*, II, Pavese's letter to Lalla Romano, April 20, 1950, p. 509: "I've been away for a month—Hades and the Elysian Fields (reread "The Lady of Beasts" in *Dialogues with Leucò* and you'll know my state of mind) and I thank you for your letter in which you were so moved. We who have been touched by the gods are much more sensitive to a caress than we let on." Almost the same expressions but with a different desperate accent are found again in the letter to Lajolo, August 25, 1950, p. 570 (already published in Lajolo, p. 371): "With the same obstinacy, with the same stoic determination of the Langhe hills, I will make my journey into the kingdom of the dead. If you want to know what I am like now,

reread "The Lady of Beasts" in *Dialogues with Leucò:* as usual, I foresaw it all five years ago." A whole chapter of the biography is entitled "The Lady with the Harsh Voice."

10. Praz, *op. cit.,* pp. 205–206. Otto Hahn, "Pavese ou la création lucide," in *Les Temps Modernes,* XVI (December, 1960–January, 1961), pp. 801–838, analyzes Pavese's masochism.

11. Aphrodite seems to emphasize Pavese's suffering; in the diary November 27, 1945, p. 283, she is described as the one who has "come from the sea," and with a simple transposition the same definition is attributed to Pavese's last woman, August 13, 1950, p. 365: "It's something very different. It is she who came from the sea." But above all, see two of the last notes before his death: "Yet even you are only a pretext. The real fault, apart from my own, lies with that '[tormented, restless one who smiles to herself]' " (August 16, 1950, p. 365), and "I have been stoical. Was that heroism? No, I made no real effort. And then, at the first onset of this '[tormented, restless one]' I have fallen back into the quicksand. Ever since March I have struggled. Names do not matter. They are only names that chanced to drift my way . . ." (August 17, 1950, p. 366); the preceding March 25, p. 361, he had written: "One does not kill oneself for love of *a* woman, but because love—any love—reveals us in our nakedness, our misery, our vulnerability, our nothingness." The motif of the smile appears in one of his first poems, called "A Memory" ("She smiles alone/ the most ambiguous smile, walking along the street"), and concludes one of his last poems "The Cats Will Know" ("You will smile alone, the sad smile/that you smile alone"). Instead, the other image, "you have come from the sea," appears in the poem "You Have a Face of Sculptured Stone."

12. Prometheus, too, says that the gods "don't know how to laugh or cry. They smile at destiny." Both Prometheus and Orpheus refer to destiny with a typically Pavesian sentence: "What has been, will be," and Oedipus asserts something similar: "What's the point of doing something that was as good as done before you were born?"

13. Solmi, *op. cit.,* p. 249: "There is, in the background, the piercing sensation of that mysterious short circuit sex-death, which finally sets fire to the narrative with a point of tragic light: that relationship in which the author is so instinctively and passionately interested, retracing its poetic and mythical incarnation in the pri-

mitive world and in life today in the city and the country, the active
essential symbol of a process of disintegration (and the awareness of
this necessarily became tragic for him even on the vital plane)."

14. "To roam the streets and find marvels, that is the great incen-
tive, yours especially": Pavese's diary, April 25, 1945, p. 280; and the
dialogue "The Friends": "That's why men drink at night. Has it ever
occurred to you that a child doesn't drink because for him death
doesn't exist? . . . What I mean is, when we were always together,
playing and hunting, and the day was short but the years never
passed, did you know then what death was, your death? A boy can
kill himself, but he doesn't know what death is. Then suddenly comes
the day when you understand, death is inside you, and from that
moment on you're a grown man. You fight and dice, you drink, you
wish the nights away. . . ."

15. Apropos of this dialogue there is an entry in Pavese's diary,
May 27, 1947, p. 306: "One also finds out what they meant when they
said that Hesperia was the land of the dead. The two faces of a
country before history passed over it and afterward resemble each
other. They are nature. 'Nature' is the kingdom of the dead." In the
same dialogue the motif of solitude is also remarkable: "Is that all,
Virbius? You want company? . . . Mortals always end by wanting
that. Why? Is it something in your blood?"

16. The "hoarse voice" is important (apart from any biographical
reference) in relation to the preceding words of Circe: "I wasn't
granted a god in my bed, and the only man was Odysseus. All the
others turn into animals at my touch; they go crazy and come after
me, like wild beasts. . . . But with them I mustn't even smile. I feel
them mount me and then run off back to their lairs. I don't lower my
eyes."

17. For example, the following description is given by Mélita as
she stands at the window with the breeze swelling the curtain: "Oh
king Jason, it's lovely from up here. The docks are crammed with
people and there's a big ship going out between the boats. It's so clear
you can see it reflected upside down in the water. Oh, look at the
flags and the prows hung with flowers—if only you could see them!
And what a lot of people! They've even climbed up the statues on the
docks. Now the sun's in my eyes." It is like a painting of Carpaccio's.
Similar descriptions reminded Giuseppe De Robertis of Massimo

Bontempelli's *Giro del Sole*. There is an echo of this dialogue in Pavese's diary, November 27, 1945, p. 282: "I watched the dawn just now, from the side windows. There was haze, stillness, and a human warmth. Astarte-Aphrodite-Melita is still sleeping. She will wake in a bad humor. For the third time, my day has come. The keenest pang of my grief is to know that grief will pass. Now it is easy to feel humiliated, but what next?"

18. The passage quoted is an echo of Leopardi's *"Aspasia."*

19. "The Poetics of Destiny," in *La letteratura americana*, p. 342, italics added.

20. In Pavese's diary, April 2, 1947, p. 305: "The gods know and see, thanks to their magic-rational nature, and with detachment. Men act, not magically, with pain. They give names; that is to say that they solve their problems in creative terms"; and in the last dialogue, "The Gods": "With a simple name they [men] told the story of the cloud, the forest, the fates."

21. "You're young, Iacchus, and you don't know that they discovered us in blood. You course restlessly through the world, and for you death is like wine: exalting, an ecstasy. But you forget that mortals have suffered every story they tell of us. . . . This is why I said they discovered us in blood. If for them death is the end and the beginning, then they have to kill us in order to see us reborn." Dionysus then tells the story of Icarius who taught the herdsmen how to grow the grapes, and they "tore him to pieces like a goat among the scrub and then buried him in order to grow more wine"; his daughter, Erigone, couldn't "round off this story except by hanging herself in the sun like a bunch of grapes."

22. Lajolo, p. 318: "Pavese, when he sent me the *Dialogues with Leucò*, wrote that, with due proportions, he had wanted to try his own *Operette morali (Short Moral Works)*." One of the most severe of Pavese's critics undoubtedly is De Robertis, who wrote in *Saggio sul Leopardi* (Florence: Vallecchi, 1960, 4th edition), p. 35: "Whoever of us, some years ago, wanted to follow Leopardi's example and compose mythical fables, discovered often that he had gone back to those juvenile essays [*"sopra gli errori popolari degli antichi"*], to that kind of pre-Leopardianism."

23. Foscolo's words, the epigraph to this chapter, are quoted by Pavese in "Adolescence," originally in *August Holiday*, now in *La*

letteratura americana, p. 315. In Pavese's diary, December 30, 1940, pp. 200ff., numerous passages from Foscolo's literary essays are mentioned. There is another reference to Foscolo in the entry for February 4, 1948, p. 318: "Falqui is a good fighter. His column 'Laboratorio' in *Fiera Letteraria* is always written with great intelligence. His idea of comparing Didimo's prose with Leopardi's, and then contrasting it with the style of the romantics who wrote in dialect is an excellent one."

24. For example, the unknown dead soldiers in *The House on the Hill* and *The Moon and the Bonfires*, and the three sisters in the latter novel. On *Dialogues with Leucò* and Foscolo's *The Sepulchres*, see Ruggero Puletti, *La maturità impossibile. Saggio critico su Cesare Pavese* (Padua: Rebellato, 1961), p. 171: "In that Romantic poem . . . poetry is made to eternalize the memory of magnanimous heroes, the echo of legendary deeds. . . . Instead, in Pavese's conception poetry is the humble tale of our past; it insures continuity between a sad present and an equally sad yesterday, which we delude ourselves into thinking was happy. Poetry does not stimulate us to "noble things," it does not exalt but rather consoles and moves us, making our days less monotonous, and our sorrow less bitter. Such poetry is closer to Pascoli's conception, which symbolized poetry in the humble lamp that 'keeps a gentle watch' over the affairs of our existence. . . ." Eugenio Corsini, *op. cit.*, p. 145, also speaks of Pavese's arrival at "a disguised and completely modern religion of the word."

25. *La letteratura americana*, p. 295. On myth, one should recall: Pavese's essay "To Tell a Story is Monotonous," in which the rhythm of the story is compared with that of swimming (*ibid.*, pp. 335–340); *Lettere*, II, the letter to Mario Untersteiner, January 12, 1948, p. 211 ("You have read the *Dialogues* exactly as I dreamed of them being read: unraveling the motifs, *interpreting* them . . . just as if it were a mytholgical document. Could I wish for more? Certainly the meaning of this confusion which the *Dialogues* are even for me, is to be found in the search for human autonomy"); and the letter to Paolo Milano, January 24, 1948, p. 218, in which Pavese, after asserting that the contemporary quality of myth justifies the dialogues, concludes: "Finally, I won't hide from you that my ambition in composing this little book was to become a part of the

illustrious Italian tradition of leisurely humanistics, from Boccaccio to D'Annunzio. Being the greatest barbarizer of our literature, . . . it was a luxury I had thought of giving myself for a long time."

26. *La letteratura americana*, p. 330. He goes on: "The poet, as such, works and studies in solitude, he is separated from the world; he knows no other duty but his own lucid and driving determination for clarity, to destroy the half-glimpsed myth, to reduce the unique and ineffable to normal human measure. The ecstasy or confusions on which his gaze is fixed must all be contained in his heart, and there filtered in an imperceptible process that goes back at least to his adolescence, like the slow agglomeration of salts and juices from which they say truffles grow. . . . The poet can only say he has done it when the clarity is evident to everyone, when it is common property and in it can be recognized the general culture of his time": thus he will have completed "his specific job as conqueror of unknown territory" (*ibid.*, pp. 332–333).

27. *Ibid.*, p. 341. In this connection in the diary there is an important entry for January 17, p. 356: "We are in this world to transform destiny into freedom (and nature into causality)."

28. *La letteratura americana*, pp. 342–343.

29. *Ibid.*, pp. 69–70.

30. *Ibid.*, p. 344.

31. *The Burning Brand*, August 16, 1950, p. 365.

Chapter 9. *The Stranger in the Hills*

1. *La letteratura americana*, p. 295.

2. There are many references to this novel in *The Burning Brand;* for example: May 13, 1948, p. 323: "Collect all your typical situations (you were born for this): violence and blood in the fields—merry-making in the hills—a walk around the summit—the sea from the shore. . . . Luckily, these situations are many. 26 Nov. '49 *Is this not the theme of The Moon and the Bonfires?*"; October 16, 1949, p. 344: "*La luna e i falò:* That is the title I have had in mind ever since the time of *Dio caprone*. Sixteen years. I must put everything into it"; the theme of return is in the entry for April 23, 1945, p. 280: "The religion of Herodotus. So many countries, so many portents. This is

not only the book of the 'grande route,' but also the book of the breathless quest for a fatherland, for the footprints left by the ancestors." Interesting notations are also in *Lettere*, II, especially in the letters to Adolfo and Eugenia Rusta, July 17, 1949, p. 399 (with the announcement of the original inspiration for the novel, "almost a wonderful vision"); to Constance Dowling, April 17, 1950, pp. 506–507 and May 19, 1950, p. 525 (with personal references to the American actress who should have been "the fittest patron saint" of *The Moon and the Bonfires*); and most of all to Lajolo, May 15, 1950, p. 524: "I know that *La luna e i falò* is my real novel, but it is good to hear someone say it, especially for its social and partisan themes, where it is so difficult to keep the tone and not make mistakes, if only political ones."

3. The quotations from *The Moon and the Bonfire[s]* in this chapter are taken from the Penguin edition, London, 1963, of the translation by Louise Sinclair, first published by John Lehmann, 1952.

4. This subject is also on pp. 24 and 107, and especially in the diary, February 13, 1949, p. 334: "Strange, the moment when (at thirteen or twelve) you left your country home, had your first glimpse of the world, and set out, buoyed up by fancies (adventures, cities, names, strong rhythms, the unknown). You did not know you were starting a long journey that, through those cities, adventures, names, delights and unknown worlds, would lead you to discover how rich in all that future was your moment of departure. . . . The world, the future is now within you as your past, as experience, skill in technique, and the rich, everlasting mystery is found to be the childish you that, at the time, you made no effort to possess."

5. Later: "What does it all mean then? That you need a village, if only for the pleasure of leaving it. Your own village means that you are not alone, that you know there's something of you in the people and the plants and the soil, that even when you are not there it waits to welcome you. But it isn't easy to stay there quietly"; and further on: "I told him that it hadn't been America that had done it so much as the rage at not being anybody, the wild desire, more than to go away, to come back one fine day after everyone had given me up as dead of hunger."

6. Fernandez, *Le roman italien et la crise de la conscience mo-*

derne, p. 198, remarks: "The family would still be the hateful 'other' and the return to one's home country would not be that return purely to oneself that it must be." Evidence of Pavese's realistic scruples in writing about a bastard is contained in his letter to Pinolo Scaglione, January 9, 1950, *Lettere*, II, p. 452, where Pavese thanks his friend for providing him with "details of the assistance given by the foundling hospitals to the families who bring up foundlings and of the salaries paid to agricultural laborers" in the region of the Langhe. Scaglione's letter with this information is reported in a footnote.

7. March 30, 1948, p. 322. Pavese's comprehension of time in its contrasting aspects can be linked to his interest in ethnology, and actually seems in line with recent conceptions of anthropologists, such as E. R. Leach's "Two Essays Concerning the Symbolic Representation of Time," in *Rethinking Anthropology* (London: London School of Economics; and New York: Humanities Press, 1966), pp. 124ff. Pavese knew Mircea Eliade's *Cosmos and History*.

8. And again: "What use is this valley to a family that comes from across the sea and knows nothing about the moon and the bonfires? You must have grown up there and have it in your bones, like wine and polenta, and then you know it without needing to speak about it and everything you have carried about inside you for so many years without knowing awakens now at the rattle of the chain on a cart, at the swish of an ox's tail, at the taste of a bowl of minestra, at the sound of a voice heard in the square at night. . . . Could I explain to anyone that what I sought was only to see something I had seen before? To see carts and haylofts, to see a wooden bucket, an iron gate, a chicory flower, a blue-checked scarf, a gourd to drink out of, the handle of a zappa. I liked the faces, too, the same as I'd always seen them; the old wrinkled women, the cautious oxen, the girls with flowers, the roofs of the dovecotes. It seemed as if only seasons had passed since I saw them last, not years"; further on: "To me the best about these days was that everything was done in its season, and each season had its own customs and its own games, which varied according to the work and the harvests and the rain or the fine weather"; finally in the diary, April 3, 1949, p. 337: "Before Christ and the Greek Logos, life was a constant close contact with nature, a continual exchange of magic between men and nature; whence came power, determination, destiny. One turned to nature and was regenerated."

9. *La letteratura americana*, p. 183. The following are some of the
innumerable examples possible: "His house stands halfway up the
slide of Salto and looks on to the highway; there is a smell of newly
sawn wood there, of flowers and shavings, which, in my first days at
La Mora, seemed to belong to another world because I came from a
poor cottage with a threshing floor—a smell which meant the main
road and the bands and the big houses at Canelli where I had never
been yet"; "And there was the smell, the smell of the house, of the
watercourse, of rotten apples, and dry grass and rosemary"; "I smelt
dry grass and a salty wind and I thought of the hills at Fresno";
"When they passed back again into the scent of the lime trees, Silvia
and her sweetheart were walking along together, whispering and
laughing. The other pair came more slowly, walking a bit apart from
each other, and sometimes they called to the pair in front and carried
on a conversation with them in a loud voice. How well I remember
these evenings, the farmhands sitting on the crossbeam, among the
strong, strong scent of the lime trees"; "For years afterwards, a gust
of perfume from lime trees in the evening had been enough to make
me feel a different being, to feel my real self, without quite knowing
why"; "I like the girl, she pleased me as the tang of the air does some
morning or the feel of the fresh fruit on the roadside stalls of the
Italians"; "I liked being in this open space among the plane trees,
hearing the sound of the trumpets and the clarinet and seeing all the
people kneeling down and running about and the Madonna coming
out of the big door, swaying on the shoulders of the sacristans. Then
came the priests, the boys in their surplices, the old women, the
gentry, the incense, and all the candles in the sunshine, the brightly
colored dresses, and the young girls."

10. Peter M. Norton, "Cesare Pavese and the American Night-
mare," in *Modern Language Notes*, LXXVII (January, 1962), pp.
24ff.

11. Gaminella is also on pp. 6–7, 71, and 148: it is the sacral hill
where "high up" there took place the sacrifice of Santa.

12. The festivals are mentioned frequently in the novel: Anguilla
came on "the Feast of the Assumption" and among the festivals he
recalls there are the one he was left out of and the one when he
accompanied his young mistresses in the gig; the bonfires on the
Feast of John the Baptist are mentioned on pp. 42 and 104; for the

mythical significance of the festival, Pavese writes in *La letteratura americana*, pp. 345–6: "The myth is that which happens and rehappens endlessly in the sublunar world and yet is unique, outside of time, like a recurring festival; each time it takes place it is as if for the first time, at a time which is the time of the festival, of the nontemporal of the myth."

13. Nuto tells how some boys had captured two gypsies who were playing a double game: ". . . instead of taking them to headquarters they take them and put them down a well and make them tell how often they'd been to the militia barracks. Then they tell one of them, who had a fine voice, to sing for his life. And he sings, sitting on top of the well, tied hand and foot, he sings like mad and puts all he has into it. While he's singing they take a mattock to them and lay them both out. . . ."

14. December 6 and 8, 1938, pp. 140–141; and December 10, 1938, p. 142: "Everything that has happened to us is of inexhaustible value; each time we think about it it makes it more far-reaching, endows it with associations, gives it a deeper significance. Childhood is not only the childhood we really had, but the impressions we formed of it in our adolescence and maturity. It seems the most important epoch because it is the one most enriched by our long succession of thoughts about it."

15. *La letteratura americana*, p. 361.

16. The figure of Candido is in *Racconti*, p. 454, quoted in Chapter 5. "Smoking Cheap Cigarettes" is in *Poesie edite e inedite*, p. 30:

"He took me to hear his band. He sits in a corner
and puts the clarinet to his mouth. . . .

                         Powerfully, my poor friend
grips everyone to the depths. And the clarinet twists,
breaks through the roaring din, goes beyond, escapes
like a lonely soul, in a dry silence.

            . . . and my friend leads them tiredly
with his hands that are hardened from swinging a sledge

                                  hammer,
and using a plane, from beating out a living."

17. For example: "When I told Nuto what I used to say to the boy,

he pursed his lips as if to put the clarinet to his mouth and shook his head hard. 'You're wrong,' he said; 'you're wrong. Why are you putting ideas into his head? As long as things don't change, he'll always have a bad time of it.'"; "Nuto listened with his lips pursed up as if he had put the clarinet to his mouth, and through the window I saw the flowers in the room and the mirrors and Irene's straight back and the effort of her arms and her fair hair against the page."

18. Cf. Pavese's diary, April 12, 1949, p. 338: "A newspaper black with headlines like a storm."

19. It is interesting to read a note made by Pavese in his diary, at Santo Stefano Belbo, July 1, 1942, pp. 226–227:

"When the moon is *old:*		When the moon is *new:*
	Sowing flowers they come	
beautiful and with thick stems		sickly and slim and elegant
	Cutting down trees, they will be	
healthy		wormeaten
	Except the pine tree which will be	
wormeaten		healthy
	Washing the sheets with ashes will make them	
clean and good		dirty—the ashes will filter through
	Pruning the vine and the buds will be	
harmful		fruitful."

Or, in the novel, another of Nuto's affirmations: "What do you expect? It's the same moon for everyone, like the rain or sickness. It doesn't matter whether they live in a hole in the ground or in a fine house, blood is red everywhere."

20. *The Burning Brand*, January 17, 1950, p. 356; and on the

following page, February 1, 1950: "Will power can be applied to myth in order to transform it into history. Destinies that become freedom."

21. Jesi, "Cesare Pavese, il mito e la scienza del mito," p. 112. Jesi's affirmation is closely related to the German poetics as found in Mann, Broch, and the expressionists.

22. John Freccero, "Mythos and Logos: The Moon and the Bonfires," in *Italian Quarterly*, IV (Winter, 1961 [actually 1960]), pp. 3–16.

23. A poem comes to mind, in *Poesie edite e inedite*, p. 15:

"On the street in front of the villa you can still see
—Sundays—little parasols passing from the village;
but the villa is far away and there are no more lads.
My sister was around twenty. They always used to come
to the terrace to find lovely little parasols,
light summer dresses, words and laughter. . . ."

24. *Poesie edite e inedite*, p. 16:

"I heard the swishing,
the swishing of the water and I turned suddenly.
How slender she was and strong in that secret body,
my girl-friend was coming down the bank, her legs bare,
dazzling. (Flora was rich and didn't work).
She scolded me a little, covering herself quickly,
but finally we laughed and I gave her my hand.
All the way back I was too happy."

It is to be noticed that in the novel, as opposed to the poem, the narrator remains hidden and observes without being seen.

25. These events are described on pp. 138–139. When he hears the news that Silvia was pregnant, Sor Matteo, depicted until now as a sanguine, merry, and affectionate landowner, reacts in a way which Brancati would have made grotesque, but which here remains essentially tragic: ". . . his head reeled and he fell to the ground. From that day he remained half-paralyzed, with his mouth awry."

26. Santa as a sacrificial victim seems to conclude the progress of Pavese's characters "from the myth of festival to the myth of sacrifice," as outlined by Jesi in his introduction to the latest edition of

Pavese's *La bella estate*, pp. vii–xx. The significance of white in relation to nothing in Melville's complex *vision du monde* is analyzed by Robert Martin Adams, *Nil: Episodes in the Literary Conquest of Void During the 19th Century* (New York: Oxford University Press, 1966), Chapter 6, especially pp. 142ff.

27. Pavese, respectively in the diary, February 9, 1950, p. 357, and in *La letteratura americana*, p. 180.

28. John Freccero, "Mythos and Logos: The Moon and the Bonfires," p. 16.

29. The meaning of this epigraph can be clarified by a passage of György Lukàcs, *Teoria del romanzo*, p. 178, which almost seems to repeat the words in a general context: "The novel is the form of virile maturity. . . . This is how time becomes the vehicle of the noble epic poetry of the novel: time is inexorably made to exist, and no one is in a position any longer to be able to move back along its current. . . . And yet there remains alive a feeling of resignation: all this must come from somewhere, must have been directed in some place; the direction of the flow certainly shows no sense, and yet it is always a direction. And from this feeling of virile resignation emanate the temporal experiences, which are legitimately noticed from an epic point of view in that they arouse actions and germinate from actions: hope and memory; temporal experiences, which at the same time are the surpassing of time: a complex vision of life as inspired unity *ante rem*, and the panoramic intuition *post rem* of life itself."

30. *La letteratura americana*, pp. 360 and 363.

31. Natalino Sapegno, "Pavese, personaggio di tragedia," in *La Stampa*, May 22, 1963, p. 7. The article continues: "The most serious obstacle to the true evaluation of Pavese's art has been the misunderstanding of the so-called 'neo-realism,' which is really the most superficial and worst part of what is left. With the distance of years it is easier to see today that his art operates in an environment of symbolic poetics, in an atmosphere of pure lyric, foreign to any measure or even ambition of realism." Alberto Moravia, too (though in a strangely ungenerous and insensitive tone), speaks of a "decadent Pavese," in *Man as an End*, translated by Bernard Wall (New York: Farrar, Straus & Giroux, 1966), while Furio Felicini, "Problemi critici dell'arte di Pavese," *Studium* (1966, no. 8–9, pp. 595–604),

denies Pavese's decadentism and stresses his "morality" and "lyricism." However, more interesting than such definitions is an entry
in Pavese's diary, May 15, 1944, p. 262: "Have you ever pondered on
the fact that those who originated the Italian novel—seeking in
despair for fluent narrative prose—are primarily lyric writers: Alfieri, Leopardi, Foscolo? The *Vita, I Frammenti di Diario,* and *Il
Viaggio Sentimentale* are the sediment of imaginative minds entirely given up to illuminating flashes of lyrical eloquence. And the
first successful novel, *I Promessi Sposi,* is the maturity of a great
lyric writer. This must have left traces upon our narrative standard."
Apart from the important references to the Romantics and Manzoni,
in this entry of Pavese's, maturity is not contrasted with lyricism:
which seems to be true too of his work, as I have tried to show in the
course of the present analysis.

32. György Lukàcs, *L'anima e le forme,* p. 108: "The essence,
though not entirely conscious, of the Romantic philosophy of life
was the predominance of a passive readiness to experience life. Its art
of living was a genial balancing of the events of life, an intensive
exploitation, and a raising to the plane of necessity all that destiny
has to offer: a poeticizing of destiny, rather than a shaping or
overcoming. The progress of spiritual life, undertaken by them [the
Romantics], could only lead to an organic fusion of the details of
events, to a beautiful harmony of images of things, but not to a
mastery of things. Yet this progress towards a spiritual life was the
only means available for satisfying their tremendous longing for the
great synthesis of unity and universality."

33. *Lettere,* I, p. 40, letter to Tullio Pinelli, October 12, 1926.

34. Michelstaedter, *Opere,* p. 630.

35. *The Burning Brand,* November 26, 1949, pp. 346–347.

36. Piero Calamandrei wrote to Pavese, August 14, 1950, *Lettere,* II,
p. 564, note: "This is great art and true poetry: confronted with
pages like these, where life's pain is filtered through the serene
contemplation of memory, the polemic over the purposes of the arts
and over the relationship between art and politics make no more
sense. True artists, without any conscious intention, always touch on
the wounds of their society, the chance accent which man's eternal
trouble takes on in their time: they are of their age and of all
ages."

37. *Lettere*, II, pp. 404–405, letter to Nicola Enrichens, July 26, 1949.

38. *La letteratura americana*, p. 351, italics added.

39. June 22, 1949, p. 340; and October 16, 1949, p. 344: "How many times in these last entries have you written 'And then??' Aren't you getting into a rut?"

40. Cf. the letter of May 30, 1950, addressed to Mario Camerino, *Lettere*, II, p. 532, already in Lajolo, p. 360: "*La luna e i falò* is the book I've carried inside me the longest and that I enjoyed writing. So much so that I don't think I'll write another for some time— maybe for ever. It's not worth tempting the gods too much."

41. The following thought is found in Pavese's diary, May 13, 1950, p. 363: "Deep, deep, deep down, did I not grab at this amazing love affair, seize upon this undreamed of, fascinating thing, to make myself revert to my old thought—*my long-standing temptation*, to have an excuse for thinking of it again . . . ? Love and Death—*this* is [an ancestral archetype]." The first italics are added.

42. *Ibid.*, May 27, 1950, p. 363; and Lajolo's confirmation, p. 368: "He was convinced that everything was useless, that he had nothing left to write, that he wasn't suited to politics, that he was worthless for women, for his friends and for himself."

43. Fernandez, *Le roman italien*, pp. 147–8; and Lajolo, p. 375: "He decided to carry out the supreme act like a human sacrifice, not so much to escape from men as to go back into himself." Pavese's longing is very well expressed in his self-portrait, which he wrote in the third person: "His basic tendency is to give to his actions a significance that transcends their actual scope; to make his days into a gallery of unmistakable and absolute moments" (in Lajolo, pp. 256–7): this is how he got to the last "act." One should also read, *ibid.*, p. 371, and in *Lettere*, II, p. 570, the last special delivery letter sent by Pavese to his friend Lajolo, the evening he killed himself: ". . . like Cortez I have burned my ships behind me. I don't know whether I'll find the treasure of Montezuma, but I know that in the high regions of Tenochtitlàn they still make human sacrifices. For many years I didn't think about these things, any more, I wrote. Now I shall never write again!"

44. In a letter to Bona Alterocca, August 23, 1950, four days before his suicide, Pavese wrote: "A cure of silence is needed. I'm sorry, but

if there is anything I understand, it is this" (in *La Stampa*, August 25, 1965, p. 7, now in *Lettere*, II, p. 567).

45. Natalia Ginzburg, "Portrait of a Friend," in *Le piccole virtù* (Turin: Einaudi, 1963, 3rd ed.), pp. 31 and 33; other passages on Pavese are in her *Lessico famigliare* (Turin: Einaudi, 1963), especially pp. 130–132 and 204–206, and in Augusto Monti, *I miei conti con la scuola* (Turin: Einaudi, 1965), pp. 248–263, especially pp. 259ff.

46. Ginzburg, "Portrait of a Friend," p. 32, italics added. One remembers the letter to Enrichens, in which Pavese, after outlining his own literary formation, concluded: "I love S. Stefano madly, because I come from far away" (in Lajolo, p. 226, now in *Lettere*, II, p. 396.) Cf. Michele Tondo, *Itinerario di Cesare Pavese* (Padua: Liviana, 1965), with the emphasis on "itinerary."

Bibliography of Pavese's Works

1936   *Lavorare stanca* (*Work Is Wearying*), untranslated.

1941   *Paesi tuoi*, written in 1939, English translation *The Harvesters* by A. E. Murch (London: Peter Owen, 1961).

1942   *La spiaggia*, written in 1940–41, English translation *The Beach* by W. J. Strachan (London: Peter Owen, 1963), and by R. W. Flint in *The Selected Works of Cesare Pavese* (New York: Farrar, Straus & Giroux, 1968).

1943   *Lavorare stanca* (*Work Is Wearying*), a new and more extensive edition, untranslated.

1946   *Feria d'agosto* (*August Holiday*), tales and essays written from 1941 to 1944, some of which appear in English translation in *Summer Storm* by A. E. Murch (London: Peter Owen, 1966).

1947   *La terra e la morte* (*Earth and Death*), poetry written in 1945, untranslated.
       Dialoghi con Leucò, written in 1945–46, English translation *Dialogues with Leucò* by William Arrowsmith and D. S. Carne-Ross (Ann Arbor: University of Michigan Press, 1965).
       Il compagno, written in 1946, English translation *The Comrade* by W. J. Strachan (London: Peter Owen, 1959).

1949   *Prima che il gallo canti* (*Before the Cock Crows*), containing: *Il carcere*, 1938–39, English translation *The Political Prisoner* by W. J. Strachan (London: Peter Owen, 1959); and *La casa in collina*, 1947–48, English translation *The House on the Hill* by W. J. Strachan (New York: Walker,

1961), and by R. W. Flint, in *The Selected Works of Cesare Pavese.*

1949   *La bella estate,* containing: *La bella estate,* 1940, English translation *The Beautiful Summer* by W. J. Strachan, in *The Political Prisoner; Il diavolo sulle colline,* 1948, English translation *The Devil in the Hills* by D. D. Paige (New York: Noonday Press, 1959), and by R. W. Flint in *The Selected Works of Cesare Pavese;* and *Tra Donne sole,* 1949, English translation *Among Women Only* by D. D. Paige (London: Peter Owen, 1953, and New York: Noonday Press, 1959), and by R. W. Flint in *The Selected Works of Cesare Pavese.*

1950   *La luna e i falò,* written at the end of 1949, English translation *The Moon and the Bonfire* by Louise Sinclair (London: John Lehmann, 1952; Penguin Books, 1963), and *The Moon and the Bonfires* by Marianne Ceconi (New York: Farrar, Straus & Giroux, 1954).

Works published posthumously:

1951   *Verrà la morte e avrà i tuoi occhi (Death Will Come and Its Eyes Will Be Yours),* poetry written in 1950, untranslated; it also contains *La terra e la morte.*

1951   *La letteratura americana e altri saggi (American Literature and Other Essays),* written in the years 1930–1950, untranslated.

1952   *Il mestiere di vivere (The Job of Living),* diary 1935–50, English translation by A. E. Murch, *The Burning Brand* (New York: Walker, 1961), and *This Business of Living* (London: Peter Owen, 1961).

1953   *Notte di festa,* short stories written in 1936–38, English translation *Festival Night* by A. E. Murch (London: Peter Owen, 1964).

1959   *Fuoco grande,* written in 1946 in collaboration with Bianca Garufi, English translation *A Great Fire* by W. J. Strachan, in *The Beach.*

1964   *8 poesie inedite e quattro lettere a un'amica,* written in
1928–29, untranslated.

In 1960 Einaudi began to publish the complete works of Cesare
Pavese, which so far include: a new edition of the diary *Il mestiere di vivere,* and of *Dialoghi con Leucò;* a volume of *Racconti,*
the short stories, containing also various fragments and previously
unpublished work; a volume of *Poesie edite e inedite,* a collection of published and unpublished poems; two volumes of *Romanzi,* the novels in chronological order; and two volumes of
Lettere, the collected letters 1924–1944 and 1945–1950.

Between 1958 and 1967 the review *Cinema Nuovo* published
Pavese's essays "Problemi critici del cinematografo" and "Di un
nuovo tipo di esteta," and his film scripts *Il diavolo sulle colline,
Due sorelle, Amore amaro,* and *Il serpente e la colomba.*

In February, 1967, the review *Il caffè* published his short story
"Congedato," written in 1931; his introduction to the Italian translation of the *Iliad* by Rosa Calzecchi Onesti (Turin: Einaudi,
1950) was not collected in his volume of essays.

(This bibliography does not list Pavese's translations into Italian.)

Index

This Index lists personal names and the titles of all Pavese's works, including single poems, short stories, essays, and dialogues quoted or analyzed in the text.